INTERNATIONAL ENCYCLOPAEDIA OF ISLAM

Vol.-1

Islamic Philosophy

INTERNATIONAL ENCYCLOPAEDIA OF ISLAM

Vol.-1

Islamic Philosophy

Editor
A.H. Qasmi

ISHA BOOKS
DELHI-110 033

International Encyclopaedia of Islam
(*Religion*)

ISBN: 81-8205-320-X (Set)

ISBN: 81-8205-321-8

Published in 2006 in India by
Isha Books, D-43, Prithviraj Road,
Adarsh Nagar, Delhi-110 033

Printed at : Rajdhani Printers, Delhi.

Contents

Preface

Man is a social creature. It is the society where he learns how to live in this vast cosmos. Apart from society, people are divided into different castes, cultures and creeds. All these factors go in developing a man's personality. Of all the factors, mentioned above, religion is most important.

There exist about more than two thousand religions in the world today. A religion is regarded as a sacred institution, which governs a man's life here and hereafter and teaches him how to lead a happy and prosperous life.

What's unique to Islam is its endowment to humanity from the divine creator or the Almighty. It is not a set of principles and dogmas scribed by a scholar or thinker. It was sent on the earth circa fifteen hundred years ago, but its principles and preachings hold good even today. Besides showing humanity a straight way to the eternal success, it also has a say in various other walks of human life, such as economy, politics, human rights, social relations, judiciary, marriage and so on and so forth.

Another distinguished feature of Islam is that apart from being the latest religion, it is also the last one. That is to say, whatever is there in Islam, it is valid upto to the doomsday. Now, there will not come any other religion till the Day of Judgement. Therefore, it is the most powerful and as well as the most human-nature-friendly.

Given the present global scenario, there was being felt a dire need to bring out such a mini-encyclopaedia of Islam which may cater to the maximum needs of man in the least possible sheet of paper.

The present series is an humble attempt in the same direction. It comprises ten volumes which cover all the major disciplines of human life like, Prayer, marriage, justice, human rights, social justice and so, on.

We are sure that the endeavour would prove to be a capsule of treasure of knowledge about Islam, prepared perfectly. Nevertheless, considering the adage 'to err is human', we would be obliged if the readers suggest some improvements for further editions.

Editor

1

Basis of Islam

Belief in One Allah

The Muhammadan rule of faith is based upon what are called the four foundations of orthodoxy, namely, the Quran, or, as it is called Kalam Ullah, the Word of God; .the Hadith (pl. Ahadith), or the traditions of the saying and practice of Muhammad; Ijma, or the consent of the Mujtahidin, or learned doctors; and Qias, or the analogical reasoning of the learned.

In studying the Muhammadan religious system it must be well understood that Islam is not simply the religion of the Quran, but that all Muhammadans, whether Sunni, Shia, or Wahabi, receive the Traditions as an authority in matters of faith and practice. The Sunni Muhammadans arrogate to themselves the title of traditionists; but the Shias also receive the Hadith as binding upon them, although they do not acknowledge the same collection of traditions as those received by their opponents. The Wahabis receive the "six correct books of the Sunnis."

The example of Muhammad is just as binding upon the Muslim, as that of Him who said, "Learn of me" is upon the Christian, and very many were the injunctions which the "Prophet" gave as to the transmission of his sayings and practice, and very elaborate is the canon whereby Muslims arrive at what they believe to be the example of their Prophet. If, therefore, the grand and elaborate system of morals as expressed in the law of Islam has failed to raise the standard of morality amongst the nations of the earth which have embraced its creed, it is not unreasonable to conclude that its failure rests in the absence of a living example of truth.

Quran : Allah's Book

The word Quran is derived from the Arabic Qara, which occurs at the commencement of Sura xcv., which is said to have been the first chapter revealed to Muhammad; and has the same meaning as the Hebrew kara, "to read," or "to recite," which is frequently used in Jeremiah xxxvi., as well as in other places in the Old Testament. It is, therefore, equivalent to the Hebrew mikra, rendered in Nehemiah viii. 18. "the reading." It is the title given to the Muhammadan Scriptures which are usually appealed to and quoted from as the "Quran Majid," or the "Glorious Quran"; the "Quran Sharif " or the "Noble Quran"; and is also called the "Furqan," or "Distinguisher," "Kalam Ullah," or the "Word of God" and "Al Kitab," or "the Book.

Muhammadans believe the Quran to be the inspired Word of God sent down to the lowest heaven complete, and then revealed from time to time to the Prophet by the Angel Jibbrail.

There is, however, only one distinct assertion in the Quran to Jibbrail having been the medium of inspiration, namely, Sura-i-Baqr (ii.), 91; and this occurs in a Medina Sura, revealed about seven years after the Prophet's rule had been established. In the Sura-i-Shura (xxvi.), 192, the Quran is said to have been given by the "Ruh ul Amin," or Faithful Spirit; and in the Sura-i-Najm. (iii.), 5, Muhammad claims to have been taught by the "Shad Eid-ul-Qua," or One terrible in power; and in the Traditions the agent of inspiration is generally spoken of as "an angel" (malak) .5 It is, therefore, not quite certain through what agency Muhammad believed himself to be inspired of God.

According to Aishah, one of the Prophet's wives, the revelation was first communicated in dreams. Aishah relates : _ "The first revelations which the Prophet received were in true dreams; and he never dreamt but it came to pass as regularly as the dawn of day. After this the Prophet was fond of retirement, and used to seclude himself in a cave in mount Hira and worship there day and night. He would, whenever he wished, return to his family at Mecca, and then go back again, taking with him the necessaries of life.

Thus, he continued to return to Khadijah from time to time, until one day the revelation came down to him, and the angel (malak) came to him and said, 'Read' (igaraa); but the Prophet said,' I am not a reader.' And the Prophet related, that he (i.e. the angel) took hold of me and squeezed me as much as I could bear, and he then let me go and said again, 'Read!' And I said,' I am not a reader.' Then he took hold to me a second time, and squeezed me as much as I could bear, and then let me go, and said 'Read!' And I said,' I am not a reader.' Then he took hold of me a third time and squeezed me as much as I could bear, and said –

"'Read! in the name of thy Lord who created;
Created man from a clot of blood in the womb.
"'Read! for thy Lord is the most beneficent,
He hath taught men the use of the pen;
He hath taught man that which he knoweth not."

"Then the Prophet repeated the words himself, and with his heart trembling he returned (i.e., from Hira to Mecca) to Khadijah, and said, 'Wrap me up, wrap me up.' And they wrapped him up in a garment till" his fear was dispelled, and he told Khadijah what had passed, and he said : 'Verily, I was afraid I should have died.' Then Khadijah said,' No, it will not be so. I swear by God, He will never make you melancholy or sad. For verily you are kind to your relatives" you speak the truth, you are faithful in trust, you bear the afflictions of the people, you spend in good works what you gain in trade, you are hospitable, and you assist your fellow men'. 'After this, Khadijah took the Prophet to Waraqa, who was the son of her uncle, and she said to him, 'O son of my uncle! hear what your brother's son says.'

Then Waraqa said to the Prophet,' O son of my brother! what do you see?' Then the Prophet told Waraqa what he saw, and Waraqa said,' That is the Namus which God sent to Moses.' Aishah also relates that Harith-bin-Hisham asked the Prophet, How did the revelation come to you?' and the Prophet said,' Sometimes like the noise of a bell, and sometimes the angle would come and converse with me in the shape of a man.'"

According to Aishah's statement, the Sura-i-Alaq (xcvi.) was the first portion of the Quran revealed; but it is more probable that the poetical Suras, in which there is no express declaration of the prophetic office, or of a divine commission, were composed at an earlier period. Internal evidence would assign the earliest date to the Suras Zilzal (xcix.), Asar (ciii.), Adiyat (c.), and Fatiha (i.), which are rather the utterances of a searcher after truth than of an Apostle of God.

The whole book was not arranged until after Muhammad's death but it is believed that the Prophet himself divided the Suras and gave most of them their present titles, which are chosen from some word which occurs in the chapter. The following is the account of the collection and arrangement of the Quran, as it stands at present, as given in traditions recorded by Bukhari.'

"Zaid-ibn-Sabit, relates:- Abu-Bakr sent a person to me, and called me to him, at the time of the battle with the people of Zemamah; and I went to him, and Umar was with him; and Abu-Bakr said to me, "Umar came to me and said, Verily, a great many of the readers of the Quran were slain on the day of the battle with the people of Zemamah; and really I am afraid that if the slaughter should be great, much will be lost from the Quran, because every person remembers something of it; and, verily, I see it advisable for you to order the Quran to be collected into one book.' I said to Umar,' How can I do a thing which the 'Prophet has not done?' He said, I swear by God, this collecting of the Quran is a good thing.' And Umar used to be constantly returning to me and saying: You must collect the Quran,' till" at length God opened my breast so to do, and I saw what Umar had been advising.' And Zaid-ibn-Sabit says that, Abu-Bakr said to me, "You are a young and sensible man, and I do not suspect you of forgetfulness, negligence, or perfidy; and, verily, you used to write for the Prophet his instructions from above; then look for the Quran in every place and collect it." I said, "I swear by God, that if people had ordered me to carry a mountain about from one place to another, it would not be heavier upon me than the order which Abu-Bakr has given for collecting the Quran." I said to Abu-Bakr, "How do you do a thing which the Prophet of God did not?" He said, "By God, this collecting of the Quran is a good act." And he used perpetually to return to me, until God put it into my heart to do the thing which the heart of Umar had been set upon. Then I sought for the Quran, and collected it from the leaves of the date, and white stones, and the breasts of people that remembered it, till" I found the last part of the chapter entitled Tauba (Repentance), with Abu-Khuzaimah Ansari, and with no other person. These leaves were in the possession of Abu-Bakr, until God caused him to die; after which Umar had them in his life-time; after that, they remained with his daughter, Hafsa; after that, Uthman compiled them into one book.'

"Anas-bin-Malik relates-Hudhaifa came to Uthman, and he had fought with the people of Syria in the conquest of Armenia; and had fought in Azurbaijan, with the people of Iraq, and he was shocked at the different ways of people reading the Quran. And Hudhaifa said to Uthman, "O Uthman, assist this people, before they differ in the Book of God, just as the Jews and Christians differ in their books." Then Uthman sent a person to Hafsa, ordering her to send those portions which she had, and saying, "I shall have a number of copies of them taken, and will then return them to you." And Hafsa sent the portions of Uthman, and Uthman ordered Zaid-ibn-Sabit, Ansari, and Abdullah-bin-Zubayr, and Saad-bin-Al Aas, and Abdullah-bin-Al-Harith-bin-Hisham; and these were all of the Quraish tribe, except Zaid-ibn-Sabit and Uthman. And he said to the three Quraishites, "When you and Zaid-ibn-Sabit differ about any part of the dialect of the Quran, then do ye write it in the Quraish dialect, because it came not down in the language of any tribe but theirs."

Then they did as Uthman had ordered; and when a number of copies had been taken, Uthman returned the leaves to Hafsa. And Uthman sent a copy to every quarter of the countries of Islam, and ordered all other leaves to be burnt, and Ibn-Shahab said, "Khadijah, son of Zaid-ibn-Sabit, informed me, saying, 'I could not find one verse when I was writing the Quran, which, verily, I heard from the Prophet; then I looked for it, and found it with Khuzaimah Ansari, and entered it into the Sura-i-Ahzab.'"

This recension of the Quran produced by Khalifah Uthman has been handed down to us unaltered; and, as Sir

William Muir remarks, "There is probably no other book in the world Which has remained twelve centuries with so pure a text."

That various readings (such as Christians understand by the term) did exist when. Uthman produced the first uniform edition is more than probable, and the Shias have always charged the Ansars with having mutilated and changed and made the Quran what they pleased;" a charge, however, which they do not attempt to prove, beyond the mere assertion that certain passages were omitted which favoured the claims of Ali to be the first Khalifah.

The various readings (Qiraat) in the Quran are not such as are usually understood by the term in English authors, but different dialects of the Arabic language. Ibn Abbas says the Prophet said, "Jibbrail taught me to read the Quran in one dialect, and when I recited it he taught me to recite it in another dialect) and so on until the number of dialects increased to seven.

Muhammad seems to have adopted this expedient to satisfy the desire of the leading tribes to have a Quran in their own dialect; for Abdul Haqq says," The Quran was first revealed in the dialect of the Quraish, which was the Prophets native tongue; but when the Prophet saw that the people of other tribes recited it with difficulty then he obtained permission from God to extend its currency by allowing it to be recited in all the chief dialects of Arabia, which were seven:- Quraish, Tay, Hawazin, Ahl-i-Yaman, Saqif, Huzail, and Bani-Tamin. Everyone of these tribes accordingly read the Quran in its own dialect, till" the time of Uthman, when these differences of reading were prohibited."

These seven dialects are called Sabata-Ahruf and the science of reading the Quran in the correct dialect is called *Ilm-i-Tajwid*.

The chronological arrangement of the chapters of the Quran is most important. In the present Urdu edition, as well as in all Arabic editions, the Suras are placed as they must have been arranged by Zaid-ibn-i-Sabit, who put them together regardless of all chronological sequence. If, therefore, we arrange them according to the order which is given in Syruty's Itqan, we shall not fail to mark the gradual development of Muhammad's mind from that of a mere moral teacher and reformer, to that of a prophet and warrior chief.

The contrast between the earlier, middle, and later Suras is very striking. He who at Mecca is the admonisher and persuader, at Medina is the legislator and the warrior, who dictates obedience, and uses other weapons than the pen of the poet and the scribe. When business pressed, as at Medina, poetry makes way for prose; and although touches of the poetical element occasionally break forth, and he has to defend himself up to a very late period against the charge of being merely a poet, yet this is rarely the case in the Medina Suras, in which we so frequently meet with injunctions to obey God and the Prophet.

To fully realize the gradual growth of Muhammad's religious system in his own mind, it is absolutely necessary to read the Quran through, not in the order in which it now stands, but that in which Muslim divines admit that it was revealed. At the same time it must be remembered that all Muhammadan doctors allow that in most of the Suras there are verses which belong to a different date from that of other portions of the chapter; for example, in the Sura-i-Alaq the first five verses belong to a much earlier date than the others; and in Sura-i-Baqr, verse 234 is acknowledged by all commentators to have been revealed after verse 240, which it abrogates.

The Quran is divided into :

1. *Harf* (pl. *Huruf*), Letters; of which there are said to be 323,671.

2. *Kalima* (pl. *Kalimat*), Words; of which there arc 77,934.
3. *Ayat* (pl. *Ayat*), Verses. Ayat is a word which signifies "signs," and it was used by Muhammad for short sections or verses of his supposed revelation. There are said to be 6,616 verses inn the whole book; but the division of verses differs in different editions of the Arabic Quran. The number of verses in the Arabic Qurans are recorded after the title of the Sura, and the verses distinguished in the text by a small cypher of circle.
4. *Sura* (pl. *Suwar*), Chapters. A word which signifies a row or series, but which is now used exclusively for the chapters of the Quran, which are one hundred and fourteen in number. These chapters are called after some word which occurs in the text, and if the Traditions are to be trusted, they were so named by Muhammad himself, although the verses of their respective Suras were undoubtedly arranged after his death, and sometimes with little regard to their sequence. Musalman doctors admit that the Khalifah Uthman arranged the chapters in the order in which they now stand in the Quran.
5. *Ruku'* (pl. *Rukuat*), Prostrations. These are of two kinds, the Ruku, of a Sura and the Ruku, of a Sipara, and are distinguished in the Arabic Quran by the letter *ain* on the margin. Muhammadans generally quote by the Ruku and not by the verse.
6. *Ruba'*, The quarter of a Sipara.
7. *Nisf*, Three-quarters of a Sipara.
8. *Suls*, Three-quarters of a Sipara.
9. *Sipara* '20 the Persian for the Arabic Juz. The Siparas or Juz, are thirty in number, and it is said that the Quran is so divided to enable the pious Muslim to

recite the whole of the Quran in the thirty days of Ramadan. Muhammadans generally quote their Quran by the Sipara and Ruku', and not by the Sura and Ayat.

10. *Manzil* (pl. *manazil*), Stages. These are seven in number, and are marked by the letters F, M, Y, B, Sh, W, and Q, which words are said to spell Famibeshauq, i.e., "My mouth with desire." They have been arranged to enable the devout Muslim to recite the whole in the course of a week.

Ilm-ul-Usul, or the Exegesis of the Quran, is a science, some knowledge of which is absolutely necessary to enable the Christian controversialist to meet a Muhammadan opponent.

The words (alfaz) of the Quran are of four classes: —*Khass, Amm, Mushtarak,* and *Muawwal.*

1. *Khass,* Words used in a special sense. These are of three kinds:- Khusus-ul-jins, Special genus; Khusus-un-nau, Special species; *Khusus-ul-ain,* Special individuality.
2. *Amm,* Collective or common, which embrace many individuals or things.
3. *Mushtarak,* Complex words which have several significations; e.g. 'ain, a word which signifies an Fye, a Fountain, the Knee, or the Sun.
4. *Muawwal,* Words which require to be explained: e.g. Salat may mean either the Liturgical daily prayer (Namaz), or simple prayer (Dud).

II. The Sentences (Ibarat) of the Quran are either Zahir or Khafi', i.e., either Obvious or Hidden.

Obvious sentences are of four classes:- *Zahir, Nass, Mufassar, Muhkam.*

1. *Zahir*-Those sentences, the meaning of which is Obvious or clear, without any assistance from the context (karina).

2. *Nass*-Those sentences the meaning of which is Manifest from the text: e.g. "Take in marriage of such other women as please you, two, three, or four." Here it is manifest that the expression "such other women as please you" is restricted.

3. *Mufassar*-Sentences which are explained by some expression in the verse: e.g. "And the angles prostrated themselves all of them with one accord save Iblis". Here it is explained that Iblis did not prostrate himself.

4. *Muhkam*-Perspicuous sentences, the meaning of which is inconvertible: e.g. *Sura-i-Maida* (v.), 98, "He (God) knoweth all things."

Hidden sentences are either *Khafi, Mushkil, Mujmal,* or *Mutashabih.*

1. *Khaji*-Sentences in which other persons or things are hidden beneath the plain meaning of a word or expression contained therein: e.g. *Sura-i-Maida.* (v), 42, "As for a thief whether male or female cut ye off their hands in recompense for their doings." In this sentence the word Sariq, "thief," is understood to have hidden beneath its literal meaning, both pickpockets and highway robbers.

2. *Mushkil*-Sentences which are ambiguous: e.g., *Sura-i-Dahr* (ixxvi.), 15, "Vessels of silver and decanters which are of glass, decanters of glass with silver whose measure they shall mete."

3. *Mujmal*-Sentences which are compendious, and have many interpretations : e.g., Sura-i-Marij (Ixx.), 19, "Man truly is by creation hasty."

4. *Mutashabih*-Intricate sentences, or expressions, the exact meaning of which it is impossible for man to ascertain until the day of resurrection, but which was known to

the Prophet: e.g., the letters Alif, Lam, Mim (A.L.M.); Alif, Lam, Ra (A.L.R.); Alif, Lam, Mim, Ra (A.L.M.R.), etc., at the commencement of different Suras or chapters. Also Sura-i-Mulk (xvii.) 1, "In whose hand is the Kingdom," i.e., Gods hand (Arabic, gad); and Sura-i-Ta Ha (xx.), "He is most merciful and sitteth on His throne," i.e., God sitteth (Arabic, istawa); and Sura-i-Baqr (ii.), 115, "The face of God" (Arabic, wajh-Ullah).

III. The use (istimal) of words in the Quran is divided into four classes. They are either Haqiqat, Majaz, Sarih, or Kinayah.

1. *Haqiqat*-Words which are used in their literal meaning: e.g., ruku, a prostration; zina, adultery.
2. *Majaz*-Words which are figurative.
3. *Sarih*-Words the meaning of which is clear and palpable; e.g., "Thou art free," "Thou art divorced."
4. *Kinayah*-Words which are metaphorical in their meaning: e.g., "Thou art separated"; by which may be meant "thou art divorced."

IV. The deduction of arguments, or istidlal, as expressed in the Quran, is divided into four sections: Ibarat, Isharat, Dalalat, and Iqtiza.

1. *Ibarat*-The plain sentence.
2. *Isharat*-A sign or hint: e.g., "Born of him;" meaning, of course, the father.
3. *Dalalat*-The argument arising from a word or expression: e.g., Sura-i-Bani Israil (xvii.), 23," Say not unto your parents fie" (Arabic, uff); from which it is argued that children are not either to abuse or beat their parents.
4. *Iqtiza*-Demanding certain conditions: e.g., Sura-i-Nisa (iv.), 91, "Whoso killeth a Mumin (believer) by mischance shall be bound to free a slave." Here the condition demanded is that the slave shall be the property of the person who frees him.

An acquaintance with the use of these expressions used in the exegetical commentaries of the Quran is of great assistance to the Bazaar-preacher, for it often happens that Maulavis interrupt the preacher by putting some difficult question, which the most able missionary will find it difficult to answer to the satisfaction of a mixed assemblage. For instance, an interesting discourse or discussion is often interrupted by a Maulavi putting the following question: "What did Jesus mean when He said, 'All that ever came before me were thieves or robbers?'

The best reply to such an one would be, "Maulavi Sahib, you know, sentences are Zahir or Khafi, hidden or evident. That is Khafi. Hidden sentences you know are of four kinds, Khafi, Mushkil, Mujmal, or Mutashabih. I consider the text you have quoted to be Mujmal, and you must admit that it would take up too much time to explain a Mujmal sentence in the midst of .my present discourse." Most probably the Maulavi -will be satisfied, for the preacher has applied a little flattering unction, in supposing that the Maulavi is learned in the principles of exegesis.

It is often painful to observe how some of our preachers will attempt to explain the sacred mysteries of our faith in the midst of an ignorant mob. Whereas learned Muslim doctors, if placed in the same position, would decline to discuss mysterious questions under such conditions. They would say, as the Christian Divine might also say, "Many things in God's word are hidden (Khafi), and cannot be explained to such a mixed audience as this, and besides this, in speaking of the nature (zat) of God, there is always some fear of blasphemy (kufr); I prefer speaking to you on that subject alone, after the preaching is over."

Shariat : Law of Islam

Muhammadan law consists of two divisions, Rawa and Narawa, i.e., Things lawful and Things unlawful.

I. That which is lawful is divided into five classes:

1. *Farz*-That which has been enjoined in the Quran.
2. *Wajib*-That of which there is some doubt as to its Divine institution.
3. *Sunnat*-The example of Muhammad, which consists of three kinds:

   Sunnat-i-Faili'-That which Muhammad himself did.

   Sunnat-i-Qauli'-That which Muhammad said should be practised.

   Sunnat-i-Taqriji'-That which was done in the presence of Muhammad and which he did not forbid.
4. *Mustahab*-That which Muhammad sometimes did and sometimes omitted.
5. *Mubah*-That which may be left unperformed without any fear of Divine punishment.

II. Things-unlawful are of three classes:-

1. *Haram*-That which is distinctly forbidden in the Quran and Hadith.
2. *Makruh*-That of which there is some doubt as to its unlawfulness, but which is generally held to be unclean or unlawful.
3. *Mufsid*-That which is corrupting and pernicious.

The divisions of lawful and unlawful do not merely apply to food, but also to ablutions and other customs and precepts.

Understanding Sin

The Muhammadan doctors divide sins into two classes, very much as the Roman Catholic divines do; the usual Roman designation being that of mortal and venial sin, whilst Muhammadans use the expressions Kabira and Saghira, "Great" and "Little". Kabira are those great sins, of which, if a Musalman do not repent, he will go to the purgatorial hell reserved for sinful Muslims. The divines of Islam are not agreed amongst themselves as to the exact number of Kabira sins, but they are generally considered to be seventeen (vide Fawaid-us-Shariat).

1. Kufr, or infidelity.
2. Constantly committing Saghira, or little sins.
3. Despairing of the mercy of God.
4. Considering one's self safe from the wrath of God.
5. False witness.
6. Qazaf, or falsely charging a Musalman with adultery.
7. Taking a false oath.
8. Magic.
9. Drinking wine.
10. Appropriation of the property of orphans.
11. Usury.
12. Adultery.
13. Unnatural crimes.
14. Theft.
15. Murder.
16. Fleeing in battle before the face of an infidel.
17. Disobedience to parents.

Sin and its Reward

Punishment is divided into three classes:-

Hadd, Tazir, and Qisas.

1. Hadd is that punishment which is said to have been ordained of God in the Quran and the Hadith, and which must be inflicted. The following belong to this class:- Adultery, for which the adulterer is stoned. Fornication, for which one hundred stripes are inflicted. Drunkenness, for which there are eighty stripes. The

slander of a married person, that is, bringing a false charge of adultery against a married person, for which the offender must receive eighty lashes. This punishment is said to have been instituted by God, when 'Aishah, the favourite wife of "the Prophet," was falsely charged with adultery! Apostacy, for which the Murtad, or Apostate, is killed, unless he repent of his error within three days. When an Apostate from Islam has been killed according to the law, or has left the country, his property goes to those of his heirs who still remain Musulmans (vide the "Al Siraji").

2. Tazir is that punishment which is said to have been ordained of God, but of which there are not special injunctions, the exact punishment being left to the discretion of the Qadi, or Judge.
3. Qisas (lit. "retaliation") is that punishment which can be remitted by the person offended against, upon the payment of a fine or compensation. The punishment for murder is of this class. The next akin to the murdered person can either take the life of his kinsman's murderer, or accept a money compensation (Diat). There is also retaliation in case of wounds. Qisas is the lex talionis of Moses, "eye for eye, tooth for tooth, hand for hand, foot for foot, burning for burning, wound for wound, stripe for stripe" (vide Exodus xxi. 24). But in allowing a money compensation for murder, Muhammad departed from the Jewish code.

Halaal Food

No animal is lawful food unless it be slaughtered according to the Muhammadan law, namely, by drawing the knife across the throat and cutting the windpipe, the carotid arteries, and the gullet, repeating at the same time the words "Bismillah Allaho Akbar, i.e. "In the name of the great God." A clean animal, so slaughtered, becomes lawful food.

In the "Sharah Waqia it is said that the following creatures are lawful (halal):-

1. Those animals that are cloven-footed and chew the cud, and are not beasts of prey.
2. Birds that do not seize their prey with their claws, or wound them with their bills, but pick up food with their bills.
3. Fish; but no other animals which move in the water.
4. Locusts.

Some commentators say that the horse is lawful; but it is generally held to be "makruh".

Fish found dead in the water is unlawful; but if it be taken out and die afterwards it is lawful.

Alligators, turtles, crabs, snakes, frogs, etc., are unlawful. Wine is expressly forbidden in the Quran; and, in the judgement of the learned, this prohibition extends to whatever has a tendency to intoxicate, such as opium, bhang, charas,' and tobacco. The Akhund of Swat his issued several "fatwahs," prohibiting the use of tobacco; but the chilam (or pipe), having become a national institution, no notice has been taken of the inhibition. The Wahabis do not permit territory, the huqqa, or chilam, is never allowed in a mosque.

Obligatory Duty

Farz-i-Kifaya are those commands which are imperative (farz); but which, if one person in eight or ten perform, it is equivalent to all having performed it.

1. To return a salutation.
2. To visit the sick, and inquire after their welfare.
3. To follow a bier on foot to the grave.
4. To accept an invitation.
5. To reply to a sneeze, e.g. if a person sneeze, and say immediately afterwards, "God be praised" (Alhamdo

lillah), it is incumbent upon at least one of the party to exclaim, "God have mercy on you" (Yarhamuk Allah).

There is an interesting chapter on the custom of saluting after sneezing in Ishaq Israeli's "Curiosities of Literature," from, which it appears that it is almost universal amongst nations.

Helping Others

Fitrat (lit. "nature") is said to be certain ancient practices of the prophets before the time of Muhammad, which have not been forbidden by him.

In the Hadith "Muslim," the customs of fitrat are said to be ten in number.

1. The clipping of the mustach, so that they do not enter the mouth.
2. Not cutting or shaving the beard.
3. Cleaning the teeth (i.e., miswak).
4. Cleansing the nostrils with water at the usual ablutions.
5. Cutting the nails.
6. Cleaning the finger-joints.
7. Pulling out the hairs under the arms.
8. Cleansing the mouth with water at the time of ablution.

Promoting Fraternity and Love

The usual Islamic salutation is "as salamu alikum," i.e. "The peace of God be with you."

When a person makes a "salam," and any of the assembly rise and return it, it is considered sufficient-for the whole company.

The lesser number should always be the first to salute the greater; he who rides should salute him who walks; he who walks, him who stands; the stander, the sitter, etc. A man should not salute a woman on the road; and it is considered very disrespectful to salute with the left hand, that hand being used for legal ablutions. The ordinary salute is made by raising the right hand either to the breast or to the forehead.

In Central Asia the salutation is generally given without any motion of the hand or body.

Pupils salute their masters by kissing, the hand or sleeve, which is the usual salutation made to men of eminent piety.

Homage is paid by kissing the feet of the ruler, or by kissing the ground or carpet.

In Afghanistan, conquered people pay homage by casting their turbans at the feel of the conqueror; and the heads of tribes often lessen the size of their turbans before appearing in the presence of their rulers.

Law of Islam

Shariat is the code of law for the Islamic way of life. The word Shariat means a clear straight path or example. It is the best system of law from Allah for humanity to follow.

Shariat, or Islamic law, is the code of conduct for Muslims and is based on two main sources: the Quran and the Sunnah of the Prophet. It aims at the success and welfare of mankind both in this life and the life-after-death.

Shariat prescribes a complete set of laws for the guidance of mankind so that Good (Maraf) is established and Evil (Munkar) is removed from society. It provides a clear and straight path which leads to progress and fulfilment in life and the attainment of Allah's pleasure.

The Quran is the main basis of Shariat. It states the principles while the Sunnah of the Prophet provides the blueprint of how to apply them. For example, the Quran says: establish Salat, observe Sawm, pay Zakat, take decisions by consultation, do not earn or spend in wrong ways — but it does not describe how to do these things. It is the Sunnah of the Prophet which shows us how to act on Allah's commands.

The Quran is the main book of guidance and the Prophet taught us how to follow it. The Prophet not only told us how to follow the guidance, he also practised it himself. Prophet Muhammad's life was the living Quran. Shariat has rules for every aspect of life. It is complete and perfect, and its application guarantees success, welfare and peace here on this earth and in the Akhirat.

Man-made laws differ from Shariat in a number of significant ways.

Man-made Law	*Shariat or Allah's Law*
1. Men make laws when they feel the need; these laws start from a few and then grow in number over the years.	Islamic Law is complete and perfect, and covers all aspects of human life. Men of learning explain and clarify Shariat for the benefit of ordinary people.
2. Laws made by men are not permanent; they are changed to suit people's wishes and desires. For example, in a particular country at a particular time, drinking alcohol may be banned; but this can change when pressure grows.	Shariat is permanent for all people all the time. It does not change with time and conditions. For example, drinking wine and gambling are not allowed under Islamic law. No one can change this; it is law that is valid for all time and for public all places. The American Government once banned all alcoholic drinks, but removed the ban after a time because it could not be enforced.

Contd...

Man-made Law	*Shariat or Allah's Law*
3. Man does not have knowledge of the future. Hence, man-made laws cannot stand the test of time.	Allah is All-knowing and All-powerful; He is the most Wise; His laws are the best and are complete.
4. Man is a created being. His laws are the creation of the created.	Allah is the Creator and His laws are for Man, His creation.
5. Man-made laws may be suitable for a particular nation or country. They cannot be universal.	Allah's laws are for all nations, all countries and for all time. They are universal.
6. Men make laws to suit their own needs. If members of parliament want to decrease the rate of tax on the rich, they can do so even if the majority of the people suffered and there was high unemployment in the country.	Allah is above all needs. He is not dependent on anything, so His laws are for the good of all people and not for a few, selfish people.

Shariah has two other sources: Ijma' (consensus) and Qiyas (analogy or reasoning on the basis of similar circumstances). These sources must still be based on the Quran and the Sunnah.

Ijma', or consensus, applies to a situation where no clear conclusion can be made from the Quran and the Sunnah. In this situation the representatives of the people who are knowledgeable and well-versed in the Quran and the Sunnah will sit together and work out an agreed formula to solve the particular problem. Ijma' developed during the period of al-Khilafatur Rashidin.

Qiyas means a reference or analogy of a comparison of one thing with a similar one. It is applied in circumstances where guidance from the Quran and the Sunnah is not directly available. A solution to a problem is reached by a process of deduction from a comparison with a similar situation in the past.

Islam and Tradition

Sunnah : The word Sunnah means a system, a path or an example. In Islam it refers to the practice of the Prophet, his life example. It is embodied in the Ahadith (plural of Hadith) which are the Prophet's sayings, actions and the actions done with his approval. Ahadith have been very carefully collected and compiled since the death of the Prophet. Six collections of Hadith are regarded as the most authentic. They are:

1. Sahih al-Bukhari (Collected and compiled by Muhammad bin Ismail known as Imam Bukhari, born 194 AH, died 256 AH/870 CE).
2. Sahih Muslim (Muslim bin al-Hajjaj, known as Imam Muslim, born 202 AH, died 261 AH/875 CE).
3. Sunan Abu Daud (Sulaiman bin Ash 'ath, known as Abu Daud, born 202 AH, died 275 AH/888/CE).
4. Sunan ibn Majah (Abu 'Abdullah Muhammad bin Yazid al-Qazwint, known as Ibn Majah, born 209 AH, died 273 AH 886 CE).
5. Jami' al-Tirmidhi (Abu Isa Muhammad bin Isa al-Tirmidhi, date of birth not recorded, died 279 AH/892 CE).

6. Sunan an-Nasai (Abu 'Abdur Rahman Ahmad bin Shoaib an-Nasa'i, born 215 AH, died 303 AH/915 CE).

In addition to this, the Muwatta' of Imam Malik (born 93 AH, died 179 AH), Musnad of Ahmad bin Hanbal (born 164 AH, died 241 AH/855 CE) and Mishkat al-Masabih of Abu Muhammad al-Hussain bin Masud (died 516 AH) are also well known. There are many more collections and commentaries.

Fiqh : Fiqh is the science of Islamic law or jurisprudence. It refers to the explanation, collection and compilation of Islamic laws based on the Quran and the Sunnah of the Prophet. The word Fiqh means knowledge and understanding.

The scholars of Islamic Law have made Shariat easier to understand and practise by the science of Fiqh. A person who has a detailed knowledge and understanding of Fiqh is called a Faqih. A person qualified to give a ruling on issues in Shariat is called a Mufti. The ruling he gives is called a fatwa (pifatawa):

Some great Muslims devoted themselves to the task of developing the science of understanding Islamic law and its practice. The four best known compilers and interpreters of Islamic law or Shariat are:

1. Abu Hanifah Numan bin Thabit, known as Imam Abu Hanifah (born 80 AH, died 150 AH/161 CE).
2. Malik bin Anas, known as Imam Malik (93-179 AH/ 795 CE).
3. Muhammad bin Idris ash-Shafi known as Imam Shafii (150-240 AH/ 820 CE).
4. Ahmad bin Hanbal, known as Imam Ibn Hanbal (164-241 AH/855 CE). Islamic law divides human activities into:

   (1) Fard or Wajib (duty or obligatory) – performance of these actions is rewarded and their omission is punished.

(2) Mandoob (recommended) – actions the performance of which is rewarded but omission of which is not punished.

(3) Mubah (silent) – actions permitted by silence.

(4) Makrah (disliked or reprehensible) – actions disapproved of but not punishable.

(5) Haram (forbidden) – actions punishable by law.

Islamic Law or Shariat embodies the ideal Islamic life. Islam is the complete way of life and Shariat is the means to arrive at the ideal life recommended by Islam. Shariat enables us to bring our life in line with the will of Allah. It is the means of achieving our goal of life.

2

Islam's Ideology

Ever since the human being has attained consciousness, moral sensibility and knowledge, a deep struggle has been going on in the human society between the forces of good and evil, knowledge and ignorance, progress and retrogression, equity and oppression, collective good and monopoly. Even in today's world this struggle is in evidence; in fact it has never abated during the whole course of human history, and will continue till such time as a just world order comes into being, through the persistent efforts of world revolutionary movements.

Prophet Muhammad (Peace be upon him) was the first person in known history who initiated a world revolution, under the banner of Islam, that stood for progress of mankind in every field of human activity, and laid down eternal principles of revolution. He established the rule that a revolution of the right kind is the prime stimulator and basic source of human development. All later revolutionary movements which helped mankind move forward have invariably followed these principles. Thus there exists a common tie between the Islamic Revolutionary Movement of Prophet Muhammad (Peace be upon him), the movements for the spread of knowledge that followed his era, and other revolutionary movements of the twentieth century that stand for progress of mankind and peace among nations. A great deal of the good we observe in the social, economic, political, cultural and spiritual advancements of the modern age is a reflection of the teachings of the Prophet. Therefore, to fight against the retrogressive and monopolist forces working against the vital interests of mankind, and to build a progressive and welfare society on the basis of the principles formulated by the Prophet with the active cooperation of the revolutionary forces of our times, is the need of the hour.

It is the common practice of the forces of monopoly and aggression to create confusion and diversion in one's mind regarding the revolutionary character of the forces of progressive change. Hence, among other things, persistent attempts continue to be made by these forces to veil the true nature of the revolutionary leadership of Prophet Muhammad (Peace be upon him). Continuous efforts are being made by the Capitalist West to deprive Islam of its revolutionary content by depicting it as a set of religious dogmas having no direct bearing upon life on this earth and its diverse problems.

The human mind is kept involved in seeking false satisfaction about the distant future of the humans (in the heavens!). Men and women are prevented from giving due importance to the world into which they are born and from participating fully in the literary, scientific and technological research so necessary for human development. The people are thus prevented from putting in their energies rightly to the building up of a society free from hunger and disease, ignorance and vice, injustice and oppression; a society in which every person could wish the others well, and work for their betterment.

Persistent attempts are also being made by the protagonists of the capitalist way of life to create misunderstandings about the revolutionary and progressive forces currently at work in the world arena. These wily attempts, spread over centuries, have brought about deprivation amongst the Muslim nations of the real intent of Islam, viz., social, economic and cultural revolution directed against the existent unjust and overbearing capitalist social orders, and have turned a number of Muslim countries into mere camp-followers and interest-servers of imperialism. The greatest tragedy that has befallen the *Muslim Ummah* is that the status of Prophet Muhammad (Peace be upon him) has been lowered and damaged to a great extent at the hands of the Muslims themselves. Very few of the Muslims look up to him on the individual as well as the national and universal level for seeking guidance in fighting the forces of destruction (according to Islamic terminology 'satanic forces') and bringing about the just world order envisaged in his teachings whereby exploitation of man by man ceases altogether.

In order, therefore, to put things in the right perspective it has now become imperative to restore the personality of Prophet Muhammad (Peace be upon him) to its true stature and grandeur in the eyes of the Muslims as well as the rest of mankind as the greatest educator and revolutionary, and the real impact of his guidance made to be felt in the reshaping of the human society of our times. In order to do so the one thing that has to be clearly understood is that the basic purpose of the Prophet's teachings is the creation of a suitable personality in the human being (through his/her own efforts as well as with the assistance of the society and the state) that can bear the burden of revolutionary action which is necessarily required to defeat the forces of reaction, and to build up a progressive Collective Order.

Prophet Muhammad (Peace be upon him) demonstrated this by his personal example. He trained a vast number of revolutionaries, and created a revolutionary group of the highest order, dedicated to the task of removing ignorance and inequity from the social structure in which he was born as well as from the world around him, of producing leaders in every sphere of life and of organizing the society and the state; thus opening the way to peace, progress and prosperity in the world. He laid down the rules of the game for creating goodwill, affectionate devotion, etiquettes, discipline, order and fruitfulness in human life, and gave firm guidelines for advancement in all spheres of human existence.

Types of Rules

For this purpose Prophet Muhammad (Peace be upon him) gave two sets of rules. The one set of rules pertains to the ideological upbringing of an individual, and includes the principle of divine worship. It enables a person to establish close relationship (in thought and action) with Allah – the Creator of the Universe and what it contains, the Sustainer of life therein, and the guiding force behind all historical events. It makes the individual intelligently aware of the fact that Allah is as good an entity as are the sun, the moon, the stars, the planets, the space, the earth, the oceans and the gravitational and other scientific truths about the universe except that He cannot be conceived; that the Laws of Nature cannot be circumvented, they can only be discovered and understood for bettering human life. Recognition of this truth, in its essence, establishes the full accountability of an individual towards the fellow-beings for all the actions in one's life. It thus relieves one of contradictory behaviour in words and actions. It provides the individual with a right purpose and the right goal and direction, and helps to improve one's knowledge, wisdom and strength of character, thus enabling one to play an active part in the reshaping of the society in which one lives.

The other set of rules pertains to the collective responsibilities of an individual – social, economic, political – which are equally binding. Being accountable before Allah in effect amounts to accountability towards the human society. Thus what Islam envisages is a balanced personality – upright, courageous, enduring, pleasant, helpful, loving, generous, truthful, knowing, intelligent and modest – capable of replacing any corrupt social structure that may be inherited by it, and of giving the supreme sacrifice by offering one's life in this process.

Thus it must be noted that all the instructions given by Prophet Muhammad (Peace be upon him) to the individual regarding divine worship are a part and parcel of the socio-economic and politico-cultural system brought about by him; one cannot exist without the other. Therefore, it has been made very clear in his sayings that any act of worship to the exclusion of genuine efforts for acquisition of knowledge and performance of Jihad (revolutionary thought and action) and other collective duties enjoined by Islam, is not acceptable to Allah (and of course to the human society as well!).

In other words, one's all acts of worship are a farce, and amount to hypocrisy and self-deception, if a person is not actively and sincerely engaged in a life-and-death struggle against the forces of monopoly and retrogression with the intention of setting up a just order in one's society, and contributing to the establishment of a world-order wherein exploitation of man by man is stopped and the final goal of bringing out and fostering all the best qualities inherent in man is achieved. All individual actions must be oriented to the furtherance of the collective cause and the common good otherwise all acts, however pious in appearance, are useless and inconsequential, rather harmful to the society.

Another relevant aspect which needs consideration is that although moral codes and ethical behaviour (if properly harnessed) are powerful factors in the spiritual unification of a society, and tend to elevate human society to a higher level, yet they could not be accomplished, nor could they play an effective role, unless a just socio-economic infrastructure exists in that society. Such is the Prophet's teaching. It must be fully understood that the real hindrance in the way of establishing such an infrastructure is the social injustice, characteristic of the feudal and capitalist systems which have come to the surface of our social life in the form of polarisation of wealth and the plundering of the productive capacity of the individual which has created demoralization on a mass scale. In order to counter this factor, a just economic order will have to be evolved through competent application of the basic principles of Islam and their useful blending with the principles developed and introduced by the scientific and technological revolution of our time, and the life- experience of the modern age.

Such an order can help in bring about the well being and happiness of the individual by affording him self-respect and equal status in society, developing his self-awareness and sense of duty, creating a healthy society of mindful individuals and establishing a lasting peace on earth. However, in order to benefit from scientific knowledge the moral maturity of an individual is a prerequisite. In other words, one must fully understand that duty must predominate over personal interests and inclinations; that good must be preferred to gain, and truth to expediency; that justice must be understood as the meaning and basis of human existence. The basic theme of social justice cannot be fully perceived by man if morality and ethics have not become a part of his consciousness.

With the passage of time deterioration and corruption tend to creep into the various institutions established by the Prophets (the greatest men of their times) or their followers. Hence, the need arises for effecting a change in the existing state of every period of history, and for initiating refreshing development of thought. The specific term used in the Islamic literature for such development is *Ijtihad,* not through the religious elite but through the collective Will of the people viz., the legislature. Now, *Ijtihad,* to be effective, can only rest upon the basic principles of life laid down by the Prophets during the course of history, and finally by Prophet Muhammad (Peace be upon him) in the light of the Holy Quran. We find these principles clearly stated in the sayings of the Prophet. We can surely define the future path for ourselves on the basis of these principles, coupled with those set in the Holy Quran, provided we are honest in our intentions, have no underpinnings, and have the will to fundamentally alter our environment and the present system of life through a revolutionary struggle. But what do we see actually? Has this vital principle of *Ijtihad* been taken seriously by the Muslim leaders, and have they applied these principles towards the development of a true and genuine socio-economic structure for the Muslim society?

In the light of what has been said above let us examine the thinking underlying a few of our institutions and concepts. First, let us examine the institution of prayer. Prayer is of two kinds.

The first kind one performs in remembrance of Allah – the Creator and Sustainer of the universe – while doing the daily jobs, thanking and praising Him, reviving and tendering his allegiance to Him, and seeking His guidance and succour while treading (to the best of one's ability) His path in the service of mankind.

The second kind are congregational prayers which are performed collectively five times a day. The real objective of prayer is to become and remain a lifelong servant of Allah serving without prejudice, and unreservedly, His creation (the human being) irrespective of creed or colour. Performance of the prayers can achieve this objective only when the Islamic principles are the dominant and ruling force guiding the state machinery as well as the society, and the human environment is charged with the spirit of mutual assistance and goodwill, not antagonism and exploitation. The teachings of Prophet Muhammad (Peace be upon him) if rightly understood clearly bring out this truth. Fidelity is the first causality at the hands of a religious person who performs his prayer not knowing the true import of his duty towards Allah and His creation.

The real purpose behind the Prophet's teachings is to nurture such human beings as are conscious of their social responsibilities; not just to produce religious beings fond of, or engrossed in, the performance of religious rites but oblivious of their duty towards the society. The moral and ethical training imparted by the Prophets is solely for the purpose of enabling a person to be useful to the collective being— the society. If an individual is not fulfilling these obligations all his professions of belief in Islam is a nullity and a mockery which should not go unchallenged. If he has to call himself a Muslim he must fully participate in the collective struggle to dismantle the unjust, monopolistic and outmoded social structure in which he is being forced to live by the wicked dominant forces of exploitation. If a person is not carrying out these essential obligations, he/she is not worthy of being called a Muslim.

Also let us examine the concept of "Islamic world" (prevalent amongst the Muslims generally, and exploited by the rulers of the Muslim and western countries particularly) meaning thereby the collective entity of nations constituting born Muslims. The Holy Quran presents Prophet Muhammad (Peace be upon him) not as a leader of the Muslim community alone that adhered to his call in his lifetime, or their descendents, but also as the leader of the whole human race, for all times to come. His clarion call "There is no deity except one Allah" (meaning thereby that all men are equal in status not subservient to one another, obeying one Allah) is addressed to all human beings, whether of the Prophet's time or of the times to come, till eternity. Whosoever accepts this call (which is couched in the simplest of words and bears manifest meaning) with his head and heart, whether born in a Muslim or a non-Muslim family and whether or not able to observe the formalities of the religious order inherited from the past by the Muslims of today, is in fact a true Muslim— a person with a purpose in life and an objective to achieve: that of creating a society of free individuals, a society without coercion and bloodshed, a society dedicated to bringing about peace, plenty and happiness for all humanity. Obviously, this cannot be achieved without outright rejection of the existing interest-based capitalist system of life which is a product of self-interest, inequity and oppression leading to the benefit of a few and bereavement of the many. It is, therefore, high time that the Muslims of today come out of their narrow concept of the so-called "Islamic World" and uphold the universal human concept of the "World Order" put forth by Prophet Muhammad (Peace be upon him) through the principles established and examples set by him.

Then there is the institution of the "wealthy elite" which has firmly dug itself into the degenerate Muslim social structure. Islam does not allow the wealthy elite to come into existence and grow at the expense of the lower sections of society. A reasonable difference in the incomes and private properties of different individuals is allowed in Islam provided it is commensurate with their working capabilities and intellectual capacities brought into play through their conscious and meritorious efforts.

Good in General

One of the important teachings of Prophet Muhammad (Peace be upon him) relating to social behaviour, passed on to us, is that whatever is left over from out of our resources and earnings after meeting the essential demands of daily living, and family requirements, should be spent for the common good. The lesson vividly imparted is that one should live a simple life, spend as little as possible on his own bare necessities and donate the rest for the collective benefit, considering the society as its rightful owner. So long as there is need and hunger, illiteracy and ignorance, deprivation and disease among the masses in a society, the spending on personal comforts and luxuries by the few is not only undesirable but also condemnable. Whoever indulges in pompous living should be neither revered nor envied, howsoever distinguished he may be and whatsoever respectful appearance he may wear. There should be equal opportunities for everyone to benefit from a country's resources, which necessarily results in equality of status in society for all persons comprising it, whether born as Muslims or otherwise. "Equality of status" is the *sine qua non* for a civilized society.

Then, let us examine the concept (or misconception shall we say) under which the intellectuals in general seem to be labouring. They believe that one should not dilate upon Islam's social order or any other aspect "without a thorough and comprehensive grasp of the Quranic and Hadith literature." They do not seem to realize that in that case an authority will have to be constituted whose certificate shall be essential for anyone to ponder upon and write about the Islamic ideology. The fact of the matter, however, is that one does not need to be an *'alim fazil'* (well-learned) to understand and tread the path of Islam! Whosoever (whether learned or otherwise) has a deep desire to know the truth about the universe, its Creator and Sustainer, and his or her personal role in life, will certainly be in a position to grasp it. The truth about everything pivotal in our lives has been clearly explained in the Quran. It is one's unhealthy desire to grab wealth and power to rule over others that keeps one afar from the Truth.

The notion, as in other fields of study, that there are certain specialists in the field of Islamic ideology (the so-called' *'Ulama')* whose rulings must be accepted unreluctantly by the ordinary Muslims, is a totally false premise; it has been invented by the Muslim despots and kings who replaced the *Khilafat-e-Rashida,* in order to safeguard their undemocratic existence and their wrongly acquired vested interests with the help and cooperation of the "religious elite". They had, therefore, relegated to themselves the right to declare whether or not any person had legitimately acquired a thorough and comprehensive grasp of the Quranic and Hadith literature. They thus created a new class of religious elite (which did not exist at all in the Islamic era) to support their un-Islamic decrees and keep the masses ignorant about the real intent of the Islamic teachings.

The truth regarding Islam is within the reach of every human being. That is why all persons are held responsible before Almighty Allah for their actions in life. The simple requirement in the days of Prophet Muhammad (Peace be upon him) was to accept the ideology put forward by him and become his companion-in-arms; in the later periods of history the requirement was to accept and follow the teachings of the Holy Quran and to seek additional guidance from the sayings of Prophet Muhammad (Peace be upon him).

The principles of Islam, as laid down in the Quran and Sunnah, are the real bases upon which human society can be built successfully. We may venture to emphatically say that all human progress really made anywhere in the world has been made on the basis of the Islamic principles. We cannot possibly deviate from the laws of nature in our life activity; to achieve success we have to discover these laws and follow them truthfully.

Thus it is imperative that we study the progress made by the developed countries in the various fields of life, in addition to studying the Islamic principles as laid down in the Quran and Sunnah, and correlate them in order to chart the future course of our social existence. Our fundamental duty as human beings, more so as Muslims, is to build the human society in such a manner as would abolish exploitation of man by man, and afford an opportunity to all human beings not only to live in peace and plenty but also to bring out and develop to the optimum level the capabilities inherent in man, on the lines determined by the laws of nature. All the directives given by Allah and His Prophets are with a view to enable man to perform this primary and all-important duty.

Truth and its Search

Life is a process of unfolding the truth, of knowing the laws of nature, and building a collective society of conscious individuals engaged in developing moral culture and high ethical consciousness based on true understanding of these laws. Such conscious living (or 'active morality' as we may call it) sets before itself the immediate task of obliterating injustice, evil and suffering. As opposed to this a passive contemplative morality, such as is current in the capitalist west and in many Muslim countries of today, makes peace with the existing evil.

Knowledge, therefore, is the chief media for consolidating morality, for moral consciousness begins with knowledge. Self awareness— both of the individual and of society — determines the development of morality. Knowledge brings out the truth which forms the basis of morality; it expands the perimeter of morality and consequently the range of conscious choice; it engenders decisiveness and consolidates will; it clarifies the real opportunities of progress and dismisses imaginary possibilities; it dispels Utopian aspirations and brings forth more realistic perspectives.

Knowledge, merged with moral strength (conscience, will, endurance, etc.), is of itself not goal-oriented. Without the right goal-orientation an individual possessed of even the highest principles and the best intentions, will be incapable of acting morally in difficult situations. It is, therefore, essential to choose real ideals and to find the real means to implement them. Knowledge (or in the modern terminology 'scientific approach') alone clarifies the reality of ideals and assists in searching the real means of achieving them.

One's moral intent, however, becomes real only when something is done for the better; intentions attain material shape only as a result of the social activities one completes. The personality is moulded as a result of the assimilation of experience of social life and consequently of knowledge. Mere reliance upon feelings (in disregard of reason) is catastrophic both for the individual and the society. Knowledge accrues from successful answers to questions such as: What events are taking place in the world? What is the meaning of these events? What is the meaning of our life activities? How are intentions and actions to be correlated? What are our social obligations? In order to apprehend these inquiries factual knowledge and true understanding is required, for which a scientific and knowledgeable approach to problems is necessary. The primary task, therefore, is education of the people with regard to the answers to these questions, because scientific knowledge emerges from the activities of the people engaged in serious efforts to ascertain the truth.

Faith based upon knowledge thus gives an individual the right direction. It develops in him/her a true conscience which persistently strives towards understanding of, and uncompromising respect for, the truth. Reason makes a person human. Assertion of blind faith in disregard of reason, on the other hand, leads a man to irrationalism and consequently to fascism; it converts the peoples into a flock which a wily shepherd (the power that rules) may lead into any convenient direction that suits it. It is precisely on account of these imperatives of life that Prophet Muhammad (Peace be upon him) has attributed overall importance to the seeking of knowledge from anywhere and everywhere.

Man is surely capable of altering his circumstances because of the creative abilities possessed by him as a gift of Nature. Cognition of the laws of nature, and conscious struggle by the individual against a social order in which one's life is in the power of others, engenders in him strength of character, respect for the human personality, a sense of responsibility (accountability) toward the society which sustains him/her, and recognition of the material needs of the individual for self-development. It is as a result of such conscious activity that man creates a new socio-economic order, and effects cultural and spiritual advancement, in every period of history.

The conscious action of Prophet Muhammad (Peace be upon him) flowing from true cognition of the Truth thus did alter the circumstances completely. Any similar activity by the individuals on a collective basis in the later stages of human development will certainly bring about alterations in their circumstances and fetch them freedom from the ruling power of the retrogressive forces. Such is the unalterable law of nature. The present-day riotous world will certainly be replaced, one day, with a world of serenity by the 'ethical man' with the help of a highly developed world-economy to an extent that would completely relieve man of unproductive labour, and useless preoccupations. True justification of the creation of the human being will then be fully and finally established. The sayings of the Prophet bear ample evidence to what has been said above.

Politics is the tool with which an agreeable shape is given to the environment of a society. Politics is the means of creating consciousness among the mass of the people and of developing the individuals in a society into creative personalities. The policies of a truly democratic government are directly concerned with creating conditions in which each individual may become a 'political being' very much concerned with the betterment and free development of all the people around him, since his/her own betterment depends on theirs.

Such a government creates unity of interest between the society and the individual by persuading the people of the rightness and the just base of its policies. It enlists conscious participation of the broadest sections of the population in the social movement for the building up of the society and the management of the state. A successful government is possible only with the active participation of the masses, that is, by bringing mass conceptions regarding goals in line with the true social objectives. A state is strong only when the people are politically conscious, that is, they know everything, can form an opinion of everything, and can do everything conscientiously. It would of course be a statement of fact to say that the people are the moving force of history.

In our modern world, where scientific and industrial development is an important landmark of history, the working class (with the help of such individuals and intellectuals from the middle and upper classes who have de-classed themselves consciously) forms the spearhead of the movement for freeing the individual conscience from the rulership of the oppressive forces, which are always at work in a society. It encompasses all those persons who contribute to the building up of a society through their physical and mental labour, and who belong to the lower and middle strata of society.

It also applies specifically to factory labour which is a product of the industrial revolution. It is the most effective of all social strata and the chief builder of a country's economy. While freeing itself, it simultaneously frees all oppressed peoples and the society as a whole, and directly contributes to the establishment of a just social order. Thus the struggle of the working people for changing the prevalent social order is tantamount to a struggle for freedom and justice; a striving against ignorance, vice and oppression. The real bearing of the teachings of Prophet Muhammad (Peace be upon him) in this respect have not been fully conveyed by the later historians. The life example of the Prophet, i.e., the revolutionary process he initiated and the methods he adopted to complete the Islamic revolution, bear ample proof of this fact of history. All revolutionary movements of the present era shall have to take cognizance of this fact of life, and the removal of injustice from the social structure in all its forms (including deprivation of workmen) must form the basis of all social movements of the Muslim World.

The raising of the standard of living of the working people by removing the handicaps imposed upon them by the vested interests of the wealthy elite should be the prime concern of all civilized nations. The upper class in a degenerate society tends to oppress and exploit the lower sections by creating vested interests for themselves. The Islamic concept of life requires the "common people" to prevent the "upper classes" from doing what is objectionable, by working for the establishment of a just social order. This is clearly reflected in this saying of Prophet Muhammad (Peace be upon him).

> "Allah most high does not punish the common people for what the upper classes do till they see what is objectionable being done publicly among them and do not forbid it though they are able to do so. When they act thus Allah will punish both the common people and the upper classes."
>
> *(Book XXIV ch.* 22 - *Mishkat Al Masabih)*

Now, to organize and energies the working people (the mass of the people) into an effective and constructive force conscious of its role of changing the unjust socio-economic structures in various countries, equipped with knowledge, understanding and strength of character, and capable of running the various institutions of the state effectively, is a gigantic task. This tremendous task cannot be achieved without a capable and dependable leadership whose words and actions are not at variance. Such a leadership, as is required for performance of the profound task ahead, can be nurtured only along the lines drawn by Prophet Muhammad (Peace be upon him).

It could be said in the final analysis that the removal of

miseries of life (ignorance, disease, hunger, injustice and oppression), promotion of economic well-being of man, and his moral and spiritual elation, through due performance of his social responsibilities, development of his political consciousness, and sound organisation of society, are the purpose and mainstay of human existence. Any firm advancement in these fields can be achieved only if serious attempts are made to raise healthy and strong leadership (answerable to the people) at all levels of the social structure. True guidance, in all its fullness, for building the edifice of such leadership is contained in the Quran and the teachings and life-example of Prophet Muhammad (Peace be upon him).

Mankind's Unity

A Message of Love and Hope : The need of our epoch is to produce individuals who could join hands to organize public life in a manner as would bring about peace and social order for humanity.

What is really needed is to restyle the worn-out life-systems and to establish classless societies all over the world, free from exploitation by the vested interests of the ordinary people. Hunger, poverty, disease, ignorance, backwardness and oppression must be eliminated and peace and tranquillity, helpful cooperation, social integration and scientific and technological advancement brought about in its place, by the people themselves.

To achieve all this we will have to approach life in a dispassionate, positive and pragmatic manner so that the talents inherent in human nature are developed to the optimum level, and the importance of human dignity is established. In the words of Robert Mugabe, Prime Minister of Zimbabwe: "We should respect all human beings whatever their race or colour. Nothing is more important than human life and dignity. We should exert to establish a free society in which people of all shades of opinion, regardless of their colour or race or creed, should be able to participate in social, economic and political life at an equal level."

The cultural, scientific and technological development of the individual, the socio-economic advancement of the society and establishment of world peace (peace between man and man) can be achieved only if the management of human affairs (local and state management) is in the hands of conscientious, hard-working and developed personalities who could play the leaders' role effectively. It must be clearly understood that the removal of miseries of life, i.e. ignorance, disease, hunger, injustice and oppression, promotion of economic well-being of human beings and their moral and spiritual elation, due performance by them of their social obligations, development of their political consciousness and sound organization of society are the purpose and mainstay of human existence. Any advancement in these fields can only be achieved if serious attempts are made to raise sound leadership fully answerable to the people, at all levels of the social structure.

The social structures of the present-day human societies of the world are stuck up in the mire of ignorance, retrogression, greed and exploitation of the masses by the vested interests. Therefore only a pragmatic approach to these problems can extricate humanity from this sad situation.

Now, when we talk about the well-being of the human species (to which category we surely belong!) we will have to, first of all, consider the meaning, importance and purpose of life itself, clarify our perception of the universe and the world we live in, study world history and, in the light of this thought process, determine our respective roles in society. These roles should of course be of improving our standards of social, cultural, economic and political performances with the clear objective of nation-building, and simultaneously contributing to unity of human beings, and world peace.

There are many impediment, however, in the way of fulfilment of the triple objectives of nation-building, unity of human beings and world peace. It will do us good to spell out these impediment. These are: (1) Lack of faith in God, (2) lack of understanding of the Laws of Nature. (3) lack of life-purpose, (4) lack of sense of accountability for our actions which results from our non-belief in life-after-death. (5) religious intolerance, which results from lack of discernment between the different notions of "faith" and "religion" (6) non-participation in the political process for changing the prevalent class-based social system (7) the desire to amass wealth by foul means for personal grandeur and lack of will to spend for the collective good.

In order to arrive at an understanding about these impediment we will have to study them in some detail.

Faith in God and Life-purpose **:** God belongs to all human beings and is not exclusive for any religious group or a section of humanity. Love for God, in effect, means love for human beings, that is, serving one another. This concept leads to a radical change in a human being, and in the society, a totally new approach to life and a new and better life style.

Such belief gives a deeper understanding of life, and brings integration, wholeness and purpose to it. If we truly love God (our Creator and Sustainer) then we will surely love each other because God dwells in each one of us. He is directly accessible to us. He is real, alive and near, guiding and comforting those who look up to Him for help. God transforms one inwardly by a complete change of heart and mind. But, for this to happen we have to approach Him for guidance in all sincerity and total honesty, just as we are, with all our faults, our intellectual doubts and concerns; He does not want a sham. Thus faith in God does move mountains. God says to us "Go forth in my strength and I will be with you". One thing is certain: when we truly take God at His word He abundantly invokes happiness on us.

The Torah, the Bible and the Gita all these Books impart the same concept of "Oneness of God" as the Quran. They present similar teachings and guide us to the same "way of life" as the Quran. The basic idea underlying the teachings of these Holy Books is that all human beings are essentially "adherents of the same faith". Thus to quote Dennis Wrigley from his book "One Lord One People", "Faith is a gift from God, equally for all human beings.

Our good works are the sign of our faith in God because faith, if it has not worked accompanying it, is dead. Walking in faith changes our approach to decision making. It leads us to associate directly with the poor, the downtrodden and the oppressed, and to prepare them mentally and physically for a better life and to work in the way of God. To the hopeless, the recognition that God has a purpose for them and they are precious in His sight, and the full knowledge that to God nothing is impossible, generates hope and confidence, and is a great turning point in their lives.

Such recognition brings men and women to full maturity by increasing their self-respect, discovering for them a new worth and a new purpose in their personal lives, changing their ways and enabling them to tread new paths and, above all, facilitating them to recognize that God knows everything about them and hence they should develop and repose full trust in Him. Thus they grow in faith and in knowledge of God and His ways of doing things and bringing about change in the world society. In a thousand different ways today, and on a global scale, God seems to be calling His people to change their ways, to take new initiatives, to explore new ways, to take risks and to see new and often bewildering horizons. A new experience of the reality of God's presence in our lives in whatever we are doing inevitably generates vitality and creativity; we come to see the way to peace and reconciliation in a divided world, and understand the root causes of aggression and alienation. Of course we do not fully understand what God is doing but the evidence of His presence is undeniable."

> Such awareness of God's presence in our lives can be experienced by us only when we develop in ourselves oneness with the hungry and the poor, the exploited and the oppressed, and be sensitive to their needs and feelings, when we experience the freshness and simplicity of love for them and a real sense of belonging to them, when we struggle on their side against the exploiting classes of *Jagirdars, Sardars,* big absentee-landlords, the filthy rich and the religious elite, against autocratic and demonic rulers and authorities, against cosmic world powers and against spiritual forces of evil. We cannot comprehend God without facing these challenges. God calls upon us to live dangerously. That is why Jesus proclaims:" I have come to set the world ablaze." *(Luke 12,49)*

Laws of Nature : It becomes evident from what has been said and explained above that the physical identities of the universe and the world have come into being and coexist under firm laws of nature that monitor their working. Among these are the law of gravity, the law of causation, the law of energy, the law of rise and fall of nations, the law of accountability, the law of spiritual development (development of human personality), etc. All these laws work simultaneously on the individual, national and universal levels.

The development of human culture and civilization depends on true understanding of these laws and their rightful application to human affairs. Such an understanding leads to the development of a mature personality which can contribute effectively to the social, economic and political advancement of human society, and to world peace.

The Accountability : Accountability of one's action in the various fields of life (individual as well as collective) on the national as well as international level is the main axis around which hinges the balance of human relations and social progress. Minus this, there is confusion, mistrust, disturbance and wars. This principle of accountability in this world actually flows from the Divine law of accountability in the next world. The more resolutely one believes in the hereafter, the more sense of accountability one develops.

As stated by Dennis Wrigley in his book, "The magnitude of destructive forces at work in the world today are enormous. The multi-billion Mafia organization operates on a global scale corrupting, degrading and killing. The sinister drug trade is now an international business in its own right, wrecking lives and bringing degradation and destruction in an unprecedented scale. Pornography has mushroomed into a multi-million business. Added to this the world powers continue to spend huge sums on arms, when millions go short of the basic necessities of life. Children and young people are immersed in violence and vulgarity." These dreadful happenings can only be checked by an elaborate and autonomous system of accountability at state level, and a deep sense of accountability in the hereafter at the individual plane.

Religious Intolerance : Religious intolerance is one of the important factors responsible for human suffering. It has a long history but the crux of it is that it is a necessary resultant of lack of comprehension among people regarding the disparity between "faith" and "religion". To quote again from Dennis Wrigley's book "So many dubious dogmatic assertions have been put forward in the name of religion; each sect or cult insists on allegiance to its claims, to the total exclusion of all others. Hence there has been a tendency for many people to conclude that they cannot be certain about anything. The frozen habits of the past prevent us from responding freely to the demands of God today. Envy prevents from genuinely loving other people, bitterness prevents from being open with other people, intolerance prevents from accepting new truths and ideas from whatever source. Instead of healthy criticism of ideas there is bitterness and despair. Religious people would resist God's mission. They would retain the outward conventions of religion but they will consistently deny its dynamic. Their modes of worship do not express the vitality of our relationship with a living God". That is why Jesus strikes out against religious hypocrisy and bigotry.

A way, therefore, must be found out to extricate ourselves from this unhappy situation. This way is to reject man-made religions and the hegemony of the religious elite and accept "faith in God and service to humanity" as the aim of life, and work on an equal footing with all human beings to shed intolerance and bring about peace, progress and prosperity in human life. A "religious institution" can justify its existence today only by contributing to unity among human beings, irrespective of caste, colour or creed, on the basis of "faith in God and service to humanity", not by working insidiously for disunity and enmity among God's people on the basis of religious differences cooked up in their interest by the religious elite.

Political Process : Political process is an instrument of change. A conscious participation in the political process of one's country is essential for changing the social structure of a society based on exploitation, oppression and injustice. The right to make laws in the interest of the dispossessed must be exercised by the majority of the people themselves and not by the vested interests of the upper class. The democratic principles must be adopted in their entirety in the various fields of life in order to build a healthy social order. This is God's Will which we dare not flout. Let us work for it sincerely and in a down-to-earth manner. For this purpose we shall have to bring together those who believe in God in the true sense, who are educated and who possess goodwill in the society, and work on a collective basis to promote awareness among the masses belonging to all religious or non-religious groups, and to spread the message of Faith, Hope and Love.

Amassing Wealth : Now, if we have to embark upon this noble mission, we shall have to pool our resources and cultivate the habit of spending (not amassing) wealth. We will have to sense the spirit of God which is alive within ourselves, amongst us and around us, and work for the fulfillment of His paramount wish of bringing out fully, through mutual cooperation, the inherent qualities endowed to the human being by Him and, on their basis, to build a world of peace and plenty in which every individual could live in dignity, as equals. All human beings are entitled to a decent living as their birth-right. Hence those who acquire wealth beyond their reasonable needs are duty bound, according to God's desire, to spend their excess wealth on the building up of their respective societies to a level where each individual could acquire the basic necessities of life, and a standard of living indicative of a civilized society.

In view of what has been said above to stand up against the oppressor (whosoever) or the oppressor classes (whichsoever) and side with the oppressed individuals or the oppressed classes (in whatever form or manner) is the end and all of faith in God, and to unite all human beings on the basis of faith in "One God" should be the end purpose of our lives.

3

Basic Philosophy

Belief in Islam

Distinction between Faith and Religion : The cultural progress of the Muslim Ummah has become marred because the distinction between the two different concepts of faith and religion have not been clearly understood. It is an established fact that the cultural harmony and solidarity of a nation is a necessary factor in the economic progress of that nation.

This cultural harmony is born out of a synthesis of cultures of the various parts of a nation that dwell in a particular geographical boundary. Hence while referring to a nation embodying a Muslim majority, the cultures of that particular nation or country will be called "Pakistani culture", "Iranian culture", "Arabian culture", "Afghani culture", "Malaysian culture", etc. Similarly for nations with a majority of non-Muslims this culture will be called "Indian culture", "Chinese culture", "Japanese culture", "Srilankan culture", etc. It would be wrong, while referring to the culture of any country, to term it as "Islamic culture" or "non-Islamic culture".

If, however, the foundation of a culture is based upon freedom, equality and the assurance of equal economic opportunities for all human beings, then a pleasant synthesis can be achieved between the existing Muslim majority and non-Muslim majority nations and this can lead to the rise of a "universal culture" that can lead man to the highest stages of progress. By "human freedom" we mean freedom from all kinds of restrictions on a human being's thought process and decision making. By "human equality" is meant equal rights and equal social status for all human beings. "Economic guarantees" mean that the state is responsible for providing basic human needs to all citizens.

These three requirements are in reality the basic values of 'faith' viz., belief in God and human brotherhood. The various religious, linguistic and ethnic groups residing in a country are actually parts of the same nation, and they possess similar rights. Different nations comprising such groups would be able to form a larger human group on the basis of human brotherhood that could work for human progress through mutual participation.

This can only happen if we put into practice the basic and common lessons of faith taught by the messengers of God. If we are to form a human fraternity on the basis of cultural integration and harmony in the coming eras, this can only be done by adopting the "faith of the Prophets" *(deen-e-ambiyaa)* not by involving ourselves in religious altercations.

The feuds and disorders that have been created in the world throughout history in the name of religion and which continue even today, and on account of which discrimination is practised in the fulfilment of basic rights of various human groups, have resulted from non-comprehension of the real meanings of the different concepts of 'faith' and 'religion'. Unless we clearly distinguish between these two concepts and make it a part of mass consciousness on the one hand, and accept the principle of religious tolerance with regard to the tenets of different religions on the other hand, it will not be possible to bring about affinity between the developed western nations and the underdeveloped and developing eastern nations on the basis of higher emotions of human fraternity. The branding of the Muslim nations as "fundamentalists" by U.S.A. and other western countries will continue with all its implications until the distinction between faith and religion is clearly made and acknowledged on a universal level.

Faith *(deen)* means "the way of life". By "faith of the Prophets" is meant the mode of life concerning which all the Prophets of God have formulated uniform principles, and which caters for the spiritual progress of humankind alongwith its economic progress. On the contrary, religion means the system consisting of specific beliefs and rituals tailored by some of the followers of different Prophets which are based upon metaphysical and supernatural concepts and modes of worship and which do not provide correct guidance regarding the issues faced in practical life.

We have, therefore, to acknowledge fully that the terms "religion" *(mazhab)* does not convey the true interpretation of the 'faith' that has been taught by the Prophets. This term is the source of discord and strife between the East and the West, and the matrix of countless religious sects. We may use the word "religion" to perceive the various distorted forms of the original faith, and to describe them, but it will be incorrect to use it as synonymous with the word "faith" or as its alternative.

When we think on these lines it becomes evident that to call people towards Islam is in reality to summon them to the basic teachings of all the Prophets, and to affirm that the peoples and the nations of the world can be united only on the basis of "the faith of the Prophets". On this foundation alone a viable system can be built bringing about cultural harmony among human beings and by setting up a society founded upon economic and social justice. At this point it should be clearly borne in mind that true Islam is not the traditional religion based on *fiqah-e-mulukiat* (laws caused to be made by the Muslim kings) which is presented by the sectarian religious leaders.

The faith presented by all the Prophets is called the faith of the Prophets, or Islam. Islam means believing in God and performing good deeds in the service of humankind. Thus invitation towards Islam means inviting all the peoples of the world, irrespective of race, language or religion, to believe in God and to do good deeds while being obedient to Him.

Belief in God means to accept God as the Creator, Owner, Sovereign and Nourisher of the whole universe and, alongwith it, to organize the structure of human life in accordance with the laws of nature which have been made by Him, and to develop a sense of an all-time accountability before Him not only in one's dealings with others but also on account of the misuse by him of material resources and intellectual capabilities granted by God. This, in fact, is the call of all the Prophets.

Almighty and Faith

All the Prophets of God, who had been deputed in all parts of the world in the various periods of history, had actually solicited and counselled mankind to believe in God and to love and fraternize with other human beings. But the privileged sections of the societies of all ages, in possession of wealth and power, had opposed the Prophets to the extent of waging war against them. It so happened that a little after the departure of the Prophets (Peace be upon them) certain self-seeking people entered the ranks of their followers and altered the essential teachings of the 'faith' preached by them and converted it into 'religions'.

They fabricated their own religious rituals and customs and made the people follow them and neglected and ignored the essential requisites of belief in God. This practice was to some extent on account of lack of foresight on the part of the people in general but chiefly because of the vested interests of particular groups. Hence the different forms of religions existing today have been shaped by the people of different ages themselves; these have not been ordained by God. Another clear difference that exists between the faith brought by the Prophets and man-made religions is that while faith invites all human beings towards peace, unity and brotherhood, religions cause discord, hate and enmity among people. 'Faith' points out positive attitudes towards life; religions, on the other hand, spurn positive attitudes in human relations.

The basic point to be remembered concerning the call of the Prophets is that there is absolutely no compulsion for others to accept it. It is left entirely upon the free will of everyone to accept or to reject it. All the Prophets of God have always proclaimed that they simply invite people towards truth, counsel them, give glad tidings to those who believe in God and do good deeds, and warn people against disbelief and the consequences of bad deeds.

Beyond this they have no other responsibility, and they have not brought any new precepts different from those of the other Prophets. The basic message of all the Prophets is the same. i.e., to remind the people of the forgotten message of the Prophets of the past of explicit belief in God and complete submission to His Commands. Ignoring this very fact regarding the message of the Prophets has resulted in the emergence of sectarian religious groups among Muslims and adherents of other Prophets, and every sect has become an inveterate bloodthirsty foe of the other on account of minor differences of creed.

In order to understand the faith of the Prophets, it is necessary to arrange a combined study of all the sacred books presented by the Prophets. As far as the Holy Quran is concerned, it is necessary for all Muslims to study it on their own, because it is a book of guidance. To seek guidance from the Holy Quran directly is the responsibility of every Muslim (this practice includes seeking guidance from those committed intellectuals who are blessed with the knowledge of the Quran).

It will be against the objective of the Holy Quran to depend upon the views and commentaries of those sectarian clerics who are followers of the traditional man-made religions (not faith). To follow the teachings of the Holy Quran is the personal responsibility of every Muslim. The Holy Quran addresses itself to all those who turn towards it for guidance. The Quran does not lay responsibility for its propagation and dissemination on any particular group or class. Instead it lays this responsibility on every Muslim individually and the whole Muslim society collectively.

It is for this very reason that Islam in order to solve the various issues that emerge in different ages, in the light of Islamic teachings, does not grant the right of interpretation *(Ijtihad)* to any person or a particular group; it grants this right collectively to the authorized-elected institutions. Such learned and wise persons who are God-fearing, in whose words and deeds there is no contradiction and who are well aware of the real message of the Quran and the methodology by which the Prophets brought about their revolutions are entitled, on their own, to exercise the right of *Ijtihad.*

But the final authority to interpret and implement such an *Ijtihad* in a country lies with the policy-making institution of the state viz. the Parliament. Those persons who are formally known as "Ulama" (the learned) cannot, either individually or collectively as a body, be given the legal right to implement their *'Ijtihad"*.

The advantage that accrues from adherence to this method is that the issues facing the country are thoroughly discussed by the people, and solved satisfactorily, the nation keeps on traversing the various stages of progress without being subjected to mental confusion, and finally achieves the distinction of becoming an accredited leader of other nations.

But what actually are we witnessing today? Everywhere the terms 'faith', 'religion' and 'Islam' are being used as a slogan to impose the worst kind of political repression and religious authoritarianism upon the masses. The true belief in God and the task of striving for human betterment having been put aside, the undemocratic and un-Islamic concepts and dogmas of traditional religions are being circulated in order to spread ignorance among the masses, to inflict them permanently with economic deprivations and to keep them completely away from the affairs of the state and government.

These sectarian religious elements have so far made use of two stratagems with considerable success. First, to get themselves acknowledged by the Muslim society as the sole spokesmen of the Quran and the Sunnah. Second, to gain for themselves the right to form political parties on sectarian basis (in which they have succeeded to a certain extent). The purpose behind this move is to gain access to state power under the guise of religion and, by making use of the authority of state institutions, to spread in the name of Islam the undemocratic and un-Islamic views that are against the vital interests of the masses.

These machinations can be foiled only by clearly stating the fact that the presence in the Muslim society of religious elements as a separate "class" is un-Islamic. The only way to nullify these designs of the religious elite is to make the intelligentsia and the masses fully conscious of the difference in meaning that exists between 'faith' and 'religion' and be conversant themselves of the Islamic values.

It has become necessary, therefore, to take effective action to frustrate relentlessly all attempts on the part of retrogressive elements (feudal lords, capitalists and their cronies the religious monopolists and other power-groups) to dampen mass consciousness by spreading obscure and mysterious concepts in the name of Islam, and to defeat the sectarian elements and other monopolists power groups in their designs. It is only thus that our nation (which includes religious minorities) could march forward towards its goals of progress.

Islam and Various Effects

In view of the clear definition of religion given above, it can be easily understood as to why there is deterioration in the political, economic and social fields and what is the real cause behind degeneration in human relationship? Among others, one major reason is non-observation of the distinction between faith and religion.

Now, first of all, we relate the effects of the wrong concept of religion regarding human life on the politics of most Muslim countries so that we can correctly estimate the extent of the damage that is being incurred by us in our individual as well as collective life. It should be borne in mind that these political effects are not limited to the formation of the assemblies, law-making and the law and order problems only. A good or a bad political process goes to make or mar the whole fabric of a society, and change in the social and economic framework can be brought about through political process alone.

In practical politics the deplorable state that we are witnessing of political parties and, because of that, of the country's politics, is because we have altogether ignored the guiding principles and personal examples which were laid down before us by the best human beings of their times (the Prophets of God). Our politicians usually have before them their personal and group interests rather than the national interests; they do not emulate the life examples of Prophet Muhammad and other Prophets (Peace be upon them).

In order to enter politics today it is not considered necessary for them to have political training or to possess any record of public service. All they need is heaps of wealth or a close link or kinship with a political leader or a ruler, and to be expert contrivers. They need not develop a positive attitude towards life or be concerned about the problems faced by their country and bear pains to collect the necessary information regarding them. They just have to have the words "Islam", "Quran", and "Shariah" on their lips even though they may be unaware of their true meanings.

They know that the Muslim masses do not possess a clear conception of Islam and its essentials and that they only have an emotional attachment to it. Therefore, by merely addressing them in an emotional way they can befool them and thus gain their own benefits. The wrong concept of religion has promoted the sectarian elements to jump into the political arena by forming political parties on the basis of religious slogans, and they with the help of their peculiar religious style and appearance attempt to win over the support of the simple and unsuspecting Muslims.

The fundamental objective of every political party should be to prepare its manifesto with reference to the national issues, to chart out a programme for solving those issues and to build the party on democratic lines. Its objective should be to gather people belonging to the different strata of the society on a platform on the basis of positive and fruitful concepts, and then by capturing state-power through an organized and sustained struggle to make use of the government machinery for the advancement of the common interests of the people in accordance with the party manifesto.

It is absolutely against the principles of politics to form separate political parties on the basis of religious slogans, sectarianism and narrow-mindedness. As far as the principles of Islam are concerned no disagreement exists in the nation regarding these though there may be different viewpoints regarding minor issues for which the doors should be kept open for dialogue. Therefore, to make Islam controversial, and on this basis to indulge in the politics of slogan-mongering, is unjustifiable. As far as the educational aspect of Islam is concerned, it is meant to nurture good attributes among the individuals of a nation so that they may work together to build such social edifice as can make human life pleasant and productive. In order to succeed in this it is necessary that party workers and political leaders serve the nation and the country while living within their own means.

Of course, if the state requires the full-time services of particular persons on account of their outstanding capabilities they can draw from the government treasury only that much as a common man needs to lead a simple and dignified life, free from want and hunger. They should not, alongwith their official pays and other necessary facilities, erect mills and factories and establish big business by using government influence thus depriving the really deserving people of their rights who possess the necessary ability but do not wield influence.

It has now become necessary, in view of such conduct of the people having vested interests, that those persons who have acquired government positions for personal gains through political influence should be forced out of the political arena, through democratic means, by developing public awareness. But this will be possible only when the conceptual difference between faith and religion is ingrained in the minds of the people to the extent that the vested interests and the exploiting classes are divested of their ability to use religion as a tool of exploitation.

The negative effects of religious thought are also cast upon the basic interests of the masses viz, political sovereignty, social equality, economic progress, education, health, employment, housing etc. The historical role played by sectarianism, built upon religion, is before us. The first blow, in the garb of religion, besets the exploited and oppressed people's right to rule.

The religious leaders by wilfully mixing up the universally accepted principle of "sovereignty of the people over a country" with the principle of "God's supreme sovereignty over the entire universe", declare people's sovereignty as a negation of the sovereignty of God; whereas without acknowledging people's sovereignty in a country the very concept of democracy is compromised and, therefore, neither the unjustified domination by an exploiting minority, group over the majority nor the oppression and injustice against the people can be ended. By not conceding the sovereignty of the people the entire democratic structure of people's representation tumbles down.

That is why the feudal lords, absentee-landlords, comparator industrialists and traders and those who have amassed wealth through smuggling, drug-trafficking and black-marketing, the civil and military bureaucracy and the religious leaders join hands to deny true representation of the people in the assemblies. All the assembly seats are grabbed by the exploiting classes on account of unhealthy collaboration of the wealthy and the sectarian clerics and the people, as usual, remain deprived of the right to legislate in furtherance of their own interests.

The central principle of the economic system given by Islam is that (particularly in circumstances when there are individuals in the society who are indigent and who get less than their needs) the persons who have accumulated more than their needs should spend to fulfill the needs of the impoverished. The hoarding of wealth, or the love of wealth in one's heart, is against the teachings of Islam. But the people with a religious bent of mind, inspite of their oral pretensions, abstain from monetary sacrifice in actual practice. It is so because the religious (doctrinal) ideology creates only a superficial relationship with Islam; it does not develop a passion for sacrifice for the betterment of humanity.

It creates a false ego in the people belonging to one religion as against those belonging to other religions but fails to create eagerness in them to make sacrifices, and offer cooperation, to the needy. Then again, by justifying the right to unlimited private property the religious classes have provided religious justification to the monopoly systems of feudalism, absentee-landlordism and rent-realization for the usurpation of the rights of those who are actually entitled to these rights. Thus uniform human rights granted by "the faith of the Prophets – Islam" have been negated. The State founded on the principles of the Islamic faith guarantees livelihood, health-care and education to all its citizens but the religious thinking negates this principle and gives secondary position to these basic human needs. It gives priority to customary worship through rituals over tangible service to each other.

The negative effects of religious thinking are also cast upon the country's judicial system. The Islamic thought hinges on judicial equity in which the wealthy and the poor, the powerful and the weak, the male and the female, the senior and the junior should get unhampered justice, free of cost, and without any discrimination. In this system no one can buy justice on the basis of wealth and influence. In a system of governance based on Islamic thought the judiciary is completely free from the influence of the executive.

Its job is to decide all matters with a living sense of accountability before God, and in conformity with the principles of Islam as laid down in the Quran, and also in the light of the precedents taken from the life examples of Prophet Muhammad (Peace be upon him), while keeping in view the collective human requirements of the people of the modern age and the laws passed by the legislature. In carrying out this duty the judiciary should not succumb to the inducements of self-interests, or to fears and temptations. In order to achieve such justice it is necessary that there should be a single judicial system in the country.

There should not be a parallel judiciary like the "Shariat Courts" constituted under the pressure of religious sectarianism or the political interests of the rulers. The appointments or demotions of the judges should not be the discretion of the President or the Prime Minister. For this purpose a separate elective system ought to be devised so that the judges should have no pressure upon them except that of accountability before their own conscience. In spite of this, if a judge does not fulfill the demands of justice deliberately, then action can be taken against him through the National Assembly or the Senate.

As a Religion

The religious approach also affects the country's educational system. The country's educational system, like the judicial system, should also be uniform. There should not be separate educational structures of the so-called *"deeni madaris"* as against the normal schools and colleges. The Islamic faith denotes a particular way of life. In order to emulate this system of life we can make use of the different sciences, and arts, but the system of religious instruction which actually divides life into different compartments cannot be accepted as part of the educational system.

The education being presently imparted in the *madaris*, schools, colleges and universities can of course be improved from the standpoint of the Islamic faith, but to produce such human breeds in the name of *"deeni madaris"* as have no positive and constructive role in the sphere of social life, and are not materially productive, can never be justified.

The educational system which is in vogue in the name of *"deeni madaris"* is a system tailored by the leaders of religious sects to promote their respective schools of thought and their personal interest. In these *"madaris"* little is taught about true Islam, the essence of belief *(iman)*, the reality of faith *(deen)* the clear verses of the Quran *(muhkamat)* and righteous deeds *(aamal-e-saleha)*; more is taught about religious dogmas, rituals, juristic hairsplitting and imparting of all sorts of meanings to those Quranic verses *(mutashabihat)* the true meanings of which are known to God alone.

In these *"madaris"* nothing is taught about science and technology. No mention is even made of those Muslim philosophers and scientists whose thoughts were utilized by Europe during the Renaissance period. By this one can fairly understand what type of human beings these *"deeni madaris"* are producing, and what kind of role they are capable of playing in the nation's academic, cultural, material and spiritual uplift.

People of religious outlook also have a peculiar viewpoint regarding women which goes to obstruct their progress. For them a woman is an inferior creature as compared to man, and should always live in servile obedience to man. They ignore the fact that women form half of the population of the whole world. They also fail to understand the fact that it is impossible for a society to develop properly unless both men and women are granted equal opportunities to develop their natural faculties and, by making use of these, to be able to vie with one another in the various walks of life.

Thus you can well understand how religious thinking has become an obstacle in the building and advancement of the society. The insecurity of women's honour and dignity at the hands of men is also the result of such thinking. The true position of women from the point of view of faith has been made clear through the teachings of the Quran as well as the practice of the last Prophet Muhammad (Peace be upon him) that, apart from the natural bodily differentiation between man and woman, and certain specific roles of each, there is no difference between the two in respect of capabilities, rights and responsibilities.

The religious thinking regarding most of the Muslim countries' religious minorities also is retrogressive. It does not accept the religious minorities as part of the nation. Religion, instead of working for the betterment of the people on human basis, compels one to adopt an inimical attitude on the basis of linguistic, religious and sectarian differences, and splits the nation into small fragments.

As a result it becomes impossible to promote human brotherhood, and the higher emotions of solidarity and compassion cannot be cultivated in society. On the contrary, the concept of faith declares the religious minorities living alongwith the religious majority as a part of the same nation, and grants equal rights to them.

A nation's culture is the criteria for judging whether it is a developed or an underdeveloped nation. Economy is the tool which contributes to a nation's material progress, while culture is the means of its spiritual progress. Culture is related to learning and competence, architecture, fine arts, folklore, festivals, carnivals and the richness of mysticism (spiritual comprehension of truth). Culture paves the way for tenderness and compassion, generosity and kindness, graceful perception and sense of beauty, chastity, mutual sympathy and cooperation in human relationship, and generates the attributes of understanding, tolerance and endurance.

As it is, culture plays a big role in adoring human life with the ornaments of peace and comfort, pleasantness of dress and elegance of beauty. Faith employs culture to promote all the higher attributes in human beings. But the exponents of religious thought, in order to maintain their hold over the simple and sincere masses, sacrifice all the higher emotions born out of the cultural influence at the altar of dry and non-rewarding religious rituals.

These religious leaders, instead of ingraining in the minds of the people God's relationship of love with man and His attributes of forgiveness of human failings, burden their minds with God's wrath and revenge, the fear of hell and greed for paradise thus pushing them into the dark abyss of ignorance. Then, they instal themselves as mediators between God and human beings ostensibly to distribute God's favours among them, provide cures to people's ailments in their own peculiar ways and distribute permits for paradise.

The entire government machinery is also affected because of the religious outlook. On account of this outlook the President and the Prime Minister, down to the ministers and high officials, all get engaged in covering up their harmful policies and manoeuvre under the screen of religion. Instead of removing their shortcomings through hard work, devotion to duty and good intentions on the basis of sense of accountability before the people and God, they make attempts to hide their anti-social thoughts and actions from the public view by such pretentious phrases as "with the grace of God", "God-willing", "God's help is with us".

They use the word God as though God belongs to them alone and that He has no relationship with the rest of humanity. In such machinations of theirs they also use and employ religious leaders too. These religious leaders keep themselves busy convincing those people who are under the spell of their influence that the government is really keen to safeguard their interests, even if that government is of the exploiting classes, and is working against the interests of the masses.

The influence of such religious thinking is cast on lower government servants also. They, instead of discharging their duties with honesty of purpose, get involved in securing undue privileges and illegal gratifications while relying falsely on Divine forgiveness of which they are assured, inspite of their wrongdoings, on account of the religious concepts fed to them. Thc purpose behind the whole discussion is to make clear that the basic point which the Prophets (who were the best of human beings) taught the people was that the way to a better life was in "having faith in God and in doing righteous deeds". It clearly means that all human beings possess equal status and are entitled to the same fundamental rights.

No human being has the right to make another human being one's vassal politically., economically or socially. All human beings should keep themselves above all kinds of social, parochial, linguistic, religious and sectarian prejudices and develop their natural capabilities through mutual cooperation.

They should help the adherents of such faith, whether of their own nation or of other nations (who are essentially tied together in human kinship) to reach the pinnacle of material and spiritual excellence, by making use of the means and resources provided by the Creator. And in order to avoid the hindrances in this path created by human weaknesses, they should always remember the fact that in the system given by the Creator of the universe and humanity, the accountability of human action is of primary importance.

In other words, when we come across other people in the social process, while traversing the highway of life, our relationship should not be based on greediness of wealth; these should instead be based on human fraternity, love and affection, forgiveness and condonation, trust and cooperation, mutual understanding, tolerance and forbearance.

This, in fact, is the end-purpose of life. As far as the rituals of worship are concerned they are a means for acknowledging God's existence, a proclamation of one's servitude to God, a means of achieving self-perfection, a way of seeking God's help for success in the life struggle one is engaged in actively, and a mode of thanksgiving at every step. Worship is a supportive power that helps to keep one on to the path of righteousness and to continue fighting against the forces of evil, provided it is performed in the light of reason and understanding, not merely as a ritualistic worship.

The way of life *(deen)* preached by the Prophets contains a dual system of worshipping God as well as performing one's social responsibilities. To become absorbed in mere rituals while not fulfilling one's social obligations, is a totally false concept, and is an adroit creation of man-made religious thought. The sooner we get out of the whirlpool of this false conception the greater will be the speed with which we will be able to tread the straight and accurate path *(sirat-e-mustaqeem)* made known to us by the Islamic faith.

4

Invisibility of Allah

Abode of Happiness

Islamic Paradise is called Jannat (garden) in Arabic and Bahisht in Persian; the word Firdaus, from which we get our English word Paradise, being restricted to one region in the celestial abodes of bliss.

There are eight different terms employed in the Quran for heaven, and although they would appear to be but different names for the same region, Muhammadan divines understand them to mean different stages of glory.

They are as follows :

1. Jannat-ul-Khuld (Sura xxv. 16), "The garden of eternity."
2. Dar-us-Salam (Sura vi. 127), "The dwelling of peace."
3. Dar-ul-Qarar (Sura xi. 42), "The dwelling which abideth."
4. Jannat-i-Adaan (Sura ix. 72), "The garden of Eden."
5. Jannat-ul-Mawa (Sura xxxii. 19), "The garden of refuge."
6. Jannat-un-Naim (Sura vi. 70), "The garden of delight."
7. Jannat-i-Illiyun (Sura xxxiii.18), "The garden of Illiyun."
8. Jannat-ul-Firdaus (Sura xviii. 107), "The garden of Paradise."

These eight stages of Paradise are spoken of as "eight doors" in the traditions (Mishkat, bk. ii. chap. i.)

The sensual delights of Muhammad's Paradise are proverbial, and they must have exercised considerable influence upon the minds of the people to whom he made known his mission. The allusions in the Quran are far too numerous to admit of quotation, but they will be found more particularly in Suras ixxvi., iv., ivi., xivii.

The descriptions of the celestial regions and the enjoyments promised to "the faithful" are still more minutely given in the traditional sayings of the Prophet (Mishkat, bk. xxiii. chap. xiii).

Apologists for Islam, Carlyle for example, have suggested that the sensual delights of Muhammad's Paradise may after all be taken figuratively, even as the Song of Solomon and the Revelation of St. John. It is quite true that such is the interpretation hinted at in the *Akhlaqi-Jalali;* and Mr. Lane in his "Modern Egyptians" says he met a Muslim of learning who considered them figurative; but such is not the view of any Muhammadan commentator. All Muslim theologians have given a literal interpretation of the sensual delights, and it is impossible for any candid mind to read the Quran and Traditions and arrive to any other conclusion on the subject.

In addition to the seven divisions of celestial bliss, there are said to be seven firmaments (asman).

1. Of pure virgin silver, which is Adam's residence.
2. Of pure gold, which is Enoch's and John Baptist's.
3. Of pearls, which is Joseph's.
4. Of white gold, which is Jesus'.
5. Of silver, which is Aaron's.
6. Of ruby and garnet, which is Moses'.
7. Of crystal, which is Abraham's.

Den of Grief

Hell, or the place of torment, is called in Arabic Jahannam, and in Persian Dozakh; and is said to have seven portals or divisions,' which the Commentator Baghawi distributes as follows :-

1. *Jahannam,* for Muhammadans; for, according to the Quran, all Muslims will pass through hell.
2. *Lazwa,* a blazing fire for Christians (Sura ixx. 15 only).
3. *Hutama,* an intense fire for Jews (Sura civ. 4 only).
4. *Sair* a flaming fire for Sabians (Sura iv. 11, and fourteen other places).
5. *Saqar,* a scorching heat for Magi (Suras liv. 58, and ixxiv. 43).
6. *Jahim,* a huge hot fire for idolaters (Sura ii. 113 and twenty other places).
7. *Hawia,* the bottomless pit for hypocrites (Sura, ci. 8).

The situation of hell is a matter of dispute.

Allah's Commandments

Taqdir, or the absolute decree and predestination of both good and evil, is the sixth article of the Muslim's creed. The orthodox belief is that whatever hath or shall come to pass in this world, whether it be good or bad, proceedeth entirely from the divine will, and is irrevocably fixed and recorded in the preserved tablet (Loh-e-Mahfuz).

The following is a translation of an Arabic treatise on the subject: "Faith in the decrees of God, is that we believe in our heart and confess with our tongue that the most High God hath decreed all things so that nothing can happen in the world, whether it respects the conditions and operations of things, or good and evil, or obedience and disobedience, or faith and infidelity, or sickness and health, or riches and poverty, or life and death, that is not contained in the written tablet of the decrees of God. But God hath so decreed good works, obedience, and faith, that He ordains and wills them, and that they may be under His decree, His salutary direction, His good pleasure and command.

On the contrary, God hath decreed, and does ordain and determine evil, disobedience, and infidelity; yet without His salutary direction, good pleasure and command, but being only by way of seduction, indignation, and prohibition. But whosoever shall say that God is not delighted with good faith, or that God hath not an indignation against evil and unbelief, he is certainly an infidel."

Allah's Army

The existence of angels (*malak*, pl. *malaik*), and their purity, are absolutely required to be believed in by the Quran, and he is reckoned an infidel who denies that there are such beings, or hates any of them or asserts any distinction of the sexes. The Muhammadans reckon four archangels:

(1) Jibbrail (Gabriel), who is God's messenger;

(2) Mikail, (Michael), who is the protector of the Jews;

(3) Israfil, who will sound the last trumpet at the resurrection;

(4) Izrail, the angle of death.

Muhammad undoubtedly obtained the names of these archangels from the Scriptures and Jewish tradition, although in the Apocryphal Book of Enoch the names of the six archangels are Uriel, Raphael, Raguel, Michael, Sarakiel, Gabriel a fact which may be cited as an additional proof, that Muhammad availed himself of Jewish traditions.

There are also the two recording angels called the *Muaqqibat*, or the angels who continually succeed each other, who record the good and evil actions of a man, one standing at his right hand and another on his left. These are also called the Kiraman Katibin (the exalted writers). The angle who has charge of Heaven is Rizwan and the angle who presides over Hell is Malik.

Munkar and Nakir are described by Muhammad as two black angels with blue eyes who visit every man in his grave, make him sit up, and examine him as to his faith in God and in Muhammad his prophet. If the answer is satisfactory, he will be allowed to sleep on in peace, but if he replies that he knows nothing of "God's Apostle," then he will be struck with an iron hammer called Mitraqat, and he animals that may be near his grave, excepting men and genii. This exciting ceremony is to take place as soon as the funeral party have proceeded forty paces from the grave!

The Devil is said to be a fallen angel who was turned out of Paradise because he refused to do homage to Adam. He is called Iblis, a word which is most probably derived from balas, a wicked or profligate person; and also Shaitan (Satan). Besides angels and devils, there are said to be a distinct order of creatures called Jinn (Genii) who were created of fire some thousands of years before Adam. According to tradition the species consists of five distinct orders:-

1. Jann;

2. Jinn;

3. Shaitan;

4. 'Ifrit;

5. Marid.

Their chief abode is the mountains of Qaf, which are supposed to encircle the world.

There are good and evil Genii. If good, they are exceedingly handsome; if evil, they are horribly hideous. The evil genii are said to have been at liberty to enter any of the seven heavens till" the birth of Jesus, when they were excluded from three of them. On the birth of Muhammad they were forbidden the other four heavens. They continue, however, to ascend to the confines of the lowest heavens, and there listen to the conversations' of the angels respecting the decrees of God, which they sometimes impart to men by means of talismans and invocations.

The good genii are Muslims, and perform all the religious duties of the faithful.

King Solomon is said to have had great power over the genii by means of his magic ring.

Students of Islam must bear in mind that most of the stories of the genii are related in the Quran, and have, therefore, received from Muhammad all the authority of all divine revelation.

Prophets before the Last Messenger

The number of prophets (rasool), which have been sent by God, are said to be 224,000, or, according to another tradition, 124,000. Of these 313 were Apostles sent with special commissions, to reclaim the world from infidelity and superstition.

Six brought new laws which successively abrogated the preceding and have special titles, or kalima :

1. Adam (Adam), Sufi-Ullah, the Chosen of God.
2. Nuh (Noah), Nabi-Ullah, the Preacher of God.
3. Ibrahim (Abraham), Khalil-Ullah, the Friend of God.
4. Musa (Moses), Kalim-Ullah, one who conversed with God.
5. 'Isa (Jesus), Ruh-Ullah, the Spirit of God.
6. Muhammad, Rasool-Ullah, the Messenger of God.

The number of sacred books delivered to man are said to have been one hundred and four, viz.

Ten, to Adam;

Fifty, to Seth (Sish);

Thirty, to Enoch (Edris);

Ten, to Ibrahim;

The Taurat, to Moses;

The Zabur, to David,

The Injil, to Jesus;

The Quran, to Muhammad.

The one hundred scriptures given to Adam, Seth, Enoch, and Abraham, are termed Sahi-fah (a pamphlet), and the other four, Kitab (a book); but all that is necessary for the Muslim to know of these books is supposed to have been retained in the Quran.

Luqman-i-Hakim (supposed to have been Aesop) and Alexander the Great are also considered by Muhammadan commentators to have been prophets. Luqman is mentioned in the thirty-first Sura of the Quran, and Zulqurnain, "the two-horned" (supposed to have been Alexander), in the eighteenth Sura; but, it is not clear as to what position the author of the Quran intended to assign to these worthies.

The Doomsday

Qiamat (lit. "standing"), or the day of resurrection and judgement, is a time which all Muslims believe is a perfect secret and known only to God. But they say that the approach of the day of judgement will be known by twenty five signs.'

1. The decay of faith among men.
2. The advancing of the meanest persons to dignity.
3. That a maid-servant shall become the mother of her mistress.
4. Tumults and seditions.
5. A war with the Turks.

6. Great distress in the world.
7. That the provinces of Iraq and Syria shall refuse to pay tribute.
8. That the buildings of Medina shall extend to Yahab.
9. The sun rising in the west.
10. The appearance of a remarkable Beast, called the Dabbat-ul-arz, which shall rise out of the earth in the temple at Mecca.
11. War with the Greeks and the taking of Constantinople by 70,000 of the posterity of Ishaq.
12. The coming of Masih-ud-Dajjal, or Antichrist.
13. The coming of Jesus Christ, who will descend upon one of the minarets of the Mosque at Damascus.
14. War with the Jews.
15. The ravages made by Yajuj and Majuj.
16. A smoke which shall fill the whole earth.
17. An eclipse of the moon.
18. The return of the Arabians to idolatry.
19. The discovery of a heap of treasure by the retreating of the river Euphrates.
20. The demolition of the temple at Mecca.
21. The speaking of beasts and inanimate things.
22. A breaking out of a fire in Yaman.
23. The appearance of a remarkable man who shall drive men before him with his staff.
24. The coming of Imam Mahdi, the director, who will come from Khurasan, his troops bearing black ensigns.
25. A mighty wind which shall sweep away the souls of all who have but a grain of faith in their hearts.

The following is a succinct account of the day of judgement, translated from a Muhammadan book:-

"Then shall God bring all men back and raise them again, and restore to them their souls, and gather them together. He will then call for the books in which have been written the -good and evil actions of all men. Then he will judge them in equity and weigh the balance (mizan) of their works, and will make retribution to every soul according to what he has done. Some shall enter Paradise through his goodness and mercy, and some shall go to hell. No Muslim shall remain in hell for ever, but shall enter into Paradise, after they have suffered according to their sins, for believers shall remain for ever in Paradise, and the unbelievers in hell fire."

Sirat is a bridge which all must pass over on the day of judgement. It is said to extend over the midst of hell, and to be sharper than the edge of a sword. In passing it the feet of the infidel will slip, and he will fall into hell fire; but the feet of the Muslim will be firm, and carry him safely to Paradise.

5

Allah, the Omnipotent

The name of the Creator of the universe in the Quran is Allah, which is the title given to the Supreme Being by Muhammadans of every race and language. It is called the special, or essential, name of God, the *ism-i-zat*; all other names being considered merely *ism-i-sifat*, or attributes, of which there are said to be ninety-nine.' It is supposed to have been derived from the word *ilah*, a deity or god, with the addition of the definite article al, thus Al-ilah, The God. But Imam Hanifa says that, just as God's essence is unchangeable so is His name, and that Allah has always been the name of the great Eternal Being (vide Ghyas-ul-Loghat). It appears to be an Arabic rendering of the Hebrew 98 e.d., God. It is expressed in Persian and Hindustani by the word Khuda, derived from the Persian Khud (self); the self-existing one.

God's Existence

The Muhammadan belief in the existence of God is expressed in the first part of the well known confession of faith, La-ilaha Illallaho, "There is no deity but God," the interpretation of which occupies so prominent a place in all treatises of divinity.

The following is an interpretation of the Muslim belief in the existence and nature of God, by the famous scholastic divine, Imam Ghazzali, in his book entitled Al Maqsud-ul-asna, an extract from which Ockley has translated from Pococks Specimen Historiae Arabum:

Allah's Glory

"Praise be to God the Creator and Restorer of all things; who does whatsoever he pleases, who is Master of the glorious throne and mighty force, and directs his sincere servants into the right way and the straight path; who favoureth them, who have once borne testimony to the unity, by preserving their confessions from the darkness of doubt and hesitation; who directs them to follow his chosen apostle, upon whom be the blessing and peace of God; and to go after his most honourable companions, to whom he hath vouchsafed his assistance and direction which is revealed to them in his essence and operations by the excellencies of his attributes, to the knowledge whereof no man attains but he that hath been taught by hearing.

To these, as touching his essence, he maketh known that he is one, and hath no partner; singular, without anything like him; uniform, having no contrary; separate, having no equal. He is ancient, having no first; eternal, having no beginning; remaining for ever, having no end; continuing to eternity, without any termination. He persists, without ceasing to be; remains without falling, and never did cease, nor ever shall cease to be described by glorious attributes, nor is subject to any decree so as to be determined by any precise limits or set times, but is the First and the Last, and is within and without.

Praise of the Almighty

He, glorified be his name, is not a body endued with form, nor a substance circumscribed with limits or determined by measure; neither does he resemble bodies, as they are capable of being measured or divided. Neither is he a substance, neither do substances exist in him; neither is he an accident, nor do accidents exist in him.

Neither is he like to anything that exists, neither is anything like to him; nor is he determinate in quantity nor comprehended by bounds, nor circumscribed by the differences of situation, nor contained in the heavens. He sits upon the throne, after that manner which he himself hath described, and in that same sense which he himself means, which is a sitting far removed from any notion of contact, or resting upon, or local situation; but both the throne itself, and whatsoever is upon it, are sustained by the goodness of his power, and are subject to the grasp of his hand.

But he is above the throne, and above all things, even to the utmost ends of the earth; but so above as at the same time not to be a whit nearer the throne and the heaven; since he is exalted by (infinite) degrees above the throne no less than he is exalted above the earth, and at the same time is near to everything that hath a being, nay, 'nearer to man than their jugular veins, and is witness to everything though his nearness is not like the nearness of bodies, as neither is his essence like the essence of bodies.

Neither both he exist in anything, neither doth anything exist in him; but he is too high to be contained in any place, and too holy to be determined by time; for he was before time and place were created, and is now after the same manner as he always was. He is also distinct from the creatures by his attributes, neither is there anything besides himself in his essence, nor is his essence in any other besides him. He is too holy to be subject to change, or any local motion; neither do any accidents dwell in him, nor any contingencies befall him; but he abides through all generations with his glorious attributes, free from all danger of dissolution.

As to the attribute of perfection, he wants no addition of his perfection. As to being, he is known to exist by the apprehension of the understanding; and he is seen as he is by an ocular intuition, which will be vouchsafed out of his mercy and grace to the holy in the eternal mansion, completing their joy by the vision of his glorious presence.

Allah, the most Powerful

He, praised be his name, is living, powerful, mighty, omnipotent, not liable to any defect or impotence; neither slumbering nor sleeping, nor being obnoxious to decay or death. To him belongs the kingdom, and the power, and the might. His is the dominion, and the excellency, and the creation, and the command thereof.

The heavens are folded up in his right hand, and all creatures are couched within his grasp. His excellency consists in his creating and producing, and his unity in communicating existence and a beginning of being. He created men and their works, and measured out their maintenance and their determined times. Nothing that is possible can escape his grasp, nor can the vicissitudes of things elude his power. The effects of his might are innumerable, and the objects of his knowledge infinite.

Knowledge of Allah

He, praised be his name, knows all things that can be understood, and comprehends whatsoever comes to pass, from the extremities of the earth to the highest heavens. Even the weight of a pismire could not escape him either in earth in heaven; but he would perceive the creeping of the black pismire in the dark night upon the hard stone, and discern the motion of an atom in the open air. He knows what is secret and conceals it, and views the conceptions of the minds, and the motions of the thoughts, and the inmost recesses of secrets, by a knowledge ancient and eternal, that never ceased to be his attribute from eternal eternity, and not by any new knowledge, super added to his essence, either inhering or adventitious.

Allah's Will

He, praised be his name, doth will those things to be that are, and disposes of all accidents. Nothing passes in the empire, nor the kingdom, neither little nor much, nor small nor great, nor good nor evil, nor profitable nor hurtful, nor faith nor infidelity, nor knowledge nor ignorance, nor prosperity nor adversity, nor increase nor decrease, nor obedience nor rebellion, but by his determinate counsel and decree, and his definite sentence and will. Nor doth he wink of him that seeth, nor the subtlety of him that thinketh, exceed the bounds of his will; but it is he who gave all things their beginning; he is the creator and restorer, the sole operator of what he pleases; there is no reversing his decree nor delaying what he hath determined, nor is there any refuge to man from his rebellion against him, but only his help and mercy; nor hath any man any power to perform any duty towards him, but through his love and will.

Though men, genii, angels and devils, should conspire together either to put one single atom in motion, or cause it to cease its motion, without his will and approbation they would not be able to do it. His will subsists in his essence amongst the rest of his attributes, and was from eternity one of his eternal attributes, by which he wiled from eternity the existence of those things that he had decreed, which were produced in their proper reasons according to his eternal will, without any before or after, and in agreement both with his knowledge and will, and not by methodising of thoughts, nor waiting for a proper time, for which reason no one thing is in him a hindrance from another.

Allah : His Power of Hearing and Sight

And he, praised be his name, is hearing and seeing, and heareth and seeth. No audible object, how still soever, escapeth his hearing; nor is any thing visible so small as to escape his sight; for distance is no hindrance to his hearing, nor darkness to his sight. He sees without pupil or eyelids, and hears without any passage or ear, even as he knoweth without a heart, and performs his actions without the assistance of any corporeal limb, and creates without any instrument, for his attributes (or properties) are not like those of men any more than his essence is like theirs.

Allah's Speech

Furthermore, he doth speak, command, forbid, promise, and threaten by an eternal, ancient word, subsisting in his essence. Neither is it like to the word of the creatures, nor doth it consist in a voice arising from the commotion of the air and the collision of bodies, nor letters which are separated by the joining together of the lips of the motion of the tongue. The Quran, the Law, the Gospel, and the Pslater, are books sent down by him to his apostles, and the Quran, indeed, is read with tongues, written in books, and kept in hearts; yet as subsisting in the essence of God, it doth not become liable to separation and division whilst it is transferred into the hearts and the papers. Thus Moses also heard the Word of God without voice or letter, even as the saints behold the essence of God without substance or accident. And that since these are his attributes, he liveth and knoweth, is powerful and willeth and operateth, and seeth and speaketh, by life and knowledge, and will and hearing, and sight and word, not by his simple essence.

Works of Allah

He, praised be his name, exists after such a manner that nothing besides him hath any being but what is produced by his operation, and floweth from his justice after the best, most excellent, most perfect, and most just model. He is, moreover, wise in his works, and just in his decrees. But his justice is not to be compared with the justice of men. For a man may be supposed to act unjustly by invading the possession of another; but no injustice can be conceived of God, inasmuch as there is nothing that belongs to any other besides himself, so that wrong is not imputable to him as meddling with things not appertaining to him.

All things, himself only excepted, genii, men, the devil, angels, heaven, earth, animals, plants, substance, accident, intelligible, sensible, were all created originally by him. He created them by his power out of mere privation, and brought them into light, when as yet they were nothing at all, but he alone existing from eternity, neither was there any other with him. Now he created all things in the beginning for the manifestation of his power, and his will, and the confirmation of his word, which was true from all eternity. Not that he stood in need of them, nor wanted them; but he manifestly declared his glory in creating, and producing, and commanding, without being under any obligation, nor out of necessity.

Loving kindness, and to show favour, and grace, and beneficence, belong to him; whereas it is in his power to pour forth upon men a variety of torments, and afflict them with various kinds of sorrows and diseases, which, if he were to do, his justice could not be arraigned, nor would he be chargeable with injustice. Yet he rewards those that worship him for their obedience on account of his promise and beneficence, not of their merit nor of necessity, since there is nothing which he can be tied to perform; nor can any injustice be supposed in him, nor can he be under any obligation to any person whatsoever. That his creatures, however, should be bound to serve him, ariseth from his having declared by the tongues of the prophets that it was due to him from them. The worship of him is not simply the dictate of the understanding, but he sent messengers to carry to men his commands, and promises, and threats, whose veracity he proved by manifest miracles, whereby men are obliged to give credit to them in those things that they relate."

6

Basic Faiths

Islam is a complete way of life. It is the guidance for all mankind from Allah, the Creator of the Universe. It covers all the things people do in their lifetime. Islam tells us the purpose of our creation, our final destiny and our place among other creatures. It shows us the best way to conduct our private and public affairs, including social, political, economic, moral and spiritual activities.

Islam is an Arabic word which means submission and obedience. Submission is acceptance of Allah's commands. Obedience means putting Allah's commands into practice. Submission and obedience to Allah bring peace, which is why Islam also means peace. A person who accepts the Islamic way of life and acts upon it is a Muslim.

Allah, another Arabic word, is the proper name of God. Muslims prefer to use the word Allah rather than the word God. Allah does not mean 'the God of the Muslims', as some people wrongly believe. Rather, it is the name the Creator has chosen for Himself. Allah is the Creator of everyone and everything. He is unique and has no son or daughter. Muslims should begin their actions by saying Bismillah, which means 'in the name of Allah'.

Islam is the way of peace and harmony. If we look around, we see that all things— the sun, the moon and the stars, the high mountains and the mighty oceans – obey a law: the Law of Allah. We find no disorder or chaos in them. Everything is in its right place. We see perfect order and total harmony in the system of Nature that Allah has created. The sun rises in the east and sets in the west and there has been no exception to this rule. The moon and the stars shine at night. Night passes, a new day comes, and so the process goes on. Flowers blossom and the trees have green leaves in the spring. Everything has a set course that cannot be violated. Have you ever noticed any violation in the Law of Allah by these objects of Nature? No, of course not. Why? Simply because they are made to obey Allah. They have no choice but to obey. This is why we find eternal peace in the system of Nature. But human beings are different: Allah has given us the knowledge and ability to choose between right and wrong. Not only this, in case we forget. He has also sent us constant reminders, by sending His prophets and books for our guidance. The final messenger of Allah is Muhammad, and the final book of guidance is the Quran.

Yet He does not force us to obey Him. He has given us the choice either to obey or disobey Him. Why? Because He wants to test us. After this test there will be a Day of reward and punishment. This is the Day of Judgement (Yawmuddin). Those who pass the test will be rewarded with everlasting happiness and peace in Paradise (al-Jannat) and those who fail will suffer terrible punishment in Hell (al-Jahannam). We can earn this reward and escape punishment by obeying and worshipping Allah.

We know there is peace and harmony in all of Nature; because nothing ever disobeys Allah. Neither the sun nor the moon, the mountains nor the trees, the animals on land or in the sea, can disobey Allah – they just behave as He has created them to behave. They have no choice.

The only exceptions are human beings and the Jinn (creatures we can't see); they have free will, which means they can choose whether to obey or disobey Allah. But if we follow the guidance given to us through the prophets, we are sure to have peace in the world we live in.

All human beings, by their very nature, like good things and dislike bad things. For example, we all like truthfulness and hate lies. Even a liar does not like to be called a liar! Why? Because we know in our hearts that telling lies is a bad thing. In the same way, helping others, showing kindness, politeness, respect for parents and teachers, honesty and all other forms of good conduct are always liked and appreciated; but rudeness, cruelty, lies, hurting others, disobedience to parents and teachers, using bad names and other bad conduct are disliked by everyone. So, we can say that human nature likes the Right and dislikes the Wrong. Right is Maroof and wrong is Munkar in Arabic – the language of the Quran.

It is also human nature to love peace and hate disorder. Peace comes from obedience to Allah's Law, whilst disorder is the outcome of disobedience. Islam establishes this peace, which is part of man's nature; so, Islam is called the Religion of Nature; in Arabic this is Dinul Fitrah.

To achieve peace in society, Islam calls upon Muslims to work together towards what is right and to keep away from what is evil. This joint effort to root out evil and establish truth is called Jihad which means to try one's utmost to see Truth prevail and Falsehood vanish from society. The aim of Jihad' is to earn the pleasure of Allah.

Doomsday in Islam

Akhirat : We have already mentioned the three most important beliefs in Islam: Tauhid (oneness of Allah), Risalat (Prophethood) and the Akhirat (life-after-death). Now we will look at the Akhirat.

Belief in Akhirat is vital for all Muslims. Our life on this earth is temporary. It is meant to prepare us for the Akhirat, which is never-ending. Life on this earth is meaningless if good actions are not rewarded and bad conduct not punished. Why attend school if bad behaviour goes unpunished and there's nothing at the end to reward all our efforts? In the same way, life on earth is meaningless if we don't face the consequences of our actions after death, standing in the majestic Court of justice of Almighty Allah on the Day of Judgement (Yawmul Akhir or Yawmuddin).

To prepare ourselves for this day, we need to follow the guidance given through the prophets. There would have been no need for prophets if there were no life-after-death.

There are people who do not care whether there is a life-after-death. Some do not even believe in it at all. These people will suffer terribly for their disbelief. A sensible person cannot possibly say there is no life-after-death. He can be doubtful but he will always be at a loss if his doubt proves untrue.

So, the safe course to follow is to believe in all that the prophets told people to believe. Not to care about Akhirat is a serious failing. We are certain that all human beings die, so it is quite reasonable to prepare for that eternal life which, no doubt, will follow death.

Doubts have been expressed by unbelievers about life-after-death. They cannot understand how Allah can raise men and women after death. But Allah can make human beings out of nothing so it is not difficult for Him to raise them after death (22:5-7; 36:77-79).

The Quran says:

> "Does man think that we shall not assemble his bones? Yes, surely, yes, we are able to restore the very shape of his fingertips." (75:3-4)

Life on this earth would not be peaceful, rather it would be horrible, if all people thought that there would be no life-after-death. There would be no restraint or control on what we do. Belief in Akhirat has a tremendous influence on the life of a Muslim. He knows that Allah is watching all his actions and he will have to account for them on the Day of Judgement. His conduct and behaviour will therefore be responsible, controlled and careful. He will always try to do those things which Allah will favour and give up those actions which will incur His punishment.

A Muslim believes that he will be rewarded in the life-after-death for all his good actions. He will live in Heaven, a place of eternal happiness and peace.

Wrong-doers will be punished on the Day of Judgement and will be sent to Hell, a place of severe punishment and suffering.

To prepare for that day and to be rewarded by Allah, the Merciful and the Kind, we need to do all that Allah demands of us and give up all bad habits and wrong actions. We can do this if we follow the guidance given to Muhammad by Allah. This is the safest course for our success in the Akhirat.

Quran : A Holy Book

The Quran is a unique book. It is guidance from our Creator for all of mankind. It is the sacred book of Muslims and the main source of Law in Islam. Every word of the Quran is from Allah'.

The Quran is the final revelation from Allah to mankind. The revelation to Prophet Muhammad began in the cave of Hira' in 610 CE. As we have said, the previous books sent to earlier prophets have not survived in their original form. Only the Quran remains unchanged. It is guidance for all of humanity until the end of the world. It is clearly very important that this book is preserved and kept free from human distortion.

No other book in the world can match the Quran in respect of its recording and preservation. The astonishing fact about this book of Allah is that it has remained unchanged even to a dot over the last fourteen hundred years. Allah the Almighty has Himself taken the responsibility of preserving the Quran. He says: "Surely, We have revealed this reminder (Dhikr) and Lo, We verily are its Guardian." (15:9) This verse shows that Allah revealed the Quran and He will protect it. Indeed, He has protected it from any change whatsoever, and His protection will Continue forever.

None except the Creator could have produced the unique verses of the Quran. Allah challenges humans and jinn together to produce anything similar to the Quran, whilst informing them that they will never be able to do it (2:23; 10:37-38; 17:88). This challenge remains, and will continue to remain, unanswered.

The Quran was recorded as soon as it was revealed under the personal supervision of Prophet Muhammad .The Quran exists today in its original form, unaltered and undistorted. It is a living miracle in the sense that it has survived so many centuries without suffering even the smallest change. Every word of it – every single letter and sound – is in the hearts and minds of thousands of Muslims who continue to memorise and recite it every day. No variation of text can be found in it. You can check this for yourself by listening to and comparing the recitation of Muslims from different parts of the world.

Arabic, the language of the Quran, unlike the languages of other revealed books, is a living, dynamic and very rich language. Millions of people all over the world use Arabic in their daily lives. This shows the relevance of the Quran and its universal usefulness even in today's world.

Through the Quran our Creator speaks to us. It is a clear proof of His Sovereignty over the universe, and that He is All-knowing, All-aware.

The subject matter of the Quran is Man and his ultimate goal in life. Its teachings cover all areas of this life and the life-after-death. It contains principles, teachings and guidance for every area of human activity. The theme of the Quran consists broadly of the three fundamental concepts of Tauhid, Risalat and Akhirat. Tauhid is the basic theme of the Quran. All the prophets of Allah called people towards Tauhid. The Quran gives a vivid description of the Paradise which will be awarded to the truly obedient servants of Allah. The severe punishment to be meted out to the evildoers is also described vividly in the Quran.

The Quran urges people to follow its guidance and teachings. The success of human beings on this earth and in the life-after-death depends on obedience to the teachings of the Quran. We cannot perform our duties as the servants of Allah and His agents if we do not follow the Quran. The Quran urges us to use our energies and wealth to establish the supremacy of Allah's Laws and remove all evils from the society in which we live.

The superb style of the Quran has a tremendous effect on its readers. It totally changes the pattern of life of those who believe and practice its teachings. It leaves a soothing effect on the mind of its reader, even if he does not fully understand its meaning. The incredible effect is hard to describe, it has to be experienced to really appreciate it.

Revelation, Collection and Compilation of the Quran **:** The Quran was revealed to Muhammad through the angel Jibbrail. It was sent down in stages and completed over a period of twenty-three years.

Each and every word of the Quran was recorded as soon as it was revealed by Allah to the Prophet through the angel Jibbrail. The verses of the Quran were sent down at different times according to the needs of the early Muslims. Jibbrail carefully instructed the Prophet in which order the verses should be put together. The Quran is not put together in the order the verses were revealed, nor according to subject matter. Its order is according to the plan of Allah, and is yet another of its striking and unique characteristics.

The Prophet's secretary, Zaid bin Thabit, used to record them exactly as the Prophet told him. He would read back to the Prophet what he had recorded.

The Quran consists of 114 chapters (sing. Sarah, pl. Suwar). The short opening chapter, Suratul Fatiha is followed by the longest chapter of the Quran, Suratul Baqarah (The Cow), with 286 verses. The chapters gradually get shorter. The shortest chapter is the 108th chapter, Suratul Kawthar (The Abundance), which has just 3 verses. There are 6236 verses (sing. Ayah, pi. Ayat) altogether. Chapters revealed when the Prophet was living in Mecca are known as Makki (Meccan) and those revealed in Medina are called Medani (Medinan).

The Quran is also divided into 30 parts (sing. Juz', pl. Ajza') of roughly equal size, which is convenient for recitation purposes. Many of the early Muslims memorised the Quran immediately after the verses were revealed. Some of the famous Huffaz (plural: persons who memorised the Quran; singular: Hafiz) were: Muadh bin Jabal, 'Ubadah bin as-Samit, Abu Darda', Abu Ayub al-Ansan and Ubay bin Kaab.

Shortly after the death of the Prophet in 632 CE, 'Umar suggested to the Khalifah, Abu Bakr, that the Quran be compiled in one volume. Up until then, the Quran was written down in separate sections. A committee was formed under Zaid bin Thabit to gather the material of the Quran into one volume.

Great care was taken to compile the Quran exactly as it had been recorded during the time of the Prophet. After careful checking and rechecking the work was completed. During the Khilafat of 'Umar, the copy was kept with Hafiah, one of the widows of the Prophet .

Later, many schools were established for the teaching of the Quran throughout the Muslim territories. During 'Umar's time, one such school in Damascus had sixteen hundred pupils under Abu Darda', one of the famous Huffaz.

As the Islamic state expanded, people in various places recited the Quran in their local dialect and accent. To avoid the possibility of any confusion or misunderstanding the Khalifah, 'Uthman, ordered the preparation of one standard version of the Quran to be written in the dialect of the Quraish. Prophet Muhammad was from the Quraish tribe. Zaid bin Thabit, 'Abdullah bin al-Zubayr, Said bin al- 'As and 'Abdur Rahman bin al-Harith were asked to prepare copies from the copy of Hafiah.

This farsighted action by 'Uthman made the uniform recitation of the Quran possible. Two original copies from the time of the Khilafat of 'Uthman still exist today – one in the Topkapi Museum in Istanbul, Turkey and the other in Tashkent, Uzbekistan. The National Library of Karachi, Pakistan has a photocopy of the Tashkent original.

The revelation of the Quran began in 610 CE at the cave Hira' on Mount Nar in Mecca. The first revealed verses are:

Iqra' bismi rabbikal ladhi khalaq,
Khalaqal insana min 'alaq.
Iqra' wa rabbukal akram,
Alladhi 'allama bil qalam.
'Allamal insana malam yalam.
"Read in the name of your Lord Who created,
Created man from something that clings.
Read, and your Lord is most generous,
Who taught by the pen,
Taught man what he did not know." (96:1-5)

The Quran was revealed over 22 years, 5 months and 14 days. The last verse of the Quran was revealed shortly before the Prophet's death:

Al yawma akmaltu lakum dinakum,
wa atmamtu 'alaikum nimaiti,
wa raditu lakumul islama dina.

"This day I have perfected your religion for you, and completed My favour upon you, and chosen for you Islam as your way of life." (5:3) Many Arabic words used in the Quran are almost impossible to translate into other languages, including English. However, with the help of the Ahadith and Surah (biography of the Prophet and his companions) translations of the Quran have been produced in many languages.

Muslims scholars have devoted years of study to explain and interpret the Quran in Arabic and other languages. These explanations and interpretations are called Tafasir (sing. Tafsir). They help us to understand the Quran. May Allah help us to understand His words and act on them.

Terms in Actual

Islam is sometimes incorrectly called 'Muhammadanism' and Muslims 'Mohammedans'. Other religions have been named after their founder or after the community in which the religion prospered. For example, Christianity has been named after Christ, Buddhism after Buddha and Judaism after the tribe of judah. But Islam has not been named after Muhammad. It is the name of Allah's Guidance for mankind revealed through all the prophets, the last of whom was Muhammad.

Islam and Muslims are words used in the Quran. The Quran says, "Surely, the way of life acceptable to Allah is Islam." (3:19) "He named you Muslims before and in this." (22:78) The message of all the prophets from Adam to Muhammad is the same: obey Allah and none other. This message, sent through prophets, was completed at the time of

Muhammad who was the last in the chain of Prophethood. This is mentioned in the Quran: "This day I have perfected your religion for you, completed my favour upon you and have chosen for you Islam as your way of life." (5:3) It is wrong, then, to call Islam 'Muhammadanism' and Muslims 'Mohammedans'.

Basic Beliefs : The basic beliefs of Islam are:

1. Allah
2. Angels of Allah (Malaikah)
3. Books of Allàh (Kutubullah)
4. Messengers of Allah (Rasoolullah)
5. The Day of Judgement (Yaumuddin)
6. Destiny (al-Qadr)
7. Life-after-death (Akhirat)

These beliefs have been stated precisely in al-Imanul Mufassal, the Faith in detail:

Amantu billahi, wa mala ikatihi, wa kutubihi, wa rusulihi, wal yawmil akhiri, wal qadri khairihi wa sharrihi minallahi taala, wal bathi badal mawt. "I believe in Allah, in His angels, in His books, in His messengers, in the Last Day (Day of Judgement) and in the fact that everything good or bad is decided by Allah the Almighty, and in the life-after-death." The seven beliefs can be grouped into three:

Tauhid (oneness and uniqueness of Allah)
Risalat (Prophethood)
Akhirat (life after death)

Tauhid, Risalat and Akhirat summarise the whole of the Islamic system of life. So, we must understand them.

Tauhid means the oneness of Allah. It is the main part oilman (Faith) and is beautifully expressed in Suratul Ikhlas in the Quran:

> "Say, He is Allah, the One. Allah is Eternal and Absolute. None is born of Him, nor is He born. And there is none like Him." (Sarah 112)

Tauhid is the most important Islamic belief. It means that everything on this earth is created by Allah, Who looks after and provides for all the needs of every creature. He is the only Source of our Guidance.

Tauhid is the belief in Allah with all His powers. Allah is All-Knowing, All-Wise and All-Powerful. He is the Merciful, the Kind and the Most-Loving. He is with us all the time. He sees us, but we do not see Him. He was, is and always will be. He is the First and the Last. He has no partner, son or daughter, nor was He born of anyone. He gives us life and takes it away. Everyone must return to Him after death.

The first duty of a Muslim is to declare his faith. To make this declaration a person must say in words and believe in his heart — la ilaha illallahu Muhammadur rasoolullah — (there is no god except Allah; Muhammad is Allah's messenger) .The saying of these Arabic words is called ash-Shahadah (Declaration of Faith). There are two parts of this declaration: (1) La ilaha illallah, (2) Muhammadur rasoolullah.

The first part, La ilaha illallah, has two aspects: Negative and Positive. La ilaha is the negative aspect, whilst illallah is the positive one.

A believer must first cleanse his heart of the idea of any other god or any other object of worship; only then can faith in the Oneness of Allah take root inside the heart.

Let us try to understand this with an example. Suppose we have a piece of land which is full of weeds and bushes where we want to grow wheat. Now, if we sow very good wheat seeds in the land without first cleaning it fully, we cannot hope to get a good wheat crop. So what must we do? We must cultivate the land, clear the weeds and bushes and prepare the soil before we sow the seeds. Then we can expect good crops.

Let us compare the land with the human heart. If the heart is full of belief in false gods, we cannot expect Tauhid to take root there. So it must be cleansed of any other god or object of worship; only then will Tauhid take root and the light of faith flow out.

Tauhid shapes and influences the entire course of our life. This is why we must have a clear understanding of its meaning.

The vast and majestic universe with its flawless system clearly indicates that there is one Creator and one Supreme Controller.

When we think about the unique system and perfect order of the universe, we find there is no chaos. The sun, the moon and the galaxy obey the same supreme Authority. The whole universe obeys the laws of this Supreme Power. There is complete cooperation and harmony in the system. Everything is nicely set in its place. No improvement can be suggested and no flaw detected. This superb and perfect combination of order and beauty is clear proof of the presence of an All-Wise and All-Powerful Creator and Regulator.

Had there been more than one Creator and Controller of the planets, for example, there would have been conflict and chaos. We notice no such disorder in the universe. The efficient running of a school and the steering of a car or a ship, calls for one headmaster, one driver or one captain. No single institution can be run problem-free with more than one leader, just as no vehicle can be driven by more than one person at the same time.

The universe, made up of many planets and stars, is a unit. All its components have a common origin and purpose because the universe was deliberately created by one Absolute Power. Everything in the universe works in harmony and cooperation as do the various parts of the human body. The limbs of the human body seem to have different functions, but they all serve the same purpose - keeping the body fit and functioning properly.

Angels in Islam

We have already mentioned belief in Angels (Malaikah) in al-Imanul Mufassal.' Who are the angels? What do they do? Can we see them? How are they different from man?

Angels are a special creation of Allah. They have been created from divine light (Nur) to perform specific duties. By comparison Adam, the first man, was created from clay, and the Jinn from fire. Iblis, the devil, is from the Jinn. Some people think Iblis was the leader of the angels. This is not true according to the Quran (18:50).

Angels have been given the qualities and powers necessary to carry out their duties, but they do not have free will. They always obey Allah and can never disobey Him. Man, on the other hand, has been given free will and can choose between right and wrong. This is why man will have to account for his actions on the Day of Judgement.

Angels do what Allah commands them. They are the sinless servants of Allah's will. They help men in the use of free will. Man decides what to do and angels help him to carry out the decision.

The duty of angels is to glorify and praise Allah. They never get tired. They are always ready to obey Allah. They do not need sleep, nor do they require the things a human being would need.

We cannot see angels unless they appear in human form. Angel Jibbrail once appeared in human form before a gathering of the companions of the Prophet. He came to teach them, but only the Prophet knew he was an angel. Angels can take any suitable appearance to carry out their duties.

There are many angels in the kingdom of Allah. Prominent among them are:

Jibbrail or Jibbrail (Gabriel)

Mikail or Mikal (Michael)

'Izrail (Malakul Mawt, also called Azrail)

Israfil : Jibbrail brought the revelation from Allah to Prophet Muhammad and to all the other prophets. 'Izrail – also called the 'Angel of Death' (Malakul Mawt) is responsible for ending our life. Israfil will blow the trumpet at the time of the end of the world and on the Day of judgement.

Some angels are busy recording all that we do. They are called the Respected Scribes (Kiraman Katibin). Not a single word we say goes unrecorded (50:18).

Allah maintains His kingdom perfectly, and angels are His obedient servants. Angels will welcome in Heaven those of us who always obey Allah's commands and will throw the wrong-doers into Hell (39:71-74).

So far we have learned that we human beings are the servants of Allah and His agents on earth. But we need guidance to carry out our duties as Allah's agents. We are unable to guide ourselves because we have many weaknesses within us and we have very limited knowledge of the past, present and future. Only Allah is above all these shortcomings and He alone has the power to give us guidance that is suitable for all times and places. We know that Allah has not left us without guidance and that He has sent prophets to show us the right path in life. In addition to this, He has also sent books of guidance through some prophets – His messengers.

Allah's blessings are countless. He provides us with all that we need. Just imagine how wonderfully He arranges our growth in the tender and affectionate care of our parents from birth to youth. Who provides us with food when we are in our mother's womb? Who fills our mother's breasts with milk to suckle as soon as we are born? Allah, the Merciful, of course. Allah's greatest favour to mankind is His guidance contained in the revealed books. The pure, perfect and most useful knowledge comes only from Allah, the Wisest and the Greatest (2:146-147,4:163,53:1-6).

A Muslim believes in all the revealed books which are mentioned in the Quran. They are: the Tawrat (Torah) of Mosa (Moses), the Zabur (Psalms) of Daud (David), the Injil (Gospel) of Isa (Jesus) and the Quran revealed to Muhammad. The Quran also mentions the Suhuf of Ibrahim (Scripture of Abraham).

Of the divine books, only the Quran remains unchanged, preserved in its original form. The original Tawrat, Zabur and Injil no longer exist. The texts available today were written by their followers many years after the death of their prophets. The writers have changed and distorted Allah's words. They have mixed divine words with those of human beings.

The Bible, which is a collection of the books of the Old Testament and the New Testament, has been translated into English from available Hebrew and Greek manuscripts. A careful reader can easily find some of the additions and alterations made to them.

The Bible, as it is available today, has many errors in it. It is not a divine revelation. It contains numerous misleading misconceptions and false accounts of the prophets. The message of Allah sent through them was either lost or distorted, because of the neglect or folly of their followers. On the other hand, the Quran contains Allah's guidance for mankind in its original form and language, unchanged and undistorted. It restates in clear and unambiguous language the message of Allah which the followers of earlier prophets have lost. The message of the Quran is valid for all times and climes.

Authority and its Absoluteness

> *Al-Qadr* : We believe that Allah has created the universe and He is its Absolute Controller and Regulator. Allah has fixed a set course for everything in the universe; this is called al-Qadr. Nothing can happen without the will and the knowledge of Allah. The destiny of every creature is already known to Allah. (25:2, 33:38)

But this does not mean that man has no freedom of will. We know that man is the Khalifah (agent) of Allah on this earth. We also know that Allah does not force us to do anything. It is up to us to obey or disobey Him. Whether we will obey or disobey is known to Him. But the fact that Allah knows what we are going to do does not affect our freedom of choice. Man does not know what his destiny is. He has the free will to choose the course he will take. We will be judged on the basis of our intentions on the Day of Judgement. If we follow Allah's guidance we will be rewarded; if not, we will be punished.

By believing in al-Qadr we testify that Allah is the Absolute Controller of all the affairs of His universe. It is He Who decides what is good and what is bad.

Allah knows already the fate of all human beings. This does not mean that we can do whatever we like, as if it would make no difference to what happens to us. We must pay attention to the Divine Guidance provided by Allah the Almighty. He gave human beings free will. We can choose between right and wrong. We will be judged for our actions on earth on the Day of Judgement.

Allah knows everything. He is the only One Who can judge His subjects. He asks mankind to follow the Divine Guidance He has provided for man's fulfilment in the life-after-death. But it depends entirely on the mercy of Allah to judge who will be rewarded and who will not.

Allah knows what will happen to everyone, but we do not know. This fore-knowledge is one of His Divine qualities (as-sifat).

Sometimes things happen that do not seem to make sense to us. Why do floods, hurricanes and earthquakes happen? Why do people starve to death in many countries around the world? Why do people suffer? What makes one man good and another a criminal?

We do not know all the answers to these questions. We have only a little knowledge of the universe, but Allah knows everything. We would be wasting time if we blamed Allah for the problems or the bad things that happen, simply because we do not seem to see the reasons behind them. We should have firm faith in the wisdom of our All-Knowing Creator, and help people in distress as much as we can.

We are unable to understand and interpret many of Allah's actions. It is meaningless to argue that human beings act without freedom and that we are forced to act the way we do. We decide for ourselves what we will do, and what we will not, and we are responsible for our own actions. This freedom of action does not contradict the foreknowledge of Allah.

What did You Learn?

Key Stage

1. What do the following Arabic words mean:

   a. Malaikah; b. Kutubullah; c. Risalat; d. Akhirat
2. What does the word Tauhid mean?
3. Carefully read the words of Suratul Ikhlas what does it tell us about Tauhid?
4. Who is the Controller of the Universe?
5. Why do you think the presence of more than one Creator would cause problems?

Key Stage

1. "Belief in Tauhid ought to change a person's life." Explain this statement, giving practical examples to clarify your answer.
2. "Tauhid, Risalat and Akhirat, summarise the whole of the Islamic system of life." Discuss this statement.
3. Group the seven basic beliefs of Islam into the three basic concepts and create a diagram of your own.
4. What is the Arabic word for each of the words listed below:

   a. Faith; b. Prophethood; c. The One; d. Oneness of Allah; e. Angels; f. Books of Allah; g. Declaration of Faith
5. Explain why belief in al-Qadr is so important in the life of a Muslim.

Key Stage

1. Discuss the significance of the positive and negative aspects of Tauhid.
2. "Belief in Tauhid has to result in action in order to be effective." Justify this statement in your own words.
3. Give an outline of the Islamic belief that al-Qadr does not contradicts person's free will to choose between right and wrong.

State of Being Prophet

Risalat is a channel of communication between Allah and mankind. Allah, the Most Merciful, has provided man with guidance to follow the right course and so make this world a happy and peaceful place to live in. There will be a great reward in the life-after-death for those who follow this guidance.

Since the beginning of the Creation, Allah has "sent His guidance for mankind through His chosen agents. These chosen people are called prophets (sing, nabi, pi. anbiyaa"). They asked the people of their time to obey and worship Allah alone. They taught, guided and trained the people to follow the way of Allah.

Prophets were human beings. We should never refer to them as the sons of Allah. Allah is One and He has no partner, son or daughter. It is a major sin to say that Allah has a son, daughter or partner.

The message of all the prophets is one and the same. As Allah is One, so is His message. The message is to worship Allah alone and to reject all false gods. "We did send Nuh (Noah) to his people, and he said 'My folk, worship Allah, you have no other god than Him. I fear for you the torment of an awful day.'" (7:59) In other words, all the prophets preached the message of:

La ilaha illallah (There is no god except Allah)

You may ask why we need guidance from Allah. The answer is simple: we human beings are weak and frail; we have no knowledge of the future and the knowledge we do have is limited. Also, we are not perfect. You can see that with so many weaknesses, we are unable to make any guidance for ourselves which can hold good for all times and all conditions. This is the reason why Allah has blessed us with guidance through prophets.

Not only this, Allah has also sent books of guidance through some of His prophets (2:213,7:52). These prophets are also called messengers (sing. rasla).The Quran is the last book of Allah's guidance. We will learn about it later.

Allah sent prophets to every nation at different times (10:47, 13:7, 35:24). It was necessary to send prophets at different times to bring forgetful human beings back to the right path (as-Siratal Mustaqim).

Concept of Death

Death is a natural event for all living things. It comes to every one of us. We will all die. The Quran says:

> "Everyone shall die." (3:185; 21:35; 29:57)

Death brings an end to our temporary life on this earth. It is an occasion of sorrow and grief for the loved ones of the deceased. In Islam, people mourn for the dead person by reciting the Quran and saying prayers (dua).

Islam asks us to keep in mind that death can arrive at any time. Only Allah knows when His servants will die. Death puts an end to our human body but it does not destroy our soul. The soul is taken away by the angel Malakul Mawt ('Izrail or Azrail) to Allah (32:11).

A person is sure to behave well and follow Allah's commands if he remembers death and the life-after-death.

In Islam, a dead body is ritually washed before it is buried. It is then covered with white sheets and fragrance is spread all over it. A funeral prayer is conducted before the burial. This prayer is called Salatul Janazah.

World's Creation

Allah created human beings to do what He wants and obey His commands. Allah says in the Quran, His final revelation to mankind:

> I have not created Jinn and mankind (for any other purpose) except to worship Me." (51:56)

'Worship' in this verse means total obedience to Allah's commands. The Quranic word for worship is 'Ibadat. Every good thing we do is 'Ibadat, if we do it for Allah's sake. The purpose of our life is to please Allah through 'Ibadat.

'Ibadat is the way to achieve success and happiness in this life and in the life-after-death.

Prophets of Islam

According to a saying of Prophet Muhammad the number of prophets is one hundred and twenty-four thousand. The Quran mentions only the twenty-five most prominent by name:

> As Muslims we must believe in all the prophets and messengers (2:285). Allah's guidance to mankind, which began with Adam was completed with Muhammad.

God's Oneness

Belief in La ilaha illallah or Tauhid has a far-reaching impact on our life:

(i) A believer in Tauhid surrenders himself completely to the Will of Allah and becomes His true servant and subject. Allah has created all that is on the earth and in the sky for the service of mankind. When a person surrenders himself to Allah's commands, he understands and appreciates that Allah has made all His Creation beneficial for him.

> The Quran confirms this when it says, "Have you not seen how Allah has made all that is in the earth subservient to you?" (22:65) "Do you not see how Allah has harnessed whatever is in Heaven and whatever is on earth for you? He has lavished His bounties on you both apparent and hidden..."
> (31:20)

These two verses clearly indicate that Allah has created everything on the earth and in the sky for the service and comfort of humans. The blessing of being served by other objects and creatures is only apparent when we believe and practise Tauhid. This means we must be totally obedient to Allah.

(ii) It produce? in the believer a high degree of self-respect, confidence and contentment. He knows that he depends on none but Allah for the fulfilment of his needs. He firmly believes that Allah alone has the power to provide all his requirements and no one else has any power to do good or harm him.

When can a believer be confident and develop self-respect? He can be so only when he feels that he depends on none but His Creator for the fulfilment of his needs. He does not become worried because he knows that Allah will take care of all his needs if he is truly obedient.

(iii) This belief makes a believer humble and modest. He is never arrogant or haughty. He is fully aware that everything on earth belongs to Allah and he gains control over the rest of the creation only by being a subject of Allah. He also knows very well that whatever he has is from Allah. So there is no reason to be proud or arrogant.

(iv) Belief in Tauhid makes a believer dutiful and upright. The believer knows that he must carry out the commands of his Creator to succeed in this life and the life hereafter. This awareness keeps him away from neglecting his duties and from other sins.

(v) It makes a person brave and courageous. It removes from his mind the fear of death or concern for safety. The believer knows that it is Allah who will cause death at the appointed time and none but He can harm the believer's safety. So, if he obeys Allah, he has nothing to worry about. He goes on doing his duty without any fear.

(vi) A believer in Tauhid consciously feels himself to be part of the whole universe. He is the best of all creations of Allah – the Powerful Master of the whole universe. This belief broadens his horizon and his outlook expands.

(vii) It produces in a believer strong determination, patience and perseverance. The believer becomes single-minded and dedicates himself to seeking the pleasure of his Creator.

Think of a boat. It has a rudder which guides the boat's movement: with the rudder under control, the boat moves forward proudly over the waves, but if the boat is not controlled by the rudder, it is tossed in any direction by every wave.

Similarly, when a believer surrenders himself to Allah alone, he can go forward in the affairs of life without fear. But if he does not obey Allah, he has to obey false gods like the fear of losing his job, fear of danger, fear of hunger and the like. When someone believes in Allah alone, his life is not ruled by such fears.

(viii) The most important effect of the belief in La ilaha illallah is that it makes a person obey Allah's commands. A believer in Tauhid is sure that Allah knows and sees everything and he cannot escape Allah's ever-watchful eye for a single moment. In fact, Allah is nearer to him than his own jugular vein (50:16). So, a true believer does not commit a sin either secretly or in the darkness of the night because he has a firm conviction that Allah sees everything all the time.

A believer in Tauhid seeks the pleasure of Allah by making his actions reflect his beliefs. Belief without practice has no place in Islam.

We Muslims are believers in Tauhid. We are Allah's servants and subjects. Our faith must be reflected in our actions.

7

Islamic Beliefs

Faith and its Declaration

Islam has five basic duties which Muslims must do. They are known as the five pillars of Islam (Arkanul Islam). These pillars are mentioned in the following Hadith (a saying of Prophet Muhammad):

> "Buniyal Islam ala khamsin: shahadati an la ilaha illallahu wa anna muhammadan rasoolullaha, wa iqamis salati, wa Itaiz zakati, wal hajji, wa sawmi ramadan."
>
> "Islam is based on five things: declaring that there is no god except Allah and that Muhammad is the Messenger of Allah, the establishment of Salat, the payment of Zakat, the Hajj and Sawm in the month of Ramadan." (al-Bukhari)

The five pillars as mentioned in the Hadith are:

Shahadah	(declaration of faith)
Salat	(five compulsory daily prayers)
Zakat	(welfare contribution)
Hajj	(pilgrimage to Mecca)
Sawm	(fasting during Ramadan)

Witness to Oneness of Allah

A Muslim declares his faith by reciting:

La ilaha illallahu Muhammadur rasoolullah.

These Arabic words mean: "There is no god except Allah; Muhammad is the messenger of Allah. "This declaration is called al-Kalimatul Taiyyibah. It contains the whole of Islamic belief. There are two parts.

The first part (La ilaha illallah) is about the Oneness of Allah (Tauhid in Arabic) while the second part (Muhammadur rasoolullah) concerns the Prophethood (Risalat) of Muhammad .The four Arabic words of the first part are: La which means no; ilaha meaning god; illa meaning except; and Allah. The second part has three words: Muhammad; rasal meaning messenger; and Allah.

The first pillar of Islam is Shahadah, which is about belief in Tauhid and Risalat of Muhammad. The other four pillars are the main duties in Islam, called 'Ibadat. 'Ibadat, an Arabic term, includes any activity which is done to gain Allah's favour. Salat, Zakat, Sawm and Hajj are the main forms of worship or 'Ibadat. If we perform them regularly and correctly we come closer to Allah, our Creator and Sustainer.

These four basic duties of Salat, Zakat, Sawm and Hajj make up the training programme which is required to shape our life around Shahadah. We already know that we belong to Allah and He is our Master. So, in order to behave like the servants of our Creator, we must practise Salat, Zakat, Sawm and Hajj honestly and faithfully.

Islam and Prayers

Salat : Salat is the second pillar of Islam. It refers to the five compulsory daily prayers. Salat is offered five times a day individually or preferably, for men and older boys, in congregation. Women and girls may also join in congregation whenever possible. We offer Salat to remember Allah. It brings us closer to Him. The Quran says:

> "Indeed, I am Allah; there is no god except Myself; so worship Me and establish Salat to remember Me."
> (20:14)

Salat is the practical proof of our faith in Allah and Islam. It has been made compulsory at certain fixed times. Allah says in the Quran: "Salat at fixed times has been enjoined on the believers." (4:103) The five daily prayers are:

Fajr	From dawn until just before sunrise
Zuhr	After midday until afternoon
Asr	From late afternoon until just before sunset
Maghrib	After sunset until daylight ends
Isha	Night until midnight or dawn

You should know at this stage how to say Salat. First, try to understand clearly why we need to offer Salat. We offer Salat to remember Allah our Creator and to be close to Him and to gain His favour.

To say your Salat you must be pure and clean. The Quran says: "Indeed Allah loves those who turn to Him in repentance and loves those who purify themselves." (2:222) Purification of the body and clothes is called Taharah, and cleanliness is called Nazafah. They are not the same, but they are connected to one another. You may be clean outwardly and still not be pure – it is especially important to remove all traces of urine or excrement from the clothes worn for Salat.

How can we have cleanliness? We can fully wash the whole body with pure and clean water or we can have a part-wash, cleaning only parts of the body. The full wash or bath is called Ghusl and the part wash is Wudu' (ablution).

Keep in mind that Muslims are not allowed to have a bath or a shower in the nude in the presence of others.

> *Wudu* : Prophet Muhammad said: "Indeed, on the Day of Resurrection, my followers will be called 'al-Ghurrul Muhajjalun' from the traces of Wudu', so whoever can increase the area of his radiance should do so (i.e. by performing ablution regularly)."
>
> (al-Bukhari)

Before we can begin to say Salat, we must first prepare ourselves. This preparation includes making sure we are clean. We do this by carrying out Wudu'.

Wudu' is essential for performing Salat. Allah says in the Quran:

> "O you who believe, when you prepare for Salat, wash your faces and your hands to the elbows; wipe over your heads and wash your feet up to the ankles."
>
> (5:6)

This verse refers to the compulsory (Fard) parts of Wudu'. The additional actions performed by Prophet Muhammad are recommended (Sunnah), and are mentioned in the books of Ahadith.

These are the steps to take:

(i) Make Niyyat (intention) saying the Tasmiyah (Basmalah or Bismillah):

Bismillahir rahmanir rahim (In the name of Allah, the Most Merciful, the Most Kind). Then wash both hands up to the wrists three times making sure that water has reached between the fingers.

(ii) Put a handful of water into the mouth and rinse it thoroughly three times.

(iii) Sniff water into the nostrils three times to clean them and then wash the tip of the nose.

(iv) Wash the face three times from right ear to left ear and from forehead to throat.

(v) Wash the right arm, and then left arm, thoroughly from wrist to elbow three times.

(vi) Move the wet palms of both hands over the head, starting from the top of the forehead to the neck.

(vii) Rub the wet fingers into the grooves and holes of both ears and also pass the wet thumbs behind the ears.

(viii) Pass the backs of the wet hands over the nape.

(ix) Wash both feet to the ankles starting from the right foot and making sure that water has reached between the toes and all other parts of the feet.

If you made a full Wudu' before putting on your socks, it is not necessary to take them off every time you repeat your Wudu'; it is enough to wipe the upper part of the socks with wet fingers. Leather socks are better for this, but any durable, untorn thick socks will also do. This type of wiping is valid for twenty-four hours only (three days in the case of a journey).

At the end of all the steps, recite:

> Ash-hadu alla ilaha illallahu wahdahu la sharika lahu wa ash-hadu anna Muhammadan abduhu wa rasooluh.

I testify that there is no god except Allah and He is One and has no partner and I testify that Muhammad is His servant and messenger.

You should repeat your Wudu' after:

1. Natural discharges (e.g. urine, stool, wind and the like).
2. Flow of blood or pus from any part of the body.
3. Full mouth vomiting.
4. Falling asleep or losing consciousness.
5. Touching the sexual organs.

Tayammum (Dry Ablution) : You can perform your Salat with Tayammum (4:43) when:

1. Water is not available at all,
2. The water available is insufficient (e.g. available water is enough for drinking only), or
3. Use of water is harmful (e.g. in sickness).

For Tayammum you are required to:

1. (a) Make Niyyat by saying: Bismillahir rahmanir rahim, then (b) place both your hands lightly on earth, sand, stone or any other object having dust on it.
2. Blow the dust off your hands and wipe your face with the hands once the same way as you do in Wudu'.
3. Repeat 1 (b) and wipe the right arm from wrist to elbow with the left hand and the left arm with the right hand.

Adaan (Call to Prayer) : Prophet Muhammad , by his practice and sayings, showed that Muslim men and older boys should offer their compulsory (Fard) Salat in congregation in a mosque (Masjid). Women and girls may offer their Salat in a mosque if they wish. All other Salat can be offered privately at home.

To call Muslims to Salat, Prophet Muhammad introduced the Adaan to signal that the time of Salat has arrived. The person who calls the Adaan is called the Muazzin (Caller). While doing so he faces the Qiblah (the direction towards the Kaaba in Mecca). He raises his hands up to his ears and calls out:

Allah-o-Akbar	Allah-o-Akbar
Allah-o- Akbar	Allah-o-Akbar
Allah is the Greatest	Allah is the Greatest
Allah is the Greatest	Allah is the Greatest

Ash-hadu alla ilaha illallah	Ash-hadu alla ilaha illallah
I testify that there is no god except Allah	I testify that there is no god except Allah
Ash-hadu anna Muhammadar rasoolullah	Ash-hadu anna Muhammadar rasoollullah
I testify that Muhammad is Allah's messenger	I testify that Muhammad is Allah's messenger
Haiya 'alas salah	Haiya 'alas salah
Rush to Salat	Rush to Salat
Haiya 'alal falah	Haiya 'alal falah
Rush to success	Rush to success
Allah-o-Akbar	Allah-o-Akbar
Allah is the Greatest	Allah is the Greatest
La ilaha Illallah	There is no god except Allah

During the Adaan for Fajr Salat the following words are added after Haiya 'alal falah:

Assalatu khairum minan nawm	Assalatu khairum minan nawm
Salat is better than sleep	Salat is better than sleep

Iqamat : Iqamah is the second call to Salat said inside the mosque at the beginning of Salat in congregation (Jamaat). When the musallins (persons saying Salat) stand in rows, the Muazzin says Iqamah which is the same as the Adaan except that after Haiya 'alal falah, the following words are added:

Qad qamatis salah	Qad qamatis salah
Salat has begun	Salat has begun

Usually, Iqamah is said in a lower voice than Adaan.

Fard (Compulsory) Salat : A Muslim must pray five times a day. The compulsory prayers are called Fard in Arabic. Each unit of prayer is called a rakat. Fard rakats are:

Fajr	....	2 rakats
Zuhr	....	4 rakats
Asr	....	4 rakats
Maghrib	....	3 rakats
Isha	....	4 rakats
	....	17 rakats
Jumuah	....	2 rakats (in place of Zuhr on Friday)

Sunnah Salat : Prophet Muhammad prayed extra rakats in addition to Fard prayers. These prayers are called Sunnah. Prophet Muhammad always prayed two rakats before the Fard of Fajr and three rakats after the Fard of 'Isha' even on a journey. The three rakats after 'Isha' are called Witr (odd number). Muslims also pray additional rakats other than Fard and Sunnah.

These are called Nafil (optional).

The Five Daily Salat

Fajr	*Zuhr*	*Asr*	*Maghrib*	*Isha*
2 Sunnah	4 Sunnah	4 Sunnah*		4 Sunnah
2 Fard	**4 Fard**	**4 Fard**	**3 Fard**	**4 Fard**
	2 Sunnah		2 Sunnah	2 Sunnah
	2 Nafl		2 Nafl	2 Nafl
				3 Witr
				2 Nafl
4	12	8	7	17

(these Sunnah before 'Asr and Isha' are Chair Mu 'akkodah, not done regularly, only occasionally.)

In addition to the five daily Salat, there are Salat for other occasions, e.g. Salatul Jumuah every Friday, Salatul 'Eid-ul-Fitr, Salatul 'Idul Adha and Salatul Tarawih in the month of Ramadan. The number of rakats in these Salat are:

Jumuah	'Eid-ul-Fitr	'Id-ul-Adha	Tarawih
4 Sunnah			20 Sunnah
2 Fard	2 Wajib	2 Wajib	
4 Sunnah			
2 Sunnah			
2 Nafl			
14	2	2	20

Wajib is a term used in Hanafi fiqh for something compulsory to a degree less than Fard. Those who follow Hanafi fiqh consider Salatul Janazah, Salatul 'Idul Fitr, Salatul 'Idul Adha and Witr Salat as Wajib.

Tarawih is offered after the two Sunnah rakats of 'Isha' but before the three of Witr.

Between 'Isha' and Fajr, a prayer called Tahajjud was regularly offered by the Prophet. It was obligatory for the Prophet . Devout Muslims try to follow the practice. Only those who wish to taste the sweetness of being closer to Allah can appreciate the benefits of the Tahajjud prayer.

Times when you must not pray:

1 From the beginning of sunrise until 15-20 minutes after full sunrise.

2 When the sun is at its height (zenith or meridian).

3 From the beginning of sunset until it is fully set.

4 For women during menstruation, and for up to 40 days during post- childbirth bleeding.

How to Perform Salat : At this stage you should be ready to start saying your Salat. Make sure you have Wudu', a clean body, clean clothes and a clean place. This is how you should do your Salat:

1 Stand upright on your prayer mat facing the direction of the Kaaba. This is called Qiyam and the direction is called the Qiblah in Arabic. In the UK the Qiblah is towards the south-east. In other countries the direction will be different. You will have to find out its direction before doing your Salat.

2 Say your Niyyat (intention) either verbally or in your mind. Niyyat is said with the words:

				Fajr	
I intend	two*	Fard*		Zuhr	
to say	three	Sunnah	rakats of Salatul	Asr	for Allah facing
	four			Maghrib	al-Kaaba
				"Isha"	

(* say the one which is relevant)

3 Raise your hands up to your ears (women and girls up to their shoulders) and say Allah-o-Akbar (Allah is the Greatest). This is called Takbiratul Ihram, meaning that all worldly things are now forbidden to you.

4 Place your right hand on your left hand just below the navel or on the chest (women and girls put their hands on their chest) and recite Titans':

Subhanaka Allahumma wa bihamdika wa tabarakasmuka wa taala jadduka wa Ia ilaha ghairuk for you may read ghaimka).

O Allah, glory and praise are for You, and blessed is Your name, and exalted is Your Majesty; there is no god but You.

Audhu billahi minash shaitanir rajim

I seek refuge in Allah from the cursed Satan (Shaitan).

Bismillahir rahmanir rahim In the name of Allah, the Most Merciful, the Most Kind.

5 Recite Suratul Fatiha (opening chapter) of the Quran:

Alhamdu lillahi rabbil 'alamin. Arrahmanir rahim. Maliki yawmid din. Iyyaka nabudu wa iyyaka nastain. Ihdinas siratal mustaqim. Siratal ladhina anamta 'alaihim, ghairil maghdubi 'alaihim wa lad dallin.

All praise is for Allah, the Lord of the Universe.

The Most Merciful, the Most Kind. Master of the Day of Judgement.

You alone we worship, from You alone we seek help. Guide us along the straight path.

The path of those whom You have favoured, not of those who earned

Your anger nor of those who went astray (or who are misguided).

Then say, quietly or loudly: Amin.

The recitation of al-Fatiha is a must in all prayers.

6 Recite any other passage from the Quran. For example:

Bismillahir rahmanir rahim

Qul huwallahu ahad. Allahus samad. Lam yalid walam yulad. Walam yakul lahu kufuwan ahad.

Say, He is Allah, the One. Allah is Eternal and Absolute. None is born of Him nor is He born. And there is none like Him. (Suratul Ikhlas 112)

7 Bow down saying Allah-o- Akbar. Place your hands on your knees and say Subhana rabbiyal 'azim (Glory to my Lord, the Great) three limes. This position is called Ruku'

8 Stand up from Ruku' saying Sami' allahu liman hamidah (Allah hears those who praise Him), followed

by Rabbana lakal hamd (Our Lord, praise be to You). This is called Itiddal as you return to the position of Qiyam (standing).

9 Prostrate saying Allah-o- Akbar, with your forehead, nose, palms of both hands, your knees and your toes touching the floor. Recite Subhana rabbiyal ala (Glory to my Lord, the Highest) three times. This position is called Sajda. Your arms should not touch the floor.

10 Get up from the floor saying Allah-o- Akbar and sit upright with your knees bent and palms placed on them. After a moment's rest prostrate again saying Allah-o- Akbar and recite Subhana rabbiyal ala three times. Get up from this position saying Allah-o- Akbar.

This completes one rakat or one unit of Salat. The second rakat is performed in the same way, except that you do not recite Subhanaka, Taawwudh (Audhu billahi...) or Tasmiyah (Bismillah...), then after the second prostration you sit upright and recite quietly at-Tashahhud:

> *At-tahiyatu lillahi was salawatu wat taiyibat.As-salamu 'alaika aiyuhan nabiyu wa rahmatullahi wa barakatuh. As-salamu 'alaina wa 'ala 'ibadillahis-salihin. Ash-hadu alla ilaha illallahu wa ash-hadu anna Muhammadan 'abduhu wa rasuluh.*
>
> All compliments are for Allah, and prayers and goodness. Peace be upon you, O Prophet! and the Mercy' of Allah and His blessings. Peace be upon us and on the righteous servants of Allah. I testify that there is no god except Allah and I testify that Muhammad is His servant and messenger.
>
> (al-Bukhari and Muslim)

In a three-rakat Salat (as in Maghrib) or a four-rakat Salat (Zuhr, 'Asr and 'Isha") you stand up for the remaining rakat after Tashahhud. But for a two-rakat Salat you remain seated after the second rakat and recite as-Safah 'alan nabi (blessings for the Prophet) or Darood:

Allahumma salli'ala Muhammadin wa'ala ali Muhammadin, kama sallaita 'ala Ibrahima wa 'ala ali Ibrahima, innaka hamidum majid, Allahumma barik 'ala Muhammadinw wa 'ala ali Muhammadin, kama barakta 'ala Ibrahima wa 'ala ali Ibrahima,

innaka hamidum majid.

O Allah! let Your blessings come on Muhammad and the family of Muhammad as You blessed Ibrahim and the family of Ibrahim.

Truly You are the Praiseworthy and Glorious.

O Allah! bless Muhammad and the family of Muhammad as You blessed Ibrahim and the family of Ibrahim.

Truly You are the Praiseworthy and Glorious. (Muslim)

After this say any of the following dua's (supplications):

Allahumma inni zalamtu nafsi zulman kathiran wa la yaghfirudh dhunaba illa anta faghfirli maghfiratan min 'indika warhamni innaka antal ghafurur rahim.

O Allah, I have been very unjust to myself and no one grants pardon against sins but You, therefore forgive me with Your forgiveness and have mercy on me. Surely, You are the Forgiver, the Merciful.

(*al-Bukhari* and *Muslim*)

Rabbijalni muqimas salati wa min dhurriyati rabbana wa taqabbal dua'.

Rabbanaghfirli wa liwalidaiya wa lilmu'minina yawma yaqumul hisab.

O Lord! make me and my children steadfast in Salat; our Lord, accept the prayer.

Our Lord, forgive me and my parents and the believers on the Day of Judgement. (*Surah Ibrahim* 14:40-41)

Now turn your face to the right saying

Assalamu 'alaikum wa rahmatullah (peace and the mercy of Allah be upon you) and then to the left repeating the words.

This completes the two-rakat Salat. In the four-rakat Salat of Zuhr, 'Asr and 'Isha', the whole procedure is repeated except that when you get up to complete the remaining two rakats (one rakat in Maghrib and Witr) after Tashahhud, you only recite al-Fatiha in Fan prayers and no other Surah. In a four-rakat Sunnah Salat you should recite another Sarah or part of the Quran after al-Fatiha.

In the first two rakats of the Fard prayer of Fajr, Maghrib and 'Isha' the Quran is recited aloud while in Zuhr and 'Asr it is recited silently. In all prayers, Tasbih (Subhana rabbiyal 'azim and *Subhana rabbiyal ala),* Tashahhud and Darood are said quietly. When the Fajr, Maghrib and 'Isha' prayers are said in congregation, only the Imam (one who leads the prayer) recites the Quran aloud. This also applies to Jumuah prayer (Friday prayer in place of Zuhr).

Salatul Witr : The Witr (odd number) prayer has three rakats. The first two rakats are said like the first two rakats of the Maghrib prayer. Then, after Tashahhud in the second rakat, stand up saying Allah-o-Akbar for the third rakat.

Recite Suratul Fatiha and some other verses from the Quran but before going to Ruku' raise your hands up to the ears saying Allah-o- Akbar and recite the following dua' after placing your hands below your navel or on the chest. This dua' is called Dua' al-Qunat:

Allahumma inna nastainuka wa nastaghfiruka wa numinu bika wa natawakkalu 'alaika wa nuthni 'alaikal khaira wa nashkuruka wa la nakfuruka wa nakhlau wa natruku maiuyafjuruk. Allahumma iyyaka nabudu, wa laka nusalli wa nasjudu wa ilaika nasa wa nahfidu wa narja rahmataka wa nakhsha 'adhabaka inna 'adhubaka bil kuffari mulhiq.

O Allah, we seek Your help and ask Your forgiveness and we believe in You and trust in You. We praise You in the best way and we thank You and we are not ungrateful and we cast off and forsake him who disobeys You. O Allah, You alone we worship and to You we pray and before You we prostrate, to You we turn in haste, and hope for Your mercy and we fear Your punishment. Your punishment overtakes the unbelievers. (al-Baihaqi)

Then say Allah-o-Akbar and bow down in Ruku' and complete the rest of the prayer like the Maghrib prayer.

The above dua' is used by Muslims who follow Hanafi fiqh. Another dua' used by some Muslims is:

Allahummahdini fiman hadait, wa 'afini fiman 'afait, wa tawallani fiman tawallait, wa barik li fima atait, wa qina sharra mna qadait , fainnaka Taadi wa la yuqda 'alaik, innahu la yadhillu man walait, tabarakta rabbana wa taalait.

O Allah, guide me along with those whom You have guided, pardon me along with those You have pardoned, be an ally to me along with those whom You are an ally to, and bless me for that for that which You have bestowed, and protect me from the evil You have decreed, for verily You decree and none can decree over You, indeed he whom You show allegiance to is never abased, O Our Lord! blessed and Exalted are You. (Abu Daud, al-Tirmidhi, Ibn Majah)

Sajdatus Sahw (Prostration of Forgetfulness) : Since we are human beings, we are not above mistakes and errors. If we forget to do something in our Salat, we can make up for it by making two extra sajda (prostrations) as we do in any rakat of Salat. This is called Sajdatus Sahw. This is done at the end of the last rakat of Salat. What you have to do is say Tashahhud (but not Darfid), then turn your face to the right and say Assalamu 'alaikum wa rahmatullah. Turn your face to the front, make two extra sajda (with Tasbih - Subhana rabbial ala), then recite Tashahhud again with Darood and dua'. Then turn your face, first to the right and then to the left, saying Assalamu 'alaikum wa rahmatullah.

A slightly different sequence is followed by some Muslims: at the end of the last rakat you say Tashahhud and Darood. Then turn your face to the right and say Assalamu 'alaikum wa rahmatullah. Turn your face to the front, make two extra sajda (with Tasbih - Subhana rabbial ala). Then turn your face, first to the right and then to the left, saying Assalamu 'alaikum wa rahmatullah.

Sajdatus Sahw is necessary if you forget to do any essentials of Salat, for example, the recitation of parts of the Quran after al-Fatiha, forgetting to say the first Tashahhud in a four-rakat Salat, or saying salam after two rakats in a four-rakat Salat.

Your Salat will not be valid if you do any of the following:

1. Miss out Niyyat (intention).
2. Miss out Takbiratul Ihram.
3. Forget to recite al-Fatiha.
4. Forget or do not make rukus' or sujud.
5. Do not face the Qiblah.
6. Do not have Wudu'.
7. Talk during Salat
8. Eat or drink during Salat.
9. Do not sit for Tashahhud.

Under these circumstances, you must repeat your Salat. Sajdatus Sahw will not be enough.

Salatul Jumuah (Friday Prayer) : Salatul Jumuah or Friday Prayer (not Jumma or Junta, as some Muslims incorrectly say) is offered in congregation. All adult Muslim men must take part. It is offered on Friday during zuhr time. It is not a must for women, but they can join this prayer if it does not upset their household duties.

People assemble for this Ṣalat immediately after noon. Upon arrival at the mosque or the prayer hall, they offer four or more rakats Sunnah prayer and then the Imam (prayer leader) delivers a Khutbah (sermon). After the Khutbah, the Imam leads two rakats Fard prayer. After the Fard prayer, six or more rakats of Sunnat and Nafil prayers are offered individually by each person.

Muslims are a community. Salatul jumuah is a community prayer. Every week, on Friday, Muslims living in an area get together to offer this prayer. This day is likened to a weekly 'Id (festival) for Muslims.

Mosques were the centre of all Islamic activity during our Prophet's time, but this is not so nowadays.

Friday prayer is an occasion for the assembly of Muslims in any given area. It gives them an opportunity to meet, discuss and solve their community problems. It develops unity, cooperation and understanding.

In an Islamic state, the Head of State or his representative or the local leader is supposed to lead the five daily prayers and the Friday prayer at the central mosque of the capital city or the central mosque of the locality, as was done by Prophet Muhammad, the first head of the Islamic state in Medina.

How nice it would be to live in a country where the Head of State or his representative or the local leader leads the prayer in the central mosque of the capital city or of the area! May Allah help us to revive this practice in all Muslim countries. Amin!

Salatul Janazah : Earlier death and Salatul Janazah have been mentioned briefly. We shall all die. When a Muslim dies, the body is given a simple ritual wash and then a funeral prayer called Salatul Janazah is offered in congregation. This Salat, unlike other Salat, has neither any Ruku' (bowing) nor any sujud (prostration) and you don't have to recite Tashahhud.

It is a collective duty (Fard-e-Kifayah) on all the Muslims of the locality of the dead person. If a number of them join in, the duty is discharged on behalf of all. If no one joins in everyone of the locality will be considered sinful before Allah. This is how the prayer is offered:

1. Make Niyyat (intention) that you are saying this prayer to Allah for the dead person.
2. Stand in rows facing the Qiblah. The coffin is placed in front of the congregation in a bier.
3. Say Allah-o-Akbar after the Imam (this takbir is Takbiratul Ibrahim and there will be three more takbirat after this) and raise your hands up to your ears; bring them down again and place them on or below your chest, putting the right hand on the left and recite the following:

   Subhanakallahumma wa bihamdika wa tabarakasmuka wa taala jadduka wajalla thanauka wa la ilaha ghairuk for you may read ghairuka). O Allah, glory and praise are for You, and blessed is Your Name, and exalted is Your Majesty and Glorious is Your Praise and there is no god but You. (Some Muslims recite Suratul Fatiha instead of this.)
4. Then the Imam will say Allah-o- Akbar loudly and you have to follow him repeating the words quietly. There is no need to raise your hands up to your ears this time. Now, recite Darood (see page 56).

5. After this, the third takbir will be said loudly by the Imam and those in the congregation will repeat it quietly. Then, if the dead person is an adult male Muslim, recite the following dua':

Allahummaghfir lihaiyina wa maiyitina wa shahidina wa gha'ibina wa saghirina wa kabirina wa dhakarina wa unthana. Allahumma man ahyaitahu minna faahyihi 'alal islami wa min tawaffaitahu minna fatawaffahu 'alal Iman.

O Allah, forgive those of us who are still alive and those who have passed away, those present and those absent, and our young and elderly, the males and the females. O Allah, he whom You wish to keep alive from among us, make him live according to Islam, and he whom You wish to die from among us, let him die in the state of Iman (faith), (al-Tirmidhi andAbu Daud).

If the dead person is an adult female Muslim then the second part of this dua' is replaced by:

Allahumma man ahyaitaha minna fa'ahyiha 'alal islami wa man tawaffaitaha minna fatawaffaha 'alal Iman.

O Allah, she whom You-wish to keep alive from among us, make her live according to Islam, and she whom You wish to die from among us, let her die in the state of Iman.

If the deceased is a boy, then recite the following:

Allahummaj' alhu lana farataw wajalhu lanaajraw wa dhukhraw wajalhu land shafiaw wa mushaffa.

O Allah, make him our forerunner and make him for us a reward and a treasure; make him one who will plead for us, and accept his pleading.

If the deceased is a girl, then recite the following:

Allahummaj'alha lana farataw wajalha lana ajraw wa dhukhraw wajalha lana shafiataw wa mushaffa.

O Allah, make her our forerunner and make her for us a reward and a treasure; make her one who will plead for us, and accept her pleading.

6. After reciting whichever dua is appropriate for the dead person, the Imam says the fourth takbir loudly and those in the congregation repeat it quietly.
7. Then the Imam turns his face first to the right saying Assalamu 'alaikum wa rahmatullah, and then to the left repeating the same words. Follow the Imam, repeating the words quietly.

This completes Salatuljanazah.

Some Dua after Salat : It is good practice to ask for forgiveness and mercy from Allah at the end of your Salat. You can make dua in your own words and in your own language but it is better for you to memorise some dua sin Arabic.

Rabbana atina fiddunya hasanah, wafil akhirati hasanah, wa qina adhabannar

Our Lord, grant us good in this world, and good in the Hereafter, and save us from the punishment of Hell-fire. (Suratul Baqarah 2:201)

Rabbana zalamna anfusana wa illam taghfirlana wa tarhamna lanakunanna minal khasirin.

Our Lord! we have wronged ourselves and if You do not forgive us and have no mercy upon us, surely we will be among those who are losers.

(Suratul Araf 7:23)

Allahumma antas salamu wa minkas salamu tabarakta ya dhal dhalali wal ikram. O Allah! You are the source of peace and from You comes peace, exalted You are, O Lord of Majesty and Honour. (Muslim)

La ilaha illallahu wahdahu la sharika lah, lahul mulku wa lahul hamdu wa huwa ala kulli shaiin qadir.

There is no god except Allah and He is One and has no partner, sovereignty is His, all praise is His and He has power over all things. O Allah, no one can stop You giving what You want to give, and no one can give what You do not want given, and no one with means (wealth, property) can do anything with their means against You. (al-Bukhari and Muslim)

Qada': making up for missed Salat : We must always try to offer Salat at the right time and make every effort not to miss our Salat. If you miss your Salat, you must do it at the first opportunity. Performing a missed Salat after its proper time is called Qada 'We must make up our Fard Salat.

Holy Quran, the Basis

1. *Suratul Fatiha (1)*

In the name of Allah, the Most Merciful, the Most Kind.

All praise is for Allah, the Lord of the Universe.

The Most Merciful, the Most Kind.

Master of the Day of Judgement.

You alone we worship, from You alone we seek help.

Guide us along the straight path.

The path of those whom You have favoured, not of those who earned.

Your anger nor of those who went astray (or who are misguided).

2. *Suratun Nas (114)*

In the name of Allah, the Most Merciful, the Most Kind.

Say, I seek refuge in the Lord of mankind,

the King of mankind,

the God of mankind,

from the mischief of the sneaking whisperer

(who whispers secretly),

who whispers into the hearts of mankind,

from among jinn and mankind.

3. Suratul Falaq (113)

In the name of Allah, the Most Merciful, the Most Kind.

Say, I seek refuge in the Lord of the Daybreak,

from the evil of what He has created,

and from the evil of the darkness when it is intense,

and from the evil of those who seek to promote discord

(who blow on knots or practise witchcraft),

and from the evil of the envier when he envies.

4. Suratul Ikhlas (112)

In the name of Allah, the Most Merciful, the Most Kind.

Say, He is Allah, the One.

Allah is Eternal and Absolute

(lives forever and is above all needs)

None is born of Him nor is He born.

And there is none like Him.

5. Suratul Lahab (111)

In the name of Allah, the Most Merciful, the Most Kind.

May the hands of Abu Lahab perish – doomed he is.

His wealth and his gains shall not help him.

He shall enter a blazing fire,

and his wife, the carrier of firewood,

shall have a rope of palm fibre around her neck.

6. *Suratun Nasr (110)*

In the name of Allah, the Most Merciful, the Most Kind.

When the help of Allah comes and the conquest,

and you see the people accepting the religion of Allah in large number,

then glorify the praises of your Lord, and seek His forgiveness.

He is ever ready to forgive.

7. *Suratul Kafirun (109)*

In the name of Allah, the Most Merciful, the Most Kind.

Say: O unbelievers!

I do not worship what you worship,

and you do not worship what I worship.

Nor will I worship what you worship,

and you will not worship what I worship.

You have your own religion and I have mine.

8. *Suratul Kawthar (108)*

In the name of Allah, the Most Merciful, the Most Kind.

Indeed we have given you the Kawthar (Fountain of Abundance).

So pray to your Lord and make sacrifice.

Surely your hater is the one cut off (i.e. without an heir).

9. Suratul Maun (107)

In the name of Allah, the Most Merciful, the Most Kind.

Have you seen him who denies the religion (the judgement)?

It is he who (harshly) pushes aside the orphan,

and does not urge others to feed the poor and the needy.

Woe to those who do their Salat

but are forgetful of their Salat,

who show off

but refuse to give even the smallest help to others.

10. Sarah Quraish (106)

In the name of Allah, the Most Merciful, the Most Kind.

For the tradition of the Quraish;

their tradition of travelling in winter and summer.

So they should worship the Lord of this house,

who has fed them and protected them from hunger,

and made them safe from fear.

11. Suratul Fit (105)

In the name of Allah, the Most Merciful, the Most Kind.

Have you not seen how your Lord dealt with the people of the elephant?

Did He not make their schemes to be nothing,

and send against them flocks of birds,

which pelted them with stones of hard-baked clay?

Thus he made them like eaten straw.

Lessons of Salat : Salat is the most important of the five basic duties of Islam after ash-Shaladali. We come closer to Allah by performing it regularly, correctly and with full awareness of its significance and meaning. At this stage, refresh your memory about the purpose of our creation and the need for performing Islamic duties. Allah has created us to worship Him. He says in the Quran: "Indeed I created Jinn and human beings for no other purpose but to worship Me." (Sdratudh Dhariyat 51:56) So, whatever duty we carry out, we must bear in mind that we are doing it for the sake of Allah. Only then can we expect to gain the desired benefits of the performance of Salat. The lessons of as-Salat are:

1. It brings men and women closer to Allah.
2. It keeps human beings away from indecent, shameful and forbidden activities. (Suratul 'Ankabut 29:45)
3. It is a training programme designed to control evil desires and passions.
4. It purifies the heart, develops the mind and comforts the soul.
5. It is a constant reminder of Allah and His greatness.
6. It develops discipline and willpower.
7. It is a guide to the most upright way of life.
8. It is a proof of true equality, solid unity and universal brotherhood.
9. It is the source of patience, courage, hope and confidence.
10. It is a means of cleanliness, purity and punctuality.
11. It develops gratitude, humility and refinement.
12. It is the demonstration of our obedience to our Creator.
13. It is a programme which prepares us to match our actions with our words.

14. It is the solid programme of preparing oneself for Jihad – striving one's utmost to please Allah.

If our Salat does not improve our conduct we must think seriously about where we are going wrong.

Alms Giving

Zakat : Zakat (welfare contribution) is the third pillar of Islam. The Arabic word Zakat means "to purify or cleanse". Zakat is to be paid once a year on savings at the rate of two and a half per cent. This rate applies to cash, bank savings and gold and silver jewellery. The rate for cattle and agricultural produce is different.

Payment of Zakat is a means of keeping our wealth clear of greed and selfishness. It also encourages us to be honest in our earnings and expenditure.

Zakat is a compulsory payment and is neither charity nor a tax. Charity is optional and taxes can be used by the state for any purpose, but Zakat has to be spent under fixed headings like helping the poor, the needy, payment of salaries to its collectors, to free captives and debtors, for travellers in need, to win over hearts of new converts and for the cause of Allah (9:60).

Zakat is an act of 'Ibadat. 'Ibadat is an Arabic term which means worship and obedience. It includes all activities of life, if we do them to please Allah. We pay Zakat to gain Allah's favour.

Zakat provides us with the opportunity of sharing our excess wealth with those less fortunate than ourselves. In fact, we and our wealth belong to Allah. He is the real owner and we are merely the trustees of His wealth. We do our duty as trustees if we pay Zakat as an obligatory part of 'Ibadat. (The words Zakat and Sadaqah are used interchangeably in the Quran)

We learned earlier that Islam is a complete code of life which includes, among other things, the economic side of life. Islam has its own economic principles. Zakat is one of the basic principles of the Islamic economy, based on social welfare and the fair distribution of wealth. In addition to the compulsory payment of Zakat, Muslims are encouraged to make voluntary contributions to help the poor and needy, and for other social welfare purposes. This voluntary contribution is called Sadaqah (charity).

Through the payment of Zakat, the rich share their wealth with the poor and thus the process of concentration of wealth is checked and fair distribution is ensured. The categories for expenditure of Zakat are mentioned in the Quran (Suratul Tawbah 9:60).

Islam and Fast

Sawm : Sawm (fasting), the fourth pillar of Islam, is another act of 'Ibadat. All adult Muslims must fast from dawn to sunset every day of Ramadan, the ninth month of the Islamic calendar. This means abstaining from eating, drinking and conjugal relations during the hours of fasting. Travellers and the sick can defer fasting during Ramadan and make up for it later. Sawm develops self-control and helps us to overcome selfishness, greed, .laziness and other faults. It is an annual training programme to refresh us for carrying out our duties towards Allah, the Creator and Sustainer. Sawm enables us to experience the pangs of hunger and thirst. We feel for ourselves what it is like to have an empty stomach. We can begin to appreciate what it must be like for the poor and the unfortunate – the millions who go hungry every day. Fasting develops self-control, and teaches us not to think just about comfort. It also helps us to restrain our sexual passions. Our appetite for food, love of comfort and sexual desires are instincts we must learn to control if we are to behave as the true servants of Allah.

Sawm helps us to remain truly obedient to Allah's

commands. That is why the Quran says: "O you who believe, fasting is prescribed for you as it was prescribed for those before you that you are expected to be truly obedient." (2:183) A truly obedient Muslim is called a muttaqi (a person with taqwa) and his true obedience or piety – developed through Sawm – is known as taqwa in Islam. Taqwa keeps a person away from sins and vices.

The month of Ramadan is a month of forgiveness, mercy and a means of avoiding the punishment of Hell.

The duty of fasting is only for Allah's sake and there is a very delightful and attractive reward for this in the life-after-death.

The following acts will break the fast if they occur during the fasting hours:

a. Deliberate eating or drinking.
b. Anything entering the body through the nose or mouth; this includes smoking or sniffing any powdered substance.
c. Having any conjugal relations (sex between husband and wife).

An injection in the muscle is allowed during fasting but not a nutritional injection. Unintentional eating or drinking due to forgetfulness or rinsing out the mouth or bathing and putting drops in the eye do not make the fast invalid.

A Muslim is expected to keep away from all bad actions during his fast. He should not tell a lie, break a promise or do any deceitful act.

The very purpose of fasting is to make a Muslim able to control his passions, so that he becomes a person of good deeds and intentions. Anger – a common human weakness – can also be brought under control by fasting.

In addition to the compulsory fasting in Ramadan, a Muslim

may fast during other times of the year. These fasts will be treated as Sunnah.

Fasting is not allowed during menstruation or post-child-birth bleeding. Women are required to make up the days lost during this period at some other time. A Muslim must not fast:

a. On the day of Eid-ul-Fitr.

b. On these days of Eid-ul-Adha.

The Quran was first revealed in the month of Ramadan. There is a night in the month which is "better than a thousand months" (97:3). This night is called Lailatul Qadr (Night of Power). According to Hadith, this night occurs during the last ten days of Ramadan (most probably the odd-numbered nights). It is a night of great importance; we should worship as much as we can on this night.

An additional prayer known as Tarawih (20 tak 'alts or 8 rakats) is offered during Ramadan after 'Isha'. This is a simnah prayer in which efforts are made to recite as much of the Quran as possible. In many mosques, the whole Quran is recited in Tarawih prayer. This prayer is generally offered in congregation. Those who cannot join a congregation should offer Tarawih at home. A pre-dawn meal known as Sahar is taken in Ramadan.

At the end of Ramadan Muslims celebrate 'Eid-ul-Fitr, a day of thanksgiving and happiness. It is one of the great occasions for the Muslim community. On this day, Muslims offer special prayers in congregation and thank Allah for His blessings and mercy.

Journey to Mecca for Hajj

Hajj is the fifth pillar of Islam. It is a visit to al-Kaaba, the house of Allah in Mecca, once in a lifetime by those Muslims who can afford to make the journey. It is performed during the period 8-13 Dhul Hijjah, the twelfth month of the Islamic calendar (3:97; 22:27-30; 2:197).

Al-Kaaba, also known as Baitullah (House of Allah), is a cube-like one-storey building which was built originally by Prophet Ibrahim (Abraham) and his son Ismail (Ishmael). It is the first house ever built for the sole purpose of the worship of Allah (3:96). Allah has blessed al-Kaaba. Muslims who can afford to make the journey and are physically fit come here every year from all over the world.

The occasion may rightly be called the Annual International Muslim Assembly. During Hajj, Islamic brotherhood becomes particularly evident and can be experienced in a special way by everyone who takes part. Barriers of language, territory, colour and race disappear and the bond of faith is uppermost. Everyone has the same status in the House of Allah -- the status of His servant.

Hajj has a number of important rituals associated with it, including:

1. Putting on Ihram (2:200).
2. Going around al-Kaaba seven times (2:200).
3. A fast walk between as-Safa and al-Marwah near al-Kaaba (2:158).
4. Visiting and staying at Mina, 'Arafat and Muzdalifah (2:198).
5. Throwing pebbles at three fixed places in Mina (2:200).
6. Shaving or trimming hair (2:200; 48:27).
7. Sacrifice of an animal (2:196, 200).

At the time of Hajj, while approaching Mecca, a pilgrim must put on Ibrahim before reaching a point called Miqat (station). For men, Ihram consists of two sheets of unsewn white cloth. This is the very simple form of dress a pilgrim must wear in place of his normal everyday clothes. For a woman, Ihram is her ordinary dress.

This change is very significant. It reminds the pilgrim of

his position in relation to Allah. He is a humble servant of his Creator. It also reminds him that after death he will be wrapped in white sheets and his favourite or expensive clothes will be left behind.

When putting on Ibrahim, pilgrims express their intention (Niyyah) by saying: "I intend to put on Ihram for Hajj."

There are then some restrictions on the pilgrim while in the state of Ihram. He or she must not:

Restriction	Purpose
a. use perfume	– to help forget enjoyment of ordinary daily life
b. kill or harm animals, even insects	– to feel that everything belongs to Allah
c. break or uproot plants	– to kill one's urge for aggression and feel a love for nature
d. hunt	– to develop mercy
e. marry or take part in a wedding	– to forget normal life and think of the Creator
f. do anything dishonest or arrogant	– to behave like a servant of Allah
g. carry arms	– to give up aggressive attitudes
h. cover the head (males)	– to express humbleness
i. cover the face (females)	– to feel a pure atmosphere
j. wear shoes covering ankles	– to express simplicity
k. cut hair or clip nails	– to express non-interference with nature
l. have conjugal relations	– to forget worldly pleasure

All these restrictions make a pilgrim think of Allah and his ultimate goal in life – success in the life-after-death – and nothing else. While in Ihram the pilgrim recites Talbiyah as follows:

Labbaik allahumma labbaik, labbaika la sharika laka labbaik, innal hamda wan nimata laka wal mulk, la sharika lak.

Here I am O Lord, here I am, here I am. You have no partner, here I am, surely praise, blessings and the kingdom are for You. You have no partner.

One of the important things pilgrims do is to drink from the well of Zam Zam, located to the south of al-Kaaba. Hajar (Hagar), the mother of Prophet Ismail (Prophet Ibrahim's eldest son), discovered the well as she ran between os-Safa and at-Marwah, desperately searching for water for baby Ismail.

Hajj has in it all the lessons of Salat, Zakat and Sawm. Do you remember why we offer Salat, pay Zakat and fast? We offer Salat to remember Allah, pay Zakat to please Him and fast only for His sake. During salah we present ourselves to Allah five times a day, but during Hajj we have to think of Allah all the time. At the time of Salat, we face towards al-Kaaba, but during Hajj we go there in person. Zakat teaches us to pay part of our savings for welfare and other good causes for Allah's sake, but during Hajj we sacrifice much more of our money for the pleasure of Allah.

Muslims from all parts of the world perform a lesser pilgrimage called 'Umrah (2:158). It can be performed at any time of the year. For 'Umrah, a person has to put on Ihram and do rituals 1,2,3 and 6 only *sawm* teaches us to control ourselves during daylight hours from eating, drinking or smoking or having conjugal relations. But in the state of Ihram there are many more restrictions. (Eating and drinking are not prohibited in the state of Ihram though.)

What do we learn from all these exercises during Hajj? We

learn that we belong to Allah, we will return to Him and we must do as He commands us. If we do, we will surely be successful in this life and in the Akhirat.

Concept of Struggle

Jihad : Jihad is the use of all our energies and resources to establish the Islamic system of life, in order to gain Allah's favour. Jihad is an Arabic word which means "to try one's utmost". It is a continuous process. In its first phase a Muslim learns to control his own passions and intentions. We need to strive hard to achieve this. This is Jihad within ourselves and is the basis for the comprehensive Jihad which is concerned with establishing Maroof" (right) and removing Munkar (evil) from our lives and from society. It demands the use of all our material and mental resources. Eventually we may be required to give our life for the cause of Islam.

The aim of Jihad is to seek the pleasure of Allah. This must not be forgotten because this purpose is the basis of all Islamic endeavours.

Earlier, we learned about the basic duties of Shahadah, Salat, Zakat, Sawm and Hajj. All these duties teach us to obey Allah and gain His favour so that we pass the test on the Day of Judgement and receive the reward of entering Paradise – the place of permanent happiness, joy and peace.

Regular and conscious performance of the four basic duties should motivate us to live and die for the cause of Islam, which we believe to be the only sure way to success in this life and in the hereafter. In other words, all Islamic duties should prepare us to engage in Jihad. Jihad is the end result of our efforts in Salat, Zakat, Sawm and Hay. We cannot think of Islam without Jihad.

We would like to see truth prevail and falsehood vanish, but we are aware that this cannot happen on its own; we have to do our utmost to achieve it. The performance of other Islamic duties will be meaningless if they do not motivate us to engage in Jihad.

The method of Jihad is the one practised by Prophet Muhammad. His life is the perfect example for us and we will learn about it later.

Our duty as Muslims is to practise Allah's commands and to urge others to do the same. This duty has been given to us by Allah in His own words in the Quran:

> "You are the best Ummah (community); you have been raised for mankind so that you command what is right and forbid what is evil, and you believe in Allah." (3:110)
>
> We should ask others to be obedient to Allah in a persuasive and convincing way. Our own life-style will count for much here. It is most important that we try hard to practise what we say. Allah does not like those who say something but do something different. The Quran says: "Why do you ask of others the right conduct and you yourselves forget?" (2:44) In another place in the Quran, Allah says, "O you who believe! Why do you say that which you do not do? It is most hateful to Allah that you say that which you do not." (61:2-3)

These verses clearly direct us to compare our own deeds with our words. To achieve this, we must do good ourselves and also urge others to do the same. This will enable us to remove our weaknesses and deficiencies. None of us is perfect, but our imperfections will gradually decrease if we do our very best to pursue our duty of Jihad.

8

Faith and its Basis

In order to appreciate the true value of the ethical system of the Arabian Prophet, it must be remembered that, in Islam, the service of man and the good of humanity constitute pre-eminently the service and worship of God Faith without work has no meaning; "this life is but a tillage (mazraa) for the next," and therefore we are told repeatedly, "do good that you may reap there." The mere recognition of a creed or formula does not constitute Islam. It is "a life to be lived in the present." "Dost thou desire to approach thy Lord, a righteously for,-the crooked path never leads to Him." It is pointed out in the language of poetry that man partakes of the nature of the beast as well as of the angel; an he is adjured to leave the nature of the beast, that he may surpass the angel. Striving for the good, the true and the pure is inculcated in the most emphatic terms, "for striving is the ordinance of God, and whatever God has ordained can only be attained by striving."

Values of Ethics

The ethical code of Islam is thus summarised in the fourth Sura of the Quran:

> "Come, I will rehearse what your Lord hath enjoined on you,-that ye assign not to Him a partner, that ye

> be good to your parents; and that ye slay not your children because of poverty: for them and for you will We provide; and that ye come not near to pollution, outward and inward, and that ye slay not a soul whom God hath forbidden, unless by right... and draw not nigh to the wealth of the orphan, save so as to better it... and when ye pronounce judgement then be just, though it be the affair of a kinsman. And God's compact fulfil ye, that is, what He hath ordained to you. Verily, this is my right way; follow it then."

And again, "Blessed are they who believe and humbly offer their thanksgiving to their Lord... who are constant in their charity, and who guard their chastity, and who observe their trust and convenants..... Verily, God bids you do justice and good, and give to kindred their due; and He forbids you to sin and to do wrong and oppress."

"Who speaketh better than he who inviteth unto God, and worketh good .... good and evil shall not be held equal. Turn away evil with that which is better."

Again, speaking of Paradise, it says, "it is prepared for the godly, who give alms in prosperity and adversity; who bridle their anger and forgive men; for God loveth the beneficent."

History has preserved, for the admiration of posterity, many examples of patience under suffering exhibited by the followers of other creeds. But the practice of the virtues of patient forgiveness is easier in adversity, when we have no power to punish the evil-doer, than in prosperity. It is related of Hussain, the grandson of the Prophet, that a slave having once thrown the contents of a scalding dish over him as he sat at dinner, fell on his knees and repeated the verse of the Quran. "Paradise is for those who bridle their anger." "I am not angry," answered Hussain.

The slave proceeded, "and for those who forgive men." "I

forgive you." The slave, however, finished the verse adding, "for God loveth the beneficent." "I give you your liberty and four hundred pieces of silver," replied Hussain.

The author of the Kashaf thus sums up the Islamic teachings: "Seek again him who drives you away; give to him who takes away from you; pardon him who injures you: for God loveth that you should cast into the depth of your souls the roots of his perfections."

Good vs Evil

The return of good for evil is preached on all occasions:

> "Think only of what is good for each, and consider not the wrong that has been done to thee: pardon others readily, and do good unto all. Fair is the dwelling-place of those who have bridled their anger and forgiven their adversaries. Return good for evil."

To the humble denizen of the earth, "with his mouth in the dust," comes the message from Him to lift up the stricken soul.

"By the noonday brightness, and by the night when it darkeneth, thy Lord hath not forsaken thee, neither hath He been displeased. Surely the future shall be better for thee than the past; and in the end He shall be bounteous to thee, and thou shalt be satisfied Did He not find thee an orphan, and give thee a home; erring and guided thee; goody and enriched thee? As to the orphan, then, wrong him not; and chide not away him that asketh of thee, and tell abroad the favours of thy Lord." "Did ye think we had Made you for sport, and that ye should not be brought back again to us?" .

To the errant sinners, turning with a true penitence to their Creator and crying out to Him,—'O our Lord, punish us not if we forget and fall into sin, blot out our sins, and forgive us,' is conveyed the promise of mercy and forgiveness:—"Come back, come back, whatever thou art, come back; hast thou denied Me or worshipped another for Me, or broken My commandments, come back. This Threshold of Mine is not the threshold of despair. If thou hast forgot thyself, turn with true penitence and come back."

It has been truly said that "the moral idea of the new gospel was set in the common sense of duty and the familiar instances of love."

"Blessed is he who giveth away his substance that he may became pure, and who offereth not favours to any one for the sake of recompense ... but only as seeking to approach the Lord Most High."

"They are the blest who, though longing for it themselves, bestowed their food on the poor and the orphan and the captive (saying), we feed you for the sake of God: we seek from you neither recompense nor thanks.'"

"Worship God alone; be kind to kindred and servants, orphans and the poor; speak righteously to men, pray, and pay alms."

"Defer humbly to your parents; with humility and tenderness say, 'O Lord, be merciful to them, even as they brought me up when I was helpless.'"

"Abandon the old barbarities, blood-vengeance, and child-murder, and be united as one flesh."

"Do thy alms openly or in secret, for both are well."

"Give of that which hath been given you before the day cometh when there shall be no trafficking, nor friendship, nor interception."

"Wouldst thou be taught the steep path? It is to ransom the captive, to feed the hungry, the kindred, the orphan, and him whose mouth is in the dust. Be of those who enjoin steadfastness and compassion on others."

"Woe to them that make a show of piety, and refuse help to the needy."

"Make not your alms void by reproaches or injury." "Forgiveness and kind speech are better than favours with annoyance." "Abandon usury." "He who spendeth his substance to be seen of men, is like a rock with thin soil over it, whereon the rain falleth and leaveth it hard. But they who expend their substance to please God and establish their souls, are like a garden on a hill, on which the rain falleth and it Yieldeth its fruit twofold; and even if the rain doth not fall, yet is there a dew."

"Judge between men with truth and follow not thy passions, lest they cause thee to err from the way of God." "Covet not another's gifts from God." "There is no piety in turning the face east or west, but in believing in God only and doing good." "Make the best of all things; enjoin justice and avoid the foolish; and if Satan stir thee to evil, take refuge in God." "Touch not the goods of the orphan." "Perform your covenant, and walk not proudly on the earth."

"The birth of a daughter brings dark shadows on a man's face... Kill not your children for fear of want: for them and for you will We provide. Verily, the killing them is a great wickedness." "God hath given you wives that ye may put love and tenderness between you."

"Commit not adultery; for it is a foul thing and an evil way."

"Know ye that this world's life is a cheat; the multiplying of riches and children is like the plants that spring up after rain, rejoicing the husbandmen, then turn yellow and wither away. In the next life is severe chastisement, or else pardon from God and his peace." "Abandon wickedness and the very semblance of it. They, verily whose only acquirement is iniquity, shall be rewarded for what they shall have gained ... .. Those who abstain from vanities and the indulgence of their passions, give alms, offer prayers, and tend well their trusts and their covenants, these shall be the heirs of eternal happiness." "Show kindness to your parents, whether one or both of them attain to old age with thee: and say not to them, 'Fie!' Neither reproach them, but speak to them both with respectful speech and tender affection." "And to him who is of kin render his due, and also to the poor and to die wayfarer, yet waste not wastefully"

"And let not thy hand be tied up to thy neck; nor yet open it with all openness, lest thou set thee down in rebuke in beggary."

"Enjoin my servants to speak in kindly sort." "Turn aside evil with that which is better." "Just balances will We set up for the day of resurrection, neither shall any soul be wronged in ought, though were a work but the weight of a grain of a mustard seed, We would bring it forth to be weighed: and our reckoning will suffice." "Seek pardon of your Lord and beturned unto Him: Verily, my Lord is merciful and loving." "And your Lord saith, 'Call upon Me, I will hearken unto you.'" "Say, 'O my servants who have transgressed to your own injury, despair not of God's mercy, for all sins doth God forgive. Gracious and merciful is He.'" "The good word riseth up to Him, and the righteous deed will He exalt." "Truly my Lord hath forbidden filthy actions, whether open or secret, and iniquity, and unjust violence."

"Call upon your Lord with lowliness and in secret, for He loveth not transgressors, and commit not disorders on the well-ordered earth after it hath been well ordered; and call on Him with fear and longing desire: verily, the mercy of God is nigh unto the righteous."

"Moreover, We have enjoined on man to show kindness to his parents. With pain his mother beareth him; with pain she bringeth him forth: and he saith, 'O my Lord! Stir me up to be grateful for Thy favours wherewith Thou hast favoured me and my parents, and to do good works which shall please Thee; and prosper me in my offspring: for to Thee am I turned, and am resigned to Thy will." "For them is a dwelling of peace with their Lord; and in recompense for their works shall He be their protector." "Lost are they who, in their ignorance, have foolishly slain their children, and have forbidden what God hath given them for food, devising an untruth against God! Now have they erred; and they were not rightly guided."

"The likeness of those who expend their wealth for the cause of God, is that of a grain of corn which produceth seven ears, and in each ear a hundred grains; they who expend their wealth for the cause of God, and never follow what they have laid out with reproaches or harm, shall have their reward with their Lord; nor fear shall come upon them, neither shall they be put to grief; .... a kind speech and forgiveness is better than alms followed by injury."

"God will not burden any soul beyond its power. It shall enjoy the good which it hath acquired, and shall bear the evil for the acquirement of which it laboured.".

"O Lord punish us not if we forget or fall into sin, O our Lord! and lay not on us a load like that which Thou hast laid on those who have been before us, O our Lord! and lay not on us that for which we have not strength: but blot out our sins and forgive us and have pity on us."

"The patient and the truthful the lowly and the charitable, and they who seek pardon at each daybreak:"... "Who give alms, alike in prosperity and in success, and who master their anger, and forgive others! God loveth the doers of good;" [Theirs a goodly home with their Lord]. "O our Lord! forgive us then our sins and hide away from us our evil deeds, and cause us to die with the righteous:" "And their Lord answereth them, 'I will not suffer the work of him among you that worketh, whether of male or female, to be lost, the one of you is the issue of the other."' "And fear ye God, in whose name ye ask mutual favours, and reverence your mothers-at their feet is paradise."

"Covet not the gifts by which God hath raised some of you above others."

"Be good to parents, and to kindred, and to orphans, and to the poor, and to a neighbour, whether kinsman or new-comer, and to a fellow-traveller, and to the wayfarer, and to the slaves whom your right hands hold; verily, God loveth not the proud, the vain boaster."

"He who shall mediate between men for a good purpose shall be the gainer by it. But he who shall mediate with an evil mediation shall reap the fruit of it. And God keepeth watch over everything."

"O ye Muslims! stand fast to justice, when ye bear witness before God, though it be against yourselves, or your parents, or your kindred, whether the party be rich or poor. God is nearer than you to both. Therefore follow not passion, lest ye swerve from truth."

Brotherhood

Brotherly love and mutual assistance are inculcated in emphatic terms:

> "Muslims are brothers in religion; and they must not oppress one another, nor abandon assisting each other, nor hold one another in contempt. The seat of righteousness is the heart; therefore, that heart, which is righteous, does not hold a Muslim in contempt; and it is wicked to hold a Muslim in contempt; and all things of one Muslim are unlawful to another, his blood, property and reputation; he must not act or speak that by which the blood of a Muslim might be spilt, and his property destroyed, and his reputation lost." "The people for Paradise are three; the first, a

just king, a doer of good to his people, endowed with virtue; the second, an affectionate man, of a tender heart to relations and others; the third, a virtuous man."

Duties of Musalmans to Each Other : Again, "The duties of Musalmans to each other are six." It was asked: "What are they O Prophet?"

He said, "When you meet a Musalman, salam to him; and when he invites you to dinner, accept it; and when he asks for advice, give it to him; and when he is sick, visit him; and when he dies, follow his bier."

But help to the suffering and the weak is not preached in an exclusive spirit, nor is it confined to Muslims, for it is declared incumbent to assist every oppressed person, whether Muslim or not. "Verily, God will say, at the Day or Resurrection, 'O sons of Adam I was sick, and ye did not visit Me,' and the sons of Adam will say, 'O our Protector how could we visit thee? for thou art Lord of the universe, and art free from sickness.' And God will say, 'O men! Did you not know that such a one of My servants was sick, and ye did not visit him? Did you not know that had you visited that servant, you would have met with favour and pleasure near Me?' And God will say, at the Resurrection, "O sons of Adam, I asked you for food, and Ye gave Me not?' And the sons of Adam will say, 'O our Lord, how could we give thee food, seeing thou art the Cherisher of the universe and art free from hunger and sating?' And God will say, 'Do not ye know that such a one of My servants asked you for bread, and you did not give 'it him? Did you know that had you given him victuals, you would have received its reward from Me.' And God will say at the Resurrection, "O sons of Adam! I asked you for water, and ye gave Me not.' They will say, 'O our Cherisher! How could we give thee water, seeing thou art the Cherisher of the universe, and not subject to thirst!' God will say, 'Such an one of My servants asked you for water, and you did not give it him: did you not know that had you given to him, you would have received its reward from Me?"'

Help of the Poor : "That person who asks, in the name of God, protection from harm by you, or from any one else, then give him protection; and that person who asks a thing from you in the name of God, then give it to him, and that person who invites you to eat, approve of and accept his invitation, and that person who does you a good and benefit, then return it, that is, do a good act to him; but if you have nothing to return him, then pray for him, till you know that you have atoned to him and performed your duty to him."

"Do not say, 'if people do good to us, we will do good to them; and if people oppress us, we will oppress them': say, on the contrary, if they oppress you, you will not oppress them."

Mercy

"Whoever is kind to His creatures, God is kind to him; therefore be kind to man on the earth, whether he be good or bad; and being kind to the bad, is to withhold them from badness, so that those who are in heaven may be kind to you."

"Strive always to excel in virtue and truth." "Help each other with generosity and piety. He who helps his fellow brethren and tries to do them good, will receive his reward from the Almighty equal to the reward of those who strive to repress wrong-doing."

"All God's creatures are His family; and he is the most beloved of God who tries to do most good God's creatures."

"The best of men is he from whom good accrues to humanity."

"He who tries to remove the wants of his brother, whether he be successful or not, God will forgive his sins."

"He who helps his brother will himself be helped on the Day of Account."

"The Prophet was asked who was the most favoured of God's creatures. He replied, 'He from whom the greatest good comes to His creatures' And then he was asked what actions are most excellent. He answered, "to gladden the heart of a human being, to feed the hungry, to help the afflicted, to lighten the sorrows of the sorrowful, and to remove the wrongs of the injured.' 'He who helps his fellow creature in the hour of need and he who helps the oppressed, God will help him in the Day of Travail.'"

"Thus saith your Lord, 'whilst living, rely on Me for I am all sufficient; do not be avaricious or covet the goods of your brethren; love for them what you love for yourself, guard yourselves from anger, passion and greed, for these are the worst of actions."'

"He who is subservient to his passions and desires, and forgets in their pursuits his duty to others, is the worst and weakest of God's creatures." "Be persistent in good actions."

"To gladden the heart of the weary, to remove the suffering of the afflicted has its own reward. In the day of trouble, the memory of the action comes like the rush of a torrent and takes away our burden."

"No man is true in the truest sense of the word, but he who is true in word,- in deed and in thought."

"He is true who protects his brother both present and absent."

"Fidelity and truth, purity and gentleness, generosity and sweetness are the best of qualities in man."

A few of the aphorisms of the first Imam, selected at random from the Ghurrar-wad-Durrar, will throw light on the teachings of the Mosque in the days of the Republic.

"He who is most dutiful to those to whom he owes duty In the wisest among you."... "He who is the most learned in the best conducted and behaved in his life. He is the most intelligent is the most virtuous"... "No evil is worse than avarice." "To be kind is one of the best of virtues; to tell falsehood one of the worst of vices. He who fulfils his word is one of the noblest of God's creations."

"A bad temper is the worst of afflictions." "To keep free from pollutions is the best of worship. To void evil actions in the best of actions."

"He who sees his own faults is the wisest of men. He who considers himself wiser than others, is the most foolish."

"The worship of God, without gratitude to man, is watering the sand of the desert."

"Fidelity is the beacon which lights the way to heaven."

"Learning is of no value without work; precept of no avail without practice."

"To be forbearing to the faults of your fellow-brethren is an act of charity."

"When you speak, speak the truth; when you attain to power, gently and beneficently with those subordinate to you. When you fall into affliction, be patient; when you have to inflict a punishment, be merciful. When you commit a fault, ask pardon. When you are placed in the seat of justice, be just. When you commit sin, be ashamed. When you see the oppressed, render help."

"Be grateful to those who benefit you. Humility increases your worth. Remembrance of God brings down His mercy."

"He who imparts learning never dies."

"Do not look at the person who speaks, but look at what he speak."

"For the envious, there is no peace. Where there is spite, there can be no true friendship."

"The untruthful knows no modesty."

"No provision [for the next world] is better than piety or doing good actions in this world."

"A man who is the slave of his passions, is the worst of all slaves; and no man has a greater enemy than his own selfishness."

"No action is good unless, the intention is good; nor any word pure unless accompanied by pure action."

"No evil is greater than evil propensities."

"Avarice kills truth."

"Knowledge is the best of blessings."

"Purity of heart is the essence of all virtues."

"Ignorance is the worst of all poverty."

"Kindness and courtesy are better than conferring an obligation."

"To overlook the faults of others is better than alms-giving."

"To forgive when it is in your power to avenge an injury, to love when you are wronged, are the best of virtues."

"Hypocrisy is the destruction of piety; to impose an obligation is destructive of charity; selfishness is destructive of wisdom."

"The good you do alone goes with you into the next world." "Good acts are the steps which take ye to God."

"The peace of the two worlds is a commentary on two words,-love for friends, charity towards enemies."

"On the tablet of my heart I have engraved from the sayings of my father, may his memory be sacred to eternity,—'My child, should you be in the company of one who is fallen, do not be impertinent and do not view him with the eyes of contempt; if, in this world, you cannot make a heart glad, yet act not so as to make the humblest soul sorrowful,'"

"O thou who hast experienced happiness and trouble from good and bad events, and who art in consequence full of thanks, and sometimes of complaints! Do not take high ground, that thy efforts be not vain; be rather like grass, that stands in the way of the wind, or like a bundle of grass, which others carry off on their shoulders."

Tenderness for Children and Respect for Age : Tenderness and affection for children and respect for age are emphatically inculcated. "He is not of us, who is not affectionate to his little ones, and does not respect the reputation of the old; and he is not of us, who does not order that which is lawful, and prohibit that which is unlawful."

"Every young person who honours the old, on account of their age, may God appoint those, in his years, to honour him." "Whoever puts his hand upon the head of an orphan, from kindness, shall have the blessings of God, for every hair his hand shall have covered; and whoever does good to a boy or girl, being orphans, he and I shall be near each other in paradise." "Whoever gives an orphan a dwelling, meat and drink, God will bestow him a place in paradise and forgive his sins."

"He who is not affectionate to God's creation, and to his own children, God will not be affectionate to him."

Sympathy with the Suffering : Sympathy with suffering and tenderness to the woe-stricken and lonely are taught as the highest duties.

"God is merciful to those who are merciful to His creatures."

"Pardon the sins of others that you may be pardoned. If you seek for mercy, be pitiful to the sufferings of mankind."

"He who is kind to an orphan will receive God's blessing on the Day of Account.".

"Verily a man's children are God's gifts."

"He who is merciful to others will himself receive mercy; he who has pity for other's wrongs will himself be pitied by the Lord of the Universe."

"He who does not forgive, will not be forgiven himself."

"'O my servants,' says the Almighty, 'if you seek My mercy, be merciful to My creatures.'"

"They will enter the abode of bliss who have a true, pure and merciful heart."

"The best of alms-giving is that which springs from the heart, and is uttered by the lips to soften the wounds of the injured."

"Modesty and chastity are parts of the Faith."

"He who is modest and chaste, nobody should find fault with him!'

"True modesty is the source of all virtues."

"Humility and courtesy are acts of piety."

"Forgive others, incite all to do good and abstain from wickedness."

"Avoid evil-doers and vain speakers and those who speak falsely."

"God loves those who suppress their anger when angry, and forgive people, and do what is right, and act piously and purely."

"The patient, the forbearing and those who forgive the faults of others, having the power to punish, will receive the reward from their Lord."

"Thus saith your Lord, 'Verily those who are patient in adversity and forgive wrongs are the doers of excellence.'"

"The faithful are those who perform their trust and fail not in their word and keep their pledge."

The Messenger

"He is not of me but a rebel at heart who, when he speaks, speaks falsely; who, when he promises, breaks his promises; and who, when trust is reposed in him, fails in his trust."

Meanness and slander, hypocrisy and untruthfulness are denounced.

"I heard the Prophet say," says one of the traditionists, "'it is better to sit alone than in company with the bad; and it is better to sit with the good than alone; and it is better to speak words to a seeker of knowledge than to remain silent; and silence is better than bad words. I advise you to be righteous to God, because it will adorn you in every work, withhold yourself from seeing the vices of mankind, and from giving them utterance.'"

Self-abnegation and patience are laid down as supreme duties:

> "Love is the abnegation of self for another; Divine love is complete self-absorption in the service of God's creatures for His pleasure."

"Patience is the recognition of God's will in the wrongs of life. Thankfulness is the overflowing of the heart with the fullness of His mercy. Acquiescence (raza) is the acceptance with thankfulness of God's will."

"He that is patient and thankful, loving and gentle to God's creatures, and returns good for evil, and subdues his passion, and forgets his own self for others-will receive a great reward in that he will approach his Lord."

The Persian moralist Saadi speaks of the virtue of patience in these terms:

> "A great river is not made turbid by a stone; the religious man who takes to heart an injury is as yet but shallow water. If any misfortune be falleth you, bear with it, that, by forgiving, others, you may yourself obtain pardon. O my brother! seeing that we are at last to return to earth, let us humble ourselves in ashes before we are changed into dust."

Fidelity and truth are most impressively inculcate:

> "When you speak, speak the truth; perform when you promise; discharge your trust; commit not fornication; be chaste; have no impure desires; withhold your hands from striking, and from taking that which is unlawful and bad. The best of God's servants are those who when seen, remind of God; and the worst of God's servants are those who carry tales about, to do mischief and separate friends, and seek for the defects of the good."

Family love and affection are recommended as highly meritorious:

> "Verily there are some of God's servants, who are neither Prophets nor Martyrs, who will emulate Prophets and Martyrs on the day of Resurrection on account of their high eminence near God. They are a family loving each other, for God's favour, befriending each other to please God and to obtain His love."

The attainment of God's love is inculcated in the following words which the Almighty addresses to mankind:

> "Whoever seeks to approach Me by that which I have given as My divine commands, is most loved by Me, and My servant is always seeking to approach Me by holiness; so that I love him: therefore, when I hold

him as a friend, I am his hearing by which he hears, and I am his sight by which he sees, and I am his hand by which he holds, and I am his feet by which he walks; if this servant supplicates Me, verily I give unto him; and, if he seeks protection with Me from harm and ills, I give him protection."

Humanity to Living Creatures : It is laid down repeatedly that not only does God reward good done to human beings, but to all living creatures.

"A woman who had sinned was passing by a dog which was holding out its tongue from thirst, and was near to dying. The woman drew off her boot and tied it to the end of her garment, and drew water for the dog, and gave it to drink; the Lord forgave her sin." The Prophet was asked, "Verily are there rewards for our doing good to quadrupeds, and giving them water to drink?" He said, "there are rewards for benefiting every living creature."

A man once came to him with a bundle and said: "O Prophet, I passed through a wood and heard the voices of the young of birds, and I took them up and put them into my carpet, and their mother came fluttering round my head." And the Prophet said: "put them down;" and when he had put them down, the mother joined the young. And the Prophet said: "Do you wonder at the affection of the mother towards her young? I swear by Him who has sent me, verily, God is more loving to His servants than the mother to these young birds. Return them to the place from which ye took them, and let their mother be with them." "Fear God with regard to animals," used he to say; "ride them when they are fit to be ridden, and get off when they are tired. Verily, there are rewards for our doing good to dumb animals, and giving them water to drink."

Charity : The Prophet's definition of charity embraced the wide circle of kindness: "Every good act," he would say, "is charity. Your smiling in your brother's face is charity; an exhortation addressed to your fellow-men to do virtuous deeds is equal to alms-giving. Putting a wanderer in the right path is charity; assisting the blind is charity; removing stones and thorns and other obstructions from the road is charity; giving water to the thirsty is charity."

"A man's true wealth hereafter is the good he does in this world to his fellow-men. When he dies, people will ask, What property has he left behind him? But the angels who examine him in the grave, will ask, What good deeds hast thou sent before thee?"

He would often tell his disciples, "Do not think any good act done to you contemptible; and I advise you, that you speak to your brother with an open countenance, because that is of the number of good acts and kindnesses. And if a man abuse you, and lay open a vice which he knows in you, then do not disclose one which you know in him, so that there may be no fault but on him."

Charity to Kindred : Charity to one's kindred is placed in the first rank.

"Giving alms to the poor has the reward of one benefaction, but that given to kindred has two rewards; one, the reward of charity, the other the reward for relationship."

The following anecdote will show the value attached to family obligations and the merit of benefactions to one's children-A man came to the Prophet and said, "I have got one dinar." He said, "Expend it upon yourself." The man said, "I have got another dinar." The Prophet said, "Expend that upon your children." The man said, "I have got another dinar." He said, "Expend that upon your wife and your parents and poor relations." He said, "I have got one other dinar." The Prophet said, "Expend that upon your servants." The man said, "I have got another dinar." "You know best the person most worthy of it; and whoever you know to be so, give it to him."

"Whatever we give" says the author of the *Akhlaq-i-Jelali*, "should be given in the fullness of zeal and goodwill, and never be the least regretted either in word or thought. For it would be the height of folly, when God, from the treasure-house of his bounty, has given a fortune to one of his servants, subject to the expenditure in a particular manner of an insignificant fraction, for him to consider the condition as burdensome to discharge. We should spend it simply to please God, and not mix up the act with any meaner motive, lest thereby it be rendered null and void.

We should bestow what we give on such as make a secret of their poverty; we should give in secret: or the ostentation of repute is folly. We find it among the Ahadith: —(the traditions of the Prophet) 'Charity that is concealed appeaseth the wrath of God.' And, again, 'The best of alms is that which the light hand giveth and the left knows not of.' From the Prophet we also have it, that when the just and holy God created the earth, it trembled and could not rest; whereupon He created the mountains to keep it still.

At this the angels marvelled and inquired whether any created thing were stronger than a mountain? He told them, yes, fire. Again, they asked whether any thing were stronger than fire? He told them, yes, water. Any thing stronger than water? Yes, wind. Any thing stronger than wind? Yes, alms concealed, which the son of Adam giveth, so that the right band gives, and the left knows it not. Of this the influence is greatest of any; for it averteth the scourge that is ready to fall."

In the battle of life men and women have always felt the need of help from a Power above and beyond themselves whose love is boundless and universal. Is not the human soul better and purer for seeking the help of its Maker in the trials of life? The following prayer shows the value attached in Islam to the outpouring of the human soul to the Giver of all good:

> "We have reached the night, and so have all other inhabitants of God's empire. Praised be God, one to whom there is no partner; for Him is dominion and praise, and He is powerful over all things. O God ! I supplicate Thee for the good of this night, and for every good that is in it; and I seek protection with Thee, from the evils of this night, and from every evil that may be in it. O Lord ! Verily, I seek protection with Thee from sickness, from age and pride; and from the contentions and calamities of the world and from the punishment of the grave. O Lord ! I have resigned my soul to Thy commands and turned to Thee. I have made over my work to Thee, and relied on Thee, and sought protection in Thee, to show my love to Thee; and for fearing Thee, there is no asylum or redemption from Thy resentment but in Thee."

"O Lord ! Pardon my faults, and the works which I may have done through ignorance; and forgive my lavishing away, and pardon my sins, which Thou knowest better than me. O Lord I Pardon me my inconsiderate speaking, and blundering; and forgive my wicked labours and intentions and all these are my characteristics. O Lord! Pardon me the faults which I have done before, and shall do after, and those which I have discovered and concealed; and those which Thou knowest better than me. Thou art the first and the last, and powerful over everything."

"O Lord ! Make me a thanks-giver to Thee, and a repeater of Thy name, and a fearer of thee, and a great obeyer of Thee, and a great humbler of myself before Thee, and complainer and repenter to Thee. O Lord! Accept my repentance and wash away my sins and approve my supplications; and strengthen my proofs, and make my tongue true; and show my heart the straight road; and remove away the wicked inclinations of my heart."

A learned critic has called the virtues of Islam, "stoical" The expression was used in an invidious sense, but if patience, forbearance, charity, truth, purity and magnanimity were the distinguishing characteristics of Stoics, I am prepared to admit that the ethical duties of Islam are stoical. In the Akhlak, magnanimity is defined thus:

> "That the soul take no note of honour or disrepute, pay no regard to affluence or adversity, but remain entirely unaffected by praise or censure, by wealth or want; from the mutations of human affairs admitting neither alteration nor transition, nor impression, nor influence: a spiritual eminence whose heights are only attainable to the most advanced on the paths of research; whose submits are not to be contemplated, but by the choicest of the accomplished."

"He is a man," says the Allamah Abul Fazl, "of high understanding and noble aspirations, who, without the help of others, recognises a ray of the divine power in the smallest things of the world; who shapes his inward and outward character accordingly, and shows due respect to himself and to others. True greatness, in spiritual and in worldly matters, does not shrink from the minute of business, but regards their performance as an act of divine worship."

"Every man of sense and understanding knows that the best way of worshipping God is in allaying the distress of the times, and in improving the condition of man."

"Have the religions of the worldly tendencies of mankind no common ground? Is there not everywhere the same enrapturing beauty which beams forth from so many thousand hidden places? Broad indeed is the carpet which God has spread, and beautiful the colours which he has given it."

Humility : At the same time men are taught to be humble.

"O men! be humble and lowly..He who guards his tongue

from detraction, God will conceal his vices; and he who suppresses his anger, God will withhold His punishments from him; and he who asks pardon of God, God will accept his supplication."

"Whatever jewels thou wearest on thy brow, only humility can give them their lustre. To that talisman paradise opens its gate, and to it opens the heart of man. Dear to all hearts is he whom lowliness exalts; his bending is the graceful droop of the branch laden with fruit."

Dignity of Labour : The dignity of labour preached in emphatic terms.

"There is a tradition from the Prophet," says Tirmidhi, "that a man of the Ansar came to him begging for some help; and the Prophet said,' Have you nothing at home?' He said, Yes, there is a large carpet, with one part of which I cover myself, and spread the other, and there is a wooden cup out of which I drink water.' The Prophet said,' Bring me the carpet and the cup.' And the man brought them, and the Prophet took them in his hands and said, who will buy them?' A man said, 'I will take them at one dirham.' 'He said, 'Who will give more?' This be repeated twice or thrice. Another man said,' I will take them for two dirhams.' Then the Prophet gave the carpet and cup to that man, and took the two dirhams, which he gave to the Ansar and said, 'Buy food with one of these dirhams and give it to your family, that they make it their sustenance for a few days; and buy a hatchet with the other dirham and bring it to me.' And the man brought it; and the Prophet put a handle to it with his own hands, and then said,' Go, cut wood and sell it; and let me not see you for fifteen days.' Then the man went cutting wood and selling it: and he came to the Prophet, when verily, he had got ten dirhams; and he bought a garment with part of them, and food with part. Them the Prophet said, "This cutting and selling of wood, and making your livelihood by it, is better for these than begging."

Idleness Reprehended : Idleness is reprehended "God is gracious to him who earns his living by his own labour and not by begging."

"He who is able and fit and does not work for himself or for others, God is not gracious to him.'

"He who works for his own living and does not beg, when he can earn, is one of God's favoured creatures."

"He who neither works for himself nor for others, will not receive the reward of God."

"Pray to God morning and evening and employ the day in your avocations."

The Charge of obscurantism can hardly be laid against Islam, when it is considered how eloquently the Founder recommended the acquisition of knowledge to his followers:

Learning and its Value

"Acquire knowledge," he used to say, "because he who acquires it in the way of the Lord performs an act of piety; who speaks of it, praises the Lord; who seeks it, adores God; who dispenses instruction in it, bestows alms; and who imparts it to its fitting objects, performs an act of devotion to God. Knowledge enables its possessor to distinguish what is forbidden from what is not; it lights the way to-Heaven; it is our friend in the desert, our society in solitude, our companion when bereft of friends; it guides us to happiness, it sustains us in misery-, it is our ornament in the company of friends; it serves as an armour against our enemies.

With knowledge, the servant of God rises to the heights of goodness and to a noble position, associates with sovereigns in this world, and attains to the perfection of happiness in the next."

"The ink of the scholar is more holy than the blood of the martyr."

"He who leaves his home in search of knowledge, walks in the path of God."

"He who travels in search of knowledge, to him God shows the way to paradise."

"One hour's meditation on the work of the Creator [in a devout spirit] is better than seventy years' prayer."

"To listen to the instruction of science and learning for one hour is more meritorious than attending the funerals of a thousand martyrs,- more meritorious than standing up in prayer for a thousand nights."

"To the student who goes forth in quest of knowledge, God will allot a high place in the mansions of bliss; every step he takes is blessed, and every lesson he receives has its retard. The seeker of knowledge will be greeted in heaven with a welcome from the angels. To listen to the words of the learned, and to instil into the heart the lessons of science, is better than religious exercises .... better than emancipating a hundred slaves. Him, who favours learning and the learned, God will favour in the next world."

"He who honours the learned, honours me."

"Eminence in science is the highest of honours. He dies not who gives life to learning. The greatest ornament of a man is erudition."

"The world is darkness; knowledge is light; but knowledge without truth is a mere shadow."

Man's responsibility was laid down in explicit terms.

"Whosoever gets to himself a sin, gets it solely at his -own responsibility."

"And let alone those who make a sport and mockery of their religion, and whom this present world has deluded, and thereby bring to remembrance that the soul perishes of what it has got to itself, and when they commit a deed of shame they say: 'We have found that our fathers did so, and God obliges us to do it:' say thou: 'Surely, God requireth not shameful doing;... they did injustice to themselves; yonder will every soul experience that which it hath bargained for;'... so then, whosoever is directed, it is solely a matter pertaining to himself-, and whosoever goes astray, he himself bears the whole responsibility of his wanderings."

In the purity of its aspirations can anything be more beautiful than the following:

> "The servants of the Merciful are they that walk upon the earth softly, and when the ignorant speak unto them, they reply 'Peace !' They that spend the light worshipping their Lord prostrate and standing and resting, those that, when they spend are neither profuse nor niggardly, but take a middle course ... those that invoke not with God any other God and slay not a soul that God hath forbidden otherwise than by right, and commit not fornication . . they who bear not witness to that which is false; and when they pass by vain sport, they pass it by with dignity, who say' Oh, our Lord, grant us of our wives and children such as shall be a comfort unto us, and make us examples unto the pious,-these shall be the rewarded, for that they persevered; and they shall, be accosted in paradise with welcome and salutation:-For ever therein,-a fair abode and resting-place !"

9

Islamic Prayer

'Prayer is the aspiration of the human soul towards God, common to every religion, from the rudest Fetishism to the most sublime Monotheism.' By performing prayer man may be qualified to live eternal life, full of bliss, in a higher scale of existence. The Holy Quran repeatedly insists upon the performance of prayer.' The prayer is related to the deep nature and inner self of the universe. The Holy Quran considers this whole universe a living organism and every part of it likes to worship. Another angle of its comprehensiveness is that merely concentration of thought is not required for this nor oral thanks giving is demanded. Rather the whole body, besides tongue, is busy in total submission while performing the prayer. And it is the complete system of worship. Prayer is the primary and last link of spiritual evolution.

It has several other important advantages which become part and parcel of an individual's character. For example, when one performs his prayer five times a day the feeling of being clean and pious will emerge in his mind. And it is obtained through ablution. Without any external effort he will inculcate this habit in him and avoid from being dirty. This was the cultural side of the prayer which made the introduction of splendid bath rooms and decorated *hamams* in Cordova and

Baghdad in the beginning of the Islamic era. It attracted Europe and the people from that Continent who began to take baths and wear clean dress. It was a turning point in their cultural history because before this the clergymen maintained that the more one's external being was dirty the more his inner self was illuminated.

The word *sa/a* means burnt. It signifies that through prayer an individual seeks to burn or kill the animal instinct within him. It signifies the liturgical form of worship, prescribed by the Holy Prophet. It is, indeed, the voice of faith. In the beginning the Muslims performed only the night prayer for fear of the infidels. This practice continued for three years. At that time there were no day prayers. After one year the compulsory night prayer was cancelled and two compulsory prayers were introduced - morning and evening prayers.' At that time each of these five compulsory prayers were only of two *Rakats.* At Medina the Zuhr, Asr, and Isha prayers were raised to four *Rakats* and Maghrib to only three. Now prayers are offered five times a day by all the Muslims, and the call of the *Muezzin,* before the daybreak, from a myriad Mosques and minarets 'Prayer is better than sleep, prayer is better than sleep' is a living witness wherever the Muslims dwell throughout the world. Life of a man begins with *adaan* and ends with prayer. It continues in the grave particularly in the case of the prophets.

The first thing Jibbrail taught Muhammad (peace be upon him) was the prayer. In one of the earliest Sura we read, "But those will prosper who purify themselves, and glorify the name of their Guardian-Lord, and (lift their hearts) in prayer."

The prayer is preceded by ablution. It is described as "half of faith and the key of prayer." Ablution means that as the purification of heart is necessary similarly the body must be clean because both are closely related with one another. Discipline is created in life after performing prayer. To get up daily at proper time and perform prayers punctually after setting aside one's routine assignments is such a habit by which routine daily business is properly disciplined. "Washing them (organs)," remarks Dr. Muhammad Hamidullah, "regret for the past and resolution for not doing the same in the future, and all this by seeking help from God."

Getting Start for Prayer

Ablution is performed as follows and during this ceremony the worshipper usually recites some verses from the Holy Quran or some other prayers. The Holy Prophet would say before and after ablutions: "In the name of God the Beneficent, the Merciful. I bear witness that there is no deity save God. He is alone. He hath no partner. And I bear witness that Muhammad is His slave and His Messenger." After performing ablutions he would say, "O God! Make me of the penitents, and make me of the purified! "First of all the worshipper washes his hands three times; then he rinses his mouth three times, throwing the water into it with his right hand.

Then he throws water up his nostrils, with his right hand, snuffing it up at the same time, and then blow it out, compressing his nostrils with the thumb and finger of the left hand. This act is also performed three times. He then washes his face three times throwing up the water with both hands. He next washes his right hand and arm, as high as the elbow, as many times, causing the water to run along his arm from the palm of the hand to the elbows, and in the same manner, he washes the left. Then he draws his wetted right hand over the upper part of his head, raising his turban or cap with his left. If he has a beard, he then combs it with the wetted fingers of is right hand, holding his hand with the palm forwards, and passing the fingers through his beard from the throat upwards. He then puts the tips of his fore-fingers into his ears and twists them round, passing his thumbs at the same time round the back of the ears from the bottom upwards. Next, he wipes his neck with the back of the fingers of both hands, making the ends of his fingers meet behind his neck, and then drawing them forward. Lastly, he washes his feet as high as the ankles, and passes his fingers between the toes."

If water is not available or it is injurious to health then the ablution may be performed with dust or sand in the above-mentioned manner. It is called tayammum.

Period of Recess

The interval between *Fajr* and *Zuhar* is at least seven or eight hours. It meant for worldly transactions. The modern world admits the wisdom underlying it. If the prayer is performed in its truest spirit then the individual and collective life is set on right path. The importance of offering prayers five times a day at appointed hours, particularly, increases in this age of psychological tension. Man has made extensive progress in different fields of life, in nature, sciences and space. His courage has helped him to reach the moon but still he is helpless in the hands of scientific culture. This culture has given birth to several new wishes. New requirements and demands have emerged in human mind. But to what an extent satisfaction and contentment have been managed for the oppressed Man ? To what an extent his burden has been lightened and psychological tension lowered ? Civilization, which is the product of science and technology, has no satisfactory answer to these questions.

In this state of nervous tension when there is a new demand every moment which has perturbed the human soul, there is no better prize than prayer which provides satisfaction for us five times a day. Through prayer we seek a communion with God and forget a continued conflict pertubing our mind. Prayer is spoken of as *munajat or confidential intercourse* with God.' Self-development is attained through prayer. It is stressed upon in its call "come to prayer" and come to *Allah.*

Prayer is a reverential expression of the soul's sincerest desires. It is highest spiritual ascent . . miraj... for a Muslim. It is through the prayer that one can ascend to the heights of moral and intellectual greatness. Five times a day throughout the Muslim world the Muslims stop their worldly business and turn their faces toward the Kaaba and stand and bow in silent communion with God. "Surely prayer keeps (one) away from indecency and evil." Prayer is pregnant with a lesson of equality. We see that Islam stresses upon that all Muslims are equal. It is the one and the only truly democratic faith in the contemporary world which has fully succeeded in putting into practice its theories about the oneness of humanity. In the Mosque all the Muslims, the lowest to the highest, kneel side by side and perform their prayers. Even a beggar in tottered rags can give the call for prayer and the Head of a State follows him. The type of democracy which Islam preaches is embodied five times a day in the Mosque where all sorts of discriminations are abolished. Its force can be used for the unification of the human race. We see the lessons of fraternity, love and concord in the Mosque in practice.

There are three aspects of the relation of a Man:

(a) Relation with God;

(b) Relation with the Apostle; and

(c) Relation with other human beings.

The prayer puts an end to arrogance and egoism through prostration. It elevates his position as a man. Prayer is not an end in itself. It is a means to an end. When a man goes into prostration Cowper's verse seems to be worth quoting:

> And Satan trembles when he sees
>
> The weakest saint upon his knees.

Elevation in Islam

This elevation of the worshipper is through the Apostle. He sends blessings on the Apostle in his prayers. After performing his prayers he sends blessings on the whole world particularly on the Muslims by salutation to right and left. It is dua which means petition or supplication addressed to God by the supplicant. It means that he promises that in the practical life he would not dare to inflict injuries on anyone. The object of prayer is to pour forth one's soul in a brief but earnest supplicatory address.

During this period he is most stripped of his worldly identities. It is in the Mosque that he concentrates his mind on the Glorification of the Almighty. But observance of solemnity is the basic requisite for it. He should absorb in prayer and manifest the profoundest reverence and humility in every gesture. His soul is washed of impure ideas by prayer. Otherwise an unmindful prayer is not accepted and it does not escape punishment. "Woe to the praying ones who are heedless of their prayers." Aishah once asked the Holy Prophet about random looks in prayer. He replied: "That is a fraud which the devil practises in the prayer of a servant." One should not have any talk or return Salam in prayer. Abdullah bin Masud is reported to have said: "We used to greet the Prophet while he was in prayer and he used to respond to us. When we returned from the Negus, we greeted him but he did not return it to us. We asked: O Messenger of Allah! We used to greet you in prayer and you to return it to us. He said: Verily there is concentration of mind in prayer."

At another time the Holy Prophet said: Verily prayer is for reading the Holy Quran and for remembering Allah. So when you are therein, let it be your engagement.

In the beginning, the worshippers, wherever they liked, used to go away in the midst of prayer and join it afterwards. This had been their practice for sometime. Once the Holy Prophet was performing the Friday prayer in the Mosque. In due course the merchandise from Syria arrived there. Except a few worshippers all others left their prayer and ran away. At once the Revelation came: "But when they see some bargain or some amusement, they disperse headlong to it, and leave thee standing. Say: The (blessing) from Presence of God is better than any amusement or bargain! And God is the Best to provide (for all needs)."

Making of rows for a congregational prayer is a practice of creating discipline. After the first row the other rows are filled by gradation of ages. The elders stand in the first and the youngers behind them. When the *Imam* bows in the prostration, all bow down following him. If the *Imam* forgets at any point he has to openly admit by undoing it. It is a check on his unlimited authority.

There are three conditions of the validity of being a valid Muslim:

(a) To believe in God;

(b) To keep up prayers;

(c) To serve the humanity.

Prayer can be performed anywhere privately or publicly. But the participation in the congregational prayer is desirable. Wherever one finds the hour of prayer he must execute it and that place is the *Masjid.* The prayer needs no Mosque rather it can be performed anywhere under the canopy of sky. But the Holy Prophet has said: "A prayer in congregation is twenty times superior to the prayer performed individually." A prayer in common is a prayer in communication and communion with all the others. A prayer rug is not necessary to perform the prayer as it is generally understood. Actually it is the space that is significant. In some countries precious and beautiful carpets are used as prayer rugs in the Mosques. And at *Eid* congregations some rich people use their own small rugs to perform their prayers. With the passage of time such a rug has become a powerful symbol and even instrument of holiness. It has a dual function: to provide a pure space to the worshipper and to indicate the orientation towards Mecca.

The prayer is performed in Arabic. It is incumbent, five times daily when the *Adaan* calls, upon every Muslim in leisure or in business, in towns or in villages, in sea or in land, in peace or in war. Before performing the prayer external impurities are washed by ablution. The prayer is not only a spiritual hymn, it is also a set of movements three dimensions - standing, kneeling and prostration. Sequence of movements denotes *rakah (pl. rakaat)* which make up a complete act of prayer. Each *rakah* consists of different movements with their appropriate recitations. They are just as the life is to the body. They are:

(a) The prayer begins with the *Niyah,* which is said standing, with the hands on either sides:

"I have purposed to offer up to God only with a sincere heart this morning (or, as the case may be), with my face Qibla wards, two (or, as the case may be) *rakah* prayers Farz *(Sunnah* or Nafil)."

(b) Then follows the *Takbir,* said with the thumbs touching the lobules of the ears and open hands on each side of the face. It is: "God is Most Great."

(c) The Qiyam, or standing position. The right hand placed upon the left, below the naval (the *Shafiis,* and the two other orthodox sects, place their hands on their breasts, as also the *Wahabis;* the *Shiehs* keep their hands on either side. In all the sects the women perform the *Qiyam* with their hands on their (breasts), and the eyes looking to the ground in self-abasement. During the *Qiyam* the *Subhan* is recited:

Holiness to Thee, O God!
And praise be to Thee!
Great is Thy name!
Great is Thy Greatness!
There is no deity but Thee!

The *Taawwuz,* or *Auzbillah,* is then said as follows:

I seek refuge from God from cursed Satan.

After which the *Tasmiyah is* repeated:

In the name of God, the Compassionate, the Merciful. Then follows the *Fatiha* which is the most essential part of the prayer. It must be repeated in each rakah. It is:

Praise be to God,
The Cherisher and Sustainer of the Worlds;
Most Gracious, Most Merciful;
Master of the Day of Judgement.
Thee do we worship,
And Thine aid we seek.
Show us the straight way;
The way of those on whom
Thou hast bestowed Thy Grace,
Those whose (portion)
Is not wrath,
And who go not astray. – Aameen.

By reciting the *Fatiha,* the worshipper praises God and shows his attitude by mind which keeps him steadfast in pleasures and sorrows. He promises to love all men to what ever creed they may belong. He promises to use his inner and outer faculties in a proper way. He seeks guidance in the straight path. He renders complete submission to God and seeks help from Him because He is the Controller of all means. Man is to struggle for peace and progress. He wishes to follow those who got the Divine favours and not those who had been the objects of the Divine displeasures.

(d) After this the worshipper can repeat as many chapters of the Holy Quran as he may wish; he should, at least, recite one long or two short verses. The following chapter is usually recited, namely, the *Suratul-Ikhlas,* or the 112th Chapter:

Say: He is God,
The One and Only;
God, the Eternal,
Absolute;
He begetteth not,
Nor is He begotten;
And there is none
Like unto Him.

(e) Bowing from the hips before which the *Takbir-i-Ruku is* said:

God is Great!

(f) The *Tasbih-i-Ruku,* said in the same posture.

I extol the holiness of my Lord, the Great!

It is repeated three times.

(g) Straightening up which is called the *Qiyam-i-Samị Ullah* or *Tasmi.* In this *Qiyam* the hands are being placed on either side. The *Imam* says aloud this sentence:

God hears him who praises Him.

The people then respond in a low voice:

O Lord, Thou art praised.

(h) Then *Takbir-i-Sijdah is* said as the worshipper drops on his knees:

God is Great.

It is followed by the prostration which brings the worshipper's brow down to the earth, below the prayer mat on which he lays his forehead in the act of reverence. It is the highest degree of submission. In the prostration he recites:

I extol the holiness of my Lord, the most High!

I extol the holiness of my Lord, the most High!

I extol the holiness of my Lord, the most High!

(i) Sitting back on the haunches, placing the hands upon his thighs, he says the *Takbir-i-Jalsah:*

God is Great!

(j) A second prostration saying the *Takbir-i-Sijdah:* God is Great!

(k) And then doing the prostration the *Tasbih-i-Sijdah* as before:

I extol the holiness of my Lord, the most High!

I extol the holiness of my Lord, the most High!

I extol the holiness of my Lord, the most High!

(1) Then if at the close of one *rakah,* he repeats the *Takbir* standing, when it is called *Takbir-i-Qiyam;* but at the end of two *rakahs,* and at the close of the prayer, he repeats it sitting, when it is called *Takbir-i-Quod.* Here ends one *rakah.* The next *rakah* begins with the *Fatiha.* At the close of every two *rakahs* he recites the *Tahyah,* which is said whilst kneeling upon the ground. His left foot bent under him he sits upon it, and places his hands upon his knees and says:

The adorations of the tongue are for God, and also the adorations of the body, and alms-giving!

Peace be on thee, O Prophet, with mercy of God and His blessing!

Peace be upon us and upon God's righteous servants!

(m) Then raising the first finger of the right hand he recites the *Tushuhhud:*

I testify that there is no deity but God and I testify that Muhammad is the servant of God, and the messenger of God!

(n) Then blessings on the Holy Prophet and his descendants are recited sitting in the same posture:

O God, have mercy on Muhammad and his descendants as Thou didst have mercy on Ibrahim and on his descendants. Thou art to be praised, and Thou art great. O God, bless Muhammad and his descendants! Thou art to be praised, and Thou art great!

(o) Then the Dua:

O God our Lord, give us the blessings of this life, and also the blessings of life everlasting. Save us from the torments of fire.

(p) He then closes with the *Salam*. He turns the head round to the left, he says:

The peace and mercy of God be with you.

At the end of the whole prayer he raises his hands and offer up a *Munaiat* or supplication. This usually consists of prayer selected from the Holy Quran or *Ahadith*.

Special Prayer on Friday

The congregational service of Friday replaces the ordinary noon service." Anyhow the regular noon-prayer remains obligatory for him who misses the congregational service of Friday. The Friday is shortened to two *rakats*. It has a wider circle of operation and brings together people of comparatively distant localities. It enhances the splendour of the day. Its special theme is the need for mutual contact in the Community for worship and understanding. On Friday in every week there is a local meeting in the central Mosque of each local centre, it may be a village, or town, or ward of a big city. Its aim is the promotion of unity and cooperation among the Muslims. During the *Juma* Prayer the economic life is suspended. It (Friday Prayer) is performed in the presence of at least forty worshippers. Its another characteristic is that the *Imam* delivers a *khutba*. It covers all the aspects of life. It is the collective duty of the Muslims to ensure the celebration of the *Juma* Prayer with due solemnity. The worshippers are prohibited to go to the Mosque at the eleventh hour when the prayer is going to be performed. Similarly they should not overstep the necks of men.

It is reported on the authority of Abu Hurrayrah that the Messenger of Allah said, "On Friday the angels wait upon the door of the Mosque recording the people in accordance with their arrival and the parable of the first-comer is like the parable of one who sends a she-camel for sacrifice to Mecca; the man who follows him next is like one who sends a cow for sacrifice; next, a ram; next, a hen; and next, an egg. When the *Imam* comes out, they close up their records and listen to the Reminder." Musab was Muhammad's emissary at Medina. He wrote to him, "Every Friday when the sun passes the meridian, I lead a congregational service of prayer of the Muslims." Before Apostle's migration to Medina Asad bin Zurara led the Friday prayer. It is remarkable that a large number of tribes embraced Islam rapidly. Their conversion made it necessary to take precautionary measures against errors both in respect of creed and ritual of these newly converts. Accordingly Umar Farooq appointed teachers in different parts of the realm, to instruct the people in the teachings of the Holy Quran and the observances of the Islamic injunctions. Besides, magistrates were ordered to see that all people were regular in their attendance at public prayers, especially on Fridays and in the month of the *Ramadan*.

In Kufa the State Treasurer was entrusted with this task." During the Abbaside reign it was a common practice that the Caliph used to lead the prayer and deliver a *khutba* on Fridays and the two *Eids*. But at the other places he appointed *Imams* as his representatives to lead the congregational prayers."

The scene of prayer performance is very effective and leaves far-reaching results even on the spectators. Said bin Hasan, an Alexandarian Jew, embraced Islam in 1298 A.C., wrote that it was the sight of the Friday Prayer which made his conversion. During a severe illness he had a vision in which a voice bade him declare himself a Muslim. "And when I entered the Mosque" (he goes on) "and saw the Muslims standing in rows like angels, I heard a voice speaking within me, 'This is the community whose coming was announced by the prophets (on whom the blessings and peace!)'; and when the preacher came forth clad in his black robe, a deep feeling of awe fell upon me................ and when he closed his sermon with the words, 'Verily God enjoineth justice and kindness and the giving of gifts to kinsfolk, and He forbiddeth wickedness and wrong and oppression. He warreth you: happy ye will be mindful." And when the prayer began, I was mightily uplifted, for the rows of the Muslims appeared to me like rows of angels, to whose prostrations and genuflactions God Almighty was revealing Himself, and I heard a voice within me saying, 'If God spake twice unto the people of Israel throughout the ages, verily He speaketh unto this community in every time of prayer.' and I was convinced in my mind that I had been created to be a Muslim."

In brief, the prayer is a source to awaken the latent energies of the human soul. It is a source of strength to the weaker, too, who gets ray of hope from the Higher Power. Islam can rightly boast of the institution of prayer. It is why that it was said that, 'between a man and infidelity, there is the abandonment of prayer only." It is a system of training. Islam lays a great stress on congregational prayers. At different junctures of history the performance of prayer had been made compulsory. In this connection Ibn Batuta (1304-78 A.C.) may be cited. He says of the inhabitants of Khawarism - Khiva, that he `never saw better bred or more liberal people, or those who were friendly to strangers. He especially approved of the whip hung up in every Mosque to chastise those who absented themselves from prayer."

10

Obligatory Tasks

Offering Prayers Five Times a Day

Prayer (Arabic Salat, Persian and Hindustani Namaz, Pushto Nmuz) is the second of the five foundations of practice in Islam. The constant round of devotion which characterizes Muhammadan nations is a very remarkable phenomenon in the system. We translate the words Salat and Namaz by the English word prayer, although this "second foundation" of the religion of Muhammad is something quite distinct from that prayer which the Christian poet so well describes as the "soul's sincere desire uttered or unexpressed." It would be more correct to speak of the Muhammadan Namaz as a service; "prayer" being more correctly rendered by the Arabic dua. In Islam prayer is reduced to a mechanical act, as distinct from a mental act; and in judging of the spiritual character of Muhammadanism, we must take into careful consideration the precise character of that devotional service which every Muslim is required to render to God at least five times a day,' and which, undoubtedly, exercises so great an influence upon the character of the followers of Muhammad.

It is absolutely necessary that the service should be performed in Arabic; and that the clothes and body of the worshipper should be clean, and that the praying place should be free from all impurity. It may be said either privately, or in company, or in a Mosque-although services in a Mosque are more meritorious than those elsewhere.

It is always preceded by ablution (Wudu),' and, if said in a Mosque, by the Adaan and Iqamat, terms which will be explained afterwards.

The regular form of prayer begins with the Niyyat, which is said standing, with the hands on either side:

> "I have purposed to offer up to God only, with a sincere heart this morning (or, as the case may be), with my face Qibla-wards, two (or, as the case may be) rakat prayers Farz (Sunnat, or Nafl)."

Then follows the *Takbir-i-Tahrimah,* said with the thumbs touching the lobules of the ears and the open hands on each side of the face.

"God is Great!"

The Qiam, or standing position. The right hand placed upon the left, below the navel and the eyes looking to the ground in self-abasement. During which is said the Subhan:

"Holiness to thee, O God!"
"And praise be to thee!"
"Great is Thy name !"
"Great is Thy greatness !"
"There is no deity but Thee !"

The Tauuz is then said as follows:-

"I seek refuge from God from cursed Satan."

After which the Tasmiyah is repeated:

"In the name of God, the compassionate, the merciful."

Then follows the Fatiha, viz., the first chapter of the Quran:

"Praise be to God, Lord of all the Worlds !"
"The compassionate, the merciful!"

"King on the day of reckoning!"

"Thee only do we worship, and to Thee only do we cry for help."

"Guide Thou us in the straight path,"

"The path of those to whom Thou hast been gracious;"

"With whom Thou art not angry,"

"And who go not astray." - Amen.

After this the worshipper can repeat as many chapters of the Quran as he may wish; he should, at least, recite one long or two short verses. The following chapter is usually recited, namely, the *Surat-ul-Ikhlas*, or the 112th chapter:

"Say: He is God alone: .

"God the eternal!"

"He begetteth not,"

"And is not begotten;"

"And there is none like unto Him."

The *Takbir-i-Ruku'*, said whilst making an inclination of the head and body and placing the hands upon the knees, separating the fingers a little.

"God is great!"

The *Tasbih-i-Ruku'*, said in the same posture.

"I extol the holiness of my Lord, the Great!"

"I extol the holiness of my Lord, the Great!"

"I extol the holiness of my Lord, the Great!"

The Qiam-i-Sami Allah or Tasmia said with the body erect, but, unlike the former Qiam, the hands being placed on either side. The Imam says" aloud,

"God hears him who praises him."

The people then respond in a low voice.

"O Lord, Thou art praised."

Takbir-i-Saidah, said as the worshipper drops on his knees.

"God is great!"

Tasbih-i-Saidah, recited as the worshipper puts first his nose and then his forehead to the ground.

"I extol the holiness of My Lord, the most High
"I extol the holiness of My Lord, the most High!"
"I extol the holiness of My Lord, the most High!"

Then raising his head and body and sinking backward upon his heels, and placing his hands upon his thighs, he says the *Takbir-i-Jalsa.*

"God is great!"

Then, whilst prostrating as before, he says the *Takbiri-Sajdah.*

"God is great!"

And then during the prostration the *Tasbih-i-Sajdah* as before.

"I extol the holiness of My Lord, the most High!"
"I extol the holiness of My Lord, the most High!"
"I extol the holiness of My Lord, the most High!"

Then, if at the close of one rakat, he repeats the Takbir standing, when it is called *Takbir-i-Qiam;* but at the end of two rakats, and at the close of the prayer, he repeats it sitting, when it is called *Takbir-i-Qaud.*

"God is great!"

Here ends one rakat or form of prayer. The next rakat begins with the Fatiha or 1st chapter of the Quran. At the close of every two rakats he recites the Attahiyat, which is said whilst kneeling upon the ground. His left foot bent under him he sits upon it and places his hands upon his knees and says":

"The adorations of the tongue are for God, and also the adorations of the body, and alms-giving.

"Peace be on thee, O Prophet, with the mercy of God and His blessing!"

"Peace be upon us and upon God's righteous servants!"

Then raising the first finger of the right hand he recites the Tashahhud:

"I testify that there is no deity but God ; and I testify that Muhammad is the servant of God, and the messenger of God!" "

The Darud is said whilst in the same posture.

"O God, have mercy on Muhammad and on his descendants, as Thou didst have mercy on Abraham and on his descendants. Thou art to be praised, and Thou are great. O God, bless Muhammad and his descendants, as Thou didst bless Abraham and his descendants!"

"Thou art to be praised, and Thou art great!"

Then the Dua

"O God our Lord, give us the blessings of this life, and also the blessings of life everlasting. Save us from the torments of fire ."

He then close with the Salam.

Turning the head round to the right, he says:

"The peace and mercy of God be with you."

Turning the head round to the left, he says:

"The peace and mercy of God be with you."

At the close of the whole set of prayers, that is, of Farz, Sunnat, Nafl, or Witr, the worshipper raises his hands and offers up a "Munajat," or supplication. This usually consists of prayers selected from the Quran or Hadith. They ought to be said in Arabic, although they are frequently offered up in the vernacular.

These daily prayers are either Farz, Sunnat, Nafl, or Witr Farz, are those number of rakats, (or forms of prayer) said to be enjoined by God. Sunnat those founded on the practice of Muhammad. Nafl, the voluntary performance of two rakats, or more, which may be omitted without sin. Witr, an odd number of rakats, either one, three, five or seven, said after the night prayer. These divisions of prayer are entirely distinct from each other. They each begin afresh with the Niyyat. The worshippers may rest for awhile between them, but not converse or worldly subjects. The Wahabis think it correct to say the Sunnat prayers in their houses and only the Farz in the mosque.

In order that our readers may be able to judge of the mechanism of this Muhammadan performance of prayer, we annex a time-table of the Muslim's common prayer showing the number of rakats or forms, from which it will be seen what is required of a pious Muhammadan. The five times of prayer are enjoined in the Quran, the other three periods of prayer are voluntary.

In addition to the daily prayers, the following are special services for special occasions:

Salat- ul-Juma—"The Friday Prayers." It consists of two rakats after the daily meridian prayer.

Salat-ul-Musafir—"Prayers for a traveller." Two rakats instead of the usual number at the meridian, afternoon, and night prayers.

Salat-ul-Khaif—"The Prayers of fear." Said in time of war. They are two rakats recited first by one regiment or company and then by the other.

Salat-ul- Tarawih—Twenty rakats recited every evening during the Ramadan, immediately after the fifth daily prayer.

Salat-ul-Istikhara —Prayers for success or guidance. The person who is about to undertake any special business, performs two rakat prayers and then goes to sleep. During his slumbers he may expect to have "Ilham," or inspiration, as to the undertaking for which he seeks guidance!

Salat-ul-Khusuf—Two rakats said at the time of an eclipse of the moon.

Salat-ul-Kusuf—Two rakats said at the time of an eclipse of the sun.

The Adaan, is the summons to prayer proclaimed by the Muazzin, or crier, in small mosques from the door or side, but in large mosques it ought to be given from the minaret (manarat). The following is a translation, "God is great! God is great! God is great! God is great! I bear witness that there is no God but God! (repeated twice) I bear witness that Muhammad is the Apostle of God! (repeated twice). Come to prayers! Come to prayers! Come to salvation! Come to salvation! God is great! There is no other God but God !"

In the early morning the following sentence is added: "Prayers are better than sleep."

The *Iqamat* (fit. "causing to stand") is a recitation at the commencement of prayers in a congregation, after the worshippers have taken up their position. It is exactly the same as the Adaan, with the addition of the words, "prayers are now ready."

The Iqamat of the Shafia' and the Wahabis is just half the length of that of the Hanifis.

Observing Fasts in the Month of Ramadan

The Ramadan is the ninth month of the Muhammadan year, which is observed as a strict fast from the dawn of day to sunset of each day in the month. The excellence of this month was much extolled by Muhammad, who said that during Ramadan "the gates of Paradise are open, and the gates of hell are shut, and the devils are chained by the leg"; and that "only those who observe it will be permitted to enter by the gate of heaven called Rayyan." Those who keep the fast "will be pardoned all their past venial sins." In the month of Ramadan, Muhammad said, the Quran began to be revealed from heaven.

The fast does not commence until some Musalman is able to state that he has seen the new moon. If the sky be overclouded and the moon cannot be seen, the fast begins upon the completion of thirty days from the beginning of the previous month.

The Ramadan must be kept by every Musalman, except the sick, the infirm, and pregnant women, or women who are nursing their children. Young children, who have not reached the age of puberty, are exempt, and also travellers on a journey. In the case of a sick person or a traveller, the month's fast must be kept as soon as they are able to perform it. This is called Qaza, or expiration.

The fast is extremely rigorous and mortifying, and when the Ramadan happens to fall in the summer and the days are long, the prohibition even to drink a drop of water to slake the thirst is a very great hardship. Muhammad speaks of this religious exercise as "easy," as most probably it was when compared with the ascetic spirit of the times. Sir William Muir thinks Muhammad did not foresee that, when he changed the Jewish intercalary year for the lunar year, that the fast would become a grievous burden instead of an easy one; but Muhammadan lexicographers say, the fast was established when the mouth occurred in the hot season.

During the month of Ramadan twenty additional rakats, or forms of prayer, are repeated after the night prayer. These are called Tarawih.

Devout Muslims seclude themselves for some time in the Mosque during this month, and abstain from all worldly conversation and engage themselves in the reading of the Quran. This seclusion is called Itiqaf. Muhammad is said to have usually observed this custom for the last ten days of Ramadan.

The Laylut- ul- Qadr, or the "night of power," is said by Muhammad to be either on the twenty first, twenty third, or twenty fifth, or twenty seventh, or twenty ninth. The exact date of this solemn night has not been discovered by any but the Prophet himself, and some of the Companions, although the learned doctors believe it to be on the twenty seventh. Of this night Muhammad says in the Quran (Surat-ul-Qadr):

> "Verily we have caused it (the Quran) to descend on the night of power.
> "And who shall teach three what the night of power is?
> "The night of power excelleth a thousand months;
> "Therein descend the angels and the spirit by permission.
> "Of their Lord in every matter;
> "And all is peace till the breaking of the morn."

By these verses commentators understand that on this night the Quran came down entire in one volume to the lowest heaven, from whence it was revealed by Jibbrail in portions as the occasion required. The excellences of this night are said to be innumerable, and it is believed that during it the whole animal and vegetable kingdom bow in humble adoration to the Almighty, and the waters of the sea become sweet in a moment of time! This night is frequently confounded' with the Shab-i-Barat; but even the Quran itself does not appear to be quite clear on the subject, for in the Surat-i-Dukhan we read, -By this clear book. See on a blessed night have we sent it down, for we would warn mankind, on the night wherein all things are disposed in wisdom."

In which it appears that the blessed night, or the Laylut-ul-Mubarak, is both the night of record and the night upon which the Quran came down from heaven, although the one is supposed to be the twenty seventh day of Ramadan, and the other the fifteenth of Shaban.

Charity in Islam

Zakat : Zakat (lit. ,purification"), the legal alms, or poor rate, is the fourth of the five foundations of practice. Zakat should be given annually of five descriptions of property, provided they have been in possession a whole year; namely, money, cattle, grain, fruit, and merchandise. There are several minor differences amongst the various sects as to the precise explanation of the law with reference to these legal alms; but the following are the general rules observed by Sunni Musalmans :

1. Money. If he is a Sahib- i-Nissab (i.e. one who has had forty rupees in his possession for a year), lie must give alms at the rate of one rupee in every forty, or two-and-a-half per cent.
2. Cattle. Should his property consist of sheep or goats, he is not obliged to give alms until they amount to forty in number. He must then give one for one hundred and twenty, and two for the next eighty, and then one for every hundred afterwards. For camels the following is the rate:-from 5 to 24, one sheep or goat; from 25 to 35, one yearling female (bint-i-mukhaz) camel; from 36 to 45, one two-year old female (bint-i-labun) camel; from 46 to 60, one three-year old female (hiqqah) camel; from 61 to 75, one four-year old female (jazah) camel; from 76 to 90, two two-year old female camels; from 91 to 120, two three-year old female camels; and from 121 and upwards, either a two-year old female camel for every forty, or a three-year old female camel for every fifty.

   For cows or bulls:-If 30 cows, a one-year old female calf-, if 40, a two-year old female calf, and so on, a one-year old female calf for every 10.

   Alms for buffaloes are the same as for sheep.

   For horses, either the same rate as for camels, or two

rupees eight annas for every horse whose value exceeds one hundred rupees. Animals used for riding, and beasts of burden, are exempt.

3. Fruits. For fruits watered by rain a tenth is given; but if irrigated, then a twentieth part.
4. Grain. The same rates as for fruits.
5. Merchandise. For the capital, as well as for the profits, Zakat is given at the rate of one in forty, provided the owner be a Sahib-i-nissab. For gold bullion, half a misqal (= 67½ grains) is given for every 20 misqal weight. For silver bullion at the rate of 2½ per cent. For whatever is found in mines, if over 240 dirhams in weight (= 2lbs. 2 oz. 2 dr.), a fifth is required; and if the money be laid out in merchandise, alms are to be given on the profits.

Wood and pearls are exempt, and also clothing; but not jewels.

The following are the classes of persons on whom it is lawful to bestow the Zakat:

1. Such pilgrims to Mecca as have not the means of defraying the expenses of the journey.
2. Religious mendicants.
3. Debtors who cannot discharge their debts.
4. Beggars.
5. Poor travellers.
6. Proselytes to Muhammadanism.

The Zakat, or legal alms, must be distinguished from the Sadaqa, or offerings, which is a term more especially applied to the offerings on the Eid- ul-Fitr (q. v.) although it is used for almsgiving in general.

Visiting the two Holy Cities : Mecca and Medina

Hajj : Hajj, or Pilgrimage to Mecca, is the fifth of the five foundations of practice. It is said, by Muhammad, to be of

Divine institution, and has the authority of the Quran for its observance . Its performance is incumbent upon those men and women who have sufficient means to meet the expenses of the journey, and to maintain their families at home during their absence.

The merits of the pilgrimage are so great, that every step taken in the direction of the Kaaba blots out a sin; and he who dies on his way to Mecca is enrolled on the list of martyrs.

The following is the orthodox way of performing the pilgrimage, founded upon the example of the "Prophet" himself.

Upon the pilgrim's, arrival at the last stage' near Mecca, he bathes himself, and performs two rakat prayers, and then divesting himself of his clothes, he assumes the pilgrim's sacred robe, which is called Ihram. This garment consists of two seamless wrappers, one being wrapped round the waist, and the other thrown loosely over the shoulder, the head being left uncovered. Sandals may also be worn, but not shoes or boots. After he has assumed the pilgrim's garb, he must not anoint his head, shave any part of his body, pare his nails, nor wear any other garment than the Ihram. Immediately on his arrival at Mecca he performs the legal ablutions, and proceeds to the Masjidul-Haram, or Sacred Mosque, and kisses the Hajr-ul-aswad, or the black stone, and then encompasses the Kaaba 4 seven times. This act, which is called Tawaf is performed by commencing on the right and leaving the Kaaba on the left.

The circuits are made thrice with a quick step or run, and four times at a slow pace.' He then proceeds to the Maqam-i-Ibrahim (the place of the prophet Abraham) and performs two rakat prayers, after which he turns to the black stone and kisses it. He then goes to the gate of the temple leading to Mount Safa, and from it ascends the hill" and runs from the summit or Mount Safa to that of Mount Marwah seven times! On the top of the hill" he remains for a few moments, and raising his hand heavenwards supplicates the Almighty.

On the eighth day, which is called Tarwiah he unites with his fellow-pilgrims at Mina in the usual services of the Muslim ritual, and stays the night.

After morning prayer he rushes to Mount Arafat, where, having said two rakat prayers with the Imam and heard the Khutbah (or oration), he remains until sunset. He then proceeds to Muzdalifah, and having said the sunset and night prayers, he stays the night at that place.

The next morning, which is the 'Eid-ul-Adha, or great feast, he comes to three places in Mind, marked by three pillars called Jamra. At each of these pillars he picks up seven small stones, or pebbles, and having said some particular prayer over each pebble and blown upon it, he throws it at one of the pillars. This ceremony is called Rami-e-Jamar, or the throwing of pebbles.

He then proceeds to the place of sacrifice at Mina, and performs the usual sacrifice of the 'Eid-ul-Adha; after this sacrifice he gets himself shaved and his nails pared. The pilgrim garb is then removed and the pilgrimage is ended, although he should rest at Mecca the three following days, which are called the Ayyam-ut-Tashriq, or the days of drying up the blood of the sacrifice. These are three days of well-earned rest after the vigorous peripatetic performances of the last four days.

The pilgrimage must be performed on three days of the month of Zul Hijja, namely from the seventh to the tenth; a visit to Mecca at any other time has not the merit of a pilgrimage.

Before he leaves Mecca the pilgrim should once more perform the circuits round the Kaaba, and throw stones at the sacred pillars, each seven times.

He then proceeds to Medina, and makes his salutations at the Shrine of Muhammad. The Wahabis do not perform the last act, as it is contrary to their principles to visit shrines.

The Musalman who has performed the pilgrimage is called Haji.

The Kaaba is also called the Qibla, or the direction to which Muslims are to pray. Mosques are, therefore, always erected Qibla wards.

The pilgrimage cannot be performed by proxy, as some English authors have stated, although it is considered a meritorious act to pay the expenses of one who cannot afford to perform it. But if a Muhammadan on his deathbed bequeathed a sum of money to be paid to a certain person to perform the pilgrimage, it is considered to satisfy the claims of the Muslim law. If a Muslim have the means of performing the pilgrimage, and omit to do so, its omission is equal to a kabira, or mortal sin.

11

Allah's Last Messenger

His Name

The earliest biographers of the Arabian Prophet, whose works are extant in Arabic, are Ibn-Ishaq (A.H. 151), Ibn-Hisham (A.H. 218), Waqidi (A.H. 207), and Tabari (A.H. 310). Ismail Abulfida, Prince of Hamah, in Syria (A.H. 733), compiled a Life of Muhammad in Arabic, which was translated by John Garnier, Professor of Arabic at Oxford (A.D. 1723), and into English by the Rev. W. Murray, Episcopal clergyman at Duffus, in Scotland.' Dr. Sprenger of Calcutta commenced a Life of Muhammad in English, and printed the first part of it at Allahabad (A.D. 1851); but it was never completed. The learned author afterwards published his work in German in 1869. The only Life of Muhammad in English, which has any pretension to original research, is that by Sir William Muir of the Bengal Civil Service.

Muhammad (lit. the praised one), son of Abdul Muttalib, by his wife Amina, was born at Mecca at, August 29th, A.D. 570. He assumed the prophetic office at the age of forty, fled from Mecca at the age of fifty four, and died at Medina, June 9th, A.D. 632, aged sixty two.

The Hijrat, or Hegira (the flight from Mecca), which is the Muhammadan era, dates from July 16th, A.D. 622.

In forming an estimate of Muhammad's prophetical pretensions, it must be remembered that he did not claim to be the founder of a new religion, but merely of a new covenant. He is the last and greatest of all God's prophets. He is sent to convert the world to the one true religion We follow the prophet in his self-asserted mission from the cave of Hira to the closing scene, when he dies in the midst of the lamentations of his harem, and the contentions of his friends-the visions of Gabriel, the period of mental depression, the contemplated suicide, the assumption of the prophetic office, his struggles with Meccan unbelief, his flight to Medina, his triumphant entry into Mecca and we wonder at the genius of the hero.

We are not insensible to the beauties of the Quran as a literary production, and we admire its conceptions of the Divine nature, its deep and fervent trust in the power of God, its frequent deep moral earnestness, and its sententious wisdom.

His Work

Ever since human beings came into being they have been subject to certain disciplines of internal impulses and extraneous order which go together to determine human behaviour. However, the internal impulses can be tamed by the application of moral and spiritual discipline while the extraneous order is subject to the exercise of ever-developing human capabilities which result in the creation of better living conditions. As social relations grow and rules of social conduct are improved upon, the extraneous order becomes more and more conducive to human development.

Another basic factor that needs to be remembered is that both positive and negative traits are embedded in the human being and that they have a pivotal role to play in the shaping of one's personality. But these too are controlled by human consciousness. The more it develops the more responsive are the positive qualities in dominating the negative aspects; the less it is developed the more negative aspects tend to dominate the positive qualities of man.

These three essential features of human life – man's internal impulses, extraneous order and the negative and positive traits – are a person's constant companion, and the success or failure of a person in life depends upon their successful or unsuccessful utilization.

In such a situation the individuals who are left alone in the maze of life with no system of guidance and relief are likely to falter or get frustrated. As a result they contribute to unbalancing the society and leading it to social disruption. In these circumstances persons who do not consider themselves answerable to society for their actions form themselves into exploiting classes by monopolizing the means of production and become unbearable in their oppression upon the weaker and poorer sections of society which, in fact, are their creation. At this stage the conscientious and daring among the people rise to the occasion and initiate a class struggle to free the lower classes from the shackles of the upper classes.

Such people are present in every society and they have been making their presence felt to a smaller or greater extent. When, however, inspite of these efforts by conscientious people deterioration exceeds certain limits, and the social structure itself becomes rotten beyond redress, Prophets are sent to restructure society on a more modern, forward-looking and enlightened pattern.

This process of re-educating humanity had been going on at various stages of history throughout the world till finally a stage arrived when, after a long process, the human intellect had developed appropriately and had shed its false notions and idiosyncrasies to quite an extent. At this stage in the pre-industrial era Prophet Muhammad (Peace be upon him) came on to the scene of history. The last of the Prophets was thus sent to perfect the system of life under Divine guidance.

The role played by Prophet Muhammad (Peace be upon him) needs to be correctly defined if we are to understand the true nature of his greatness, and if we wish to follow, in the right spirit and with devotion to his august person, his teachings and the directions set by him.

In the past many centuries not much has been done in this regard by the Muslims in general and the religious elite in particular except to eulogise the Prophet's person and pay lip-service to his achievements. The true intent and bearing of his teachings have not been spelt out by the 'religious' guides and Muslim rulers because they were not true to their faith and had their own vested interests to serve, which they had deceitfully created. Their interests required that the people be kept ignorant about the revolutionary character of these teachings. Thus they tailored Islam to their own requirements and to their personal benefit. They formed it into a protective barrier to safeguard the interests of the few *jagirdars* and moneyed barons as against many poor people who were being suppressed by them. They created an upper class who seized the means of production, which was state property, and deprived the masses of education, good health and decent living. They dispossessed the people of their ownership of the means of production, their share in state power and their right to administer their own affairs. Our present social structure stands at this very level. The greatness of Prophet Muhammad (Peace be upon him), and for that matter of all the Prophets, lies in that they stood for the oppressed as against the oppressors, for the exploited as against the exploiters, for the interests of the masses as against those of the vested interests, for collective benefit as against individual advantages.

Having gone through this basic premise in the introductory study made above we would now venture to elucidate some of the important features of the Prophets' call to Islam which stand as part of his personality and which must be emulated by all human beings, Muslims as well as others.

The foremost feature of Prophethood is truthfulness and consistency between words and actions. The other features are: simple living as against pompous life-style; making full use of one's intellectual capabilities and sense of understanding in day-to-day affairs while not being led away by emotional viewpoints and slogans; developing collective wisdom among the people and acquiring as well as spreading knowledge to the utmost; standing up against all kinds of tyranny and siding with the oppressed poor; doing justice to everybody and in all circumstances; doing a good turn to as many people as one can by helping them to stand upon their own feet and helping those in distress with no desire for any benefit in return; freeing oneself from the influence of those forefathers who were wrongdoers and instead finding fresh solutions to modern requirements; not following the evil path of immodesty, injustice and violence.

Thus the solutions to modern problems have to be framed in the light of the Holy Quran, the Prophet's Sunnah, other Holy Scriptures and the scientific literature produced in later periods of history. Prophet Muhammad's objective was clearly to evolve a system of life by which the human race would live in peace, harmony and freedom and that social equality and universal fraternity could become a reality.

We must, however, understand that the exemplary qualities of Prophet Muhammad (Peace be upon him) enumerated above cannot be imbibed unless we first of all demolish the existing social structure of our country which is based on economic and political exploitation of the masses by initiating a thorough struggle at the people's level; it is not enough to resort to mere reformatory measures. This is necessary because otherwise this socio-economic set-up will not allow any room for the suppressed people to work for amelioration of their lot, and to develop their personalities, through material, moral and spiritual advancement.

His Prayers

This is precisely why Prophet Muhammad (Peace be upon him) concentrated on three things: First and foremost he put forth the message of Truth that Allah Almighty is the Creator of the universe, that He is the absolute ruler and lawgiver as well as the Sustainer of the whole living world and that He should be accepted as such by the human beings.

They should strive to come nearer to Him and earn His love by assimilating to some extent a few of His attributes such as love, forgiveness, providing sustenance to the needy, alleviating suffering and illness and improving things around them in order to serve their fellow-beings. His second message was that the purpose of creation of humankind is to evolve a system of life that will be instrumental in establishing a just social order in which each person will be a source of succour, enlightenment and peace of mind for the other.

Such a productive and orderly life could only be fostered by shedding selfishness, lust for power and wealth and the urge to usurp others' rights. The third message that was translated into action by him was to change the existing social order based upon exploitation of the labour of the numerous downtrodden by the few who had appropriated the means of production which, legitimately, is the common property of the people.

Such social structure had curtailed the opportunities of economic development from reaching the hands of the majority of the people, and denied their basic human rights. This third message, in fact, constitutes the programme for realizing the first two objectives.

In view of what has been explained above it can be said authoritatively that Prophet Muhammad (Peace be upon him) was a "Prophet of Revolution". The salient features of this revolution are:

1. Breaking up of the grip of exploiter landed and moneyed classes, and their accomplices the religious elite, over the oppressed poor.
2. Eradicating poverty and ignorance.
3. The State guaranteeing basic human rights and freedoms.
4. Doing away with religious intolerance and inculcating instead the spirit of cooperation, fraternity and mutual understanding at the human level.
5. Organizing the society on progressive lines while keeping in view the principle that exploitation of the weak, and oppression against them in any form whatsoever, was not to be allowed.
6. Carrying out all human affairs, be they family or state affairs, on the basis of mutual consultation and consensus.
7. Granting equal rights and uniform social status and dignity to every one while considering no one inferior to the other on account of wealth or position in society. The sole criterion for determining a higher status in society was to be one's contribution towards betterment of society.
8. Developing the individual into a beacon of excellence, both morally and spiritually, so that he or she is able to contribute in a committed manner to the building up of society.
9. Spreading this message of Islam to the four corners of the world and working for a world-revolution in the realm of intellect and learning.

It is thus imperative on us to follow this path set for humanity by Muhammad and other Prophets (Peace be upon them) and by the Holy Books, irrespective of caste, colour or creed. This is the only way we can make this earthly abode of ours into an abode of peace and piousness and, in the long run, convert it into a heaven of bliss, beauty and serenity.

This path can be followed by us only by getting rid of the dogmatic, fanatical and sectarian interpretation of Islam, that goes to divide rather than unite people and creates gruesome monopolies to the detriment of the common man, by pulling down the overbearing feudal structure and replacing it with a just socio-economic order. This great task can only be accomplished by setting up an organization consisting of scrupulous and dedicated persons of all denominations who expressly believe in Allah, who accept the Quran and the life-example of Prophet Muhammad (Peace be upon him) as their guide in all matters and are prepared to carry out a long struggle for bringing about a democratic revolution in order to put back the downtrodden people on the seat of power.

His Heirs to Power

The Caliph, or Khalifa (i.e., the vicegerent of the Prophet), is the sovereign dignity amongst Muhammadans, vested with absolute power. The word more frequently used for the office in Muhammadan works of jurisprudence is Imam (leader), or Imam-ul-Azam (the great leader). It is held to be an essential principle in the establishment of the office, that there shall be only one Caliph at the same time; for the Prophet said: -"When two Caliphs have been set up, put the last to death and preserve the second, for the last is a rebel" (vide Mishkat, bk. xvi. chap. i.) According to all Sunni Muhammadan books, it is absolutely necessary that the Caliph be "a man, an adult, a sane person, a free man, a learned divine, a powerful ruler, a just person, and one of the Quraish" (i. e. of the tribe to which the Prophet himself belonged). The Shias, of course, hold that he should be one of the descendants of the Prophet's own family; but this is rejected by the Sunnis and Wahabis. The condition that the Caliph should be of the Quraish, is very important; for thereby the present Ottoman Sultans fail to establish their claims to the Caliphate.

After the deaths of the first five Caliphs, - Abu Bakr, Umar, Uthman, Ali, and Hasan,-the Caliphate, which is allowed by all parties to be elective, and not hereditary, passed successively to the Umayyads and Abbasides. The temporal power of the Abbaside Caliphs was overthrown by Houlakon Khan, son of the celebrated Chengiz Khan, A.D. 1258; but, for three centuries, the descendants of the Abbaside, or Baghdad, Caliphs resided in Egypt, and asserted their claim to the spiritual power.

The founder of the dynasty of Ottoman Sultans was Uthman, the son of a tribe of Oghouz Turks, a powerful chief, whose descendant, Bazazet I, is said to have obtained the title of Sultan from one of the Abbaside Caliphs in Egypt, A.D. 1389. When Salim I, conquered Egypt (A.D. 1516), it is asserted that he obtained a transfer of the title of Caliph to himself from one of the successors of the old Baghdad Caliphs. It is, however, a mere assertion; for the title and office being elective, and not hereditary, it was not in the power of any Caliph to transfer it to another. Force of circumstances alone compelled the ruler of the Ottoman Empire to assume the position, and has induced his subjects to acquiesce in the usurpation.

12

Pearls of Wisdom

Quran's Verses

Surely, this Quran guides to that which is most just, and gives good news to believers who practise good and they will get a great reward." (17:9)

"And He (commands you, saying): This is my straight path, so follow it. Do not follow other paths, which will separate you from His path. Thus He has ordered you so that you may be truly obedient (Muttaqun)." (6:153) Tauhid

"Allah! There is none worthy of worship except Him,

the Living, the Ever Lasting!

Slumber does not overtake Him nor does sleep,

Whatever is in the Heavens and in the Earth belongs to Him.

Who is there to plead to Him except with His permission?

He knows what lies before them and what is behind them, while they

grasp nothing of His knowledge except what He wills.

His Authority (Kursi) extends over Heaven and Earth;

Preserving them both does not overburden Him.

He is the Most High, the Most Great.' (2:255)'

(*This verse is called Ayatul Kursi*)

Risalat : "And surely, We have sent a messenger to every nation (proclaiming) serve Allah (Alone) and turn away from false gods (Taghat)...' (16:36)

"Allah has favoured the believers by sending them a messenger from among themselves, to recite His verses to them, to purify them, and teach them the book and wisdom whereas previously they were in clear error." (3:164)

"He it is Who has sent His messenger with the guidance and the religion of truth, that He make it victorious over every other religion, however much the idolaters may dislike." (61:9)

Akhirat : "O mankind! If you are in doubt about the Resurrection then consider that We have created you from dust, then from a drop of seed, then from something that clings, then from a lump of flesh shapely and shapeless, so that We may make (our power) clear to you. And We cause what We wish to remain in the wombs for an appointed time, and afterwards We bring you forth as babies, then (give you growth) that you attain your full strength. And among you there is he who dies (young), and among you there is he who is brought to the most pitiable time of life (senility), so that, after knowledge, he knows not (because of infirmity). And you (Muhammad) see the earth barren, but when We send down rain thereon, it thrills and swells and puts forth every lovely kind of growth. This is all because of Allah. He is the Truth. Surely, He makes the dead alive and surely He has the power to do everything; there is no doubt that the Hour will come and truly Allah will raise those who are in graves." (22:5-1)

"Those who disbelieve say: when we have become dust like our forefathers, shall we truly be raised up again?" (27:67)

"Do you think then that We have created you for nothing and that you would not be returned to Us?" (23:115)

"Allah has created the Heavens and Earth with truth and that everyone may be repaid what it has earned. And they will not be wronged." (45:22)

Qualities of a Mumin **:** "Successful indeed are the believers, who are humble in their prayers (Salat), who avoid vain talk, And who practise the system of Zakat;

And who guard their modesty except from their wives or the (slaves) that their right hands possess for then they are not blameworthy, But whoever wants beyond that such are the transgressors :

> And who faithfully observe their trusts and undertakings,
>
> And who are mindful of their prayers (Salat).
>
> These are indeed the inheritors
>
> Who will inherit the Paradise wherein they will live forever." (23:1-11)
>
> "O believers, fear Allah as He should be feared and do not die except as Muslims." (3:102)

Luqman's Advice to his Son **:** "And (remember) when Luqman said to his son when he was advising him: 'O my son! Do not make any partner to Allah. Truly, making anyone partner to Allah is a terrible sin (great zulm).' (31:13)

"'O my son! Establish Salat and command for the right and forbid the evil and persevere in whatever difficulty you are in. Surely, this is one of those things which have been strongly recommended. Do not turn your face in disgust from people, nor walk arrogantly on the land. Allah does not love the arrogant boasters. Be modest in your behaviour and lower your voice. Truly the harshest of all voices is the voice of the ass.' (31:17-19)

Duties and Obligations : "...Be kind to your parents and the relatives and the orphans, arid these in need and speak nicely to people...." (2:83)

"And We have made it a duty for man to be good to his parents. His mother bears him with one fainting spell after another fainting spell, while his weaning takes two years. Thank Me as well as your parents; towards Me lies the final destination." (31:14)

"Your Lord has ordered that you worship none but Him and (show) kindness to your parents, whether either of them or both of them attain old age in your life, never say to them, 'Ough' nor be harsh to them, but speak to them kindly. And serve them with tenderness and humility and say: My Lord, have mercy on them, just as they cared for me as a little child. " (17:23-24)

"We have made it a duty on man to be kind to his parents, but if they try to make you associate anything with Me which you have no knowledge of, do not obey them. To Me is your return and I shall tell you what you used to do." (29:8)

Luqman was famous for his sound intelligence and wisdom in Arabia. He was most probably an Arabic-speaking African.

Relatives, Neighbours and the Needy

"Give your relatives their due and also the needy and the traveller in need and do not squander (your wealth) irresponsibly." (17:26)

"Allah commands justice, kindness and giving (their due) to near relatives..." (16:90)

"And when near relatives, orphans and the needy are present at the division (of inheritance), provide for them out of it and speak politely to them." (4:8)

"...And (show) kindness to (your) parents and to near

relatives, orphans, the needy and to the neighbour who is your relative and the neighbour who is not your relative..." (4:36)

"Have you seen him who rejects the Judgement? That is the person who pushes the orphan aside and does not encourage feeding the needy." (107:1-3)

Orphans : "Therefore, do not treat the orphan with oppression." (93:9)

"Those who live on orphans' property without having any right to do so only suck up fire into their bellies, and they will (eventually) roast in a blaze." (4:10)

"Give orphans their property and do not exchange something bad for something good..." (4:2)

"Do not approach an orphan's estate before he comes of age except to improve it..." (6:152 and 17:34)

Brotherhood : "Believers are but brothers, so set things right between your brothers and observe your duty to Allah so that you may obtain mercy." (49:10)

Greetings : "When those who believe in Our signs come to you, say: peace be upon you..." (6:54)

"When you are welcomed with a greeting, then answer back with something finer than it or (at least) return it. Truly Allah takes count of all things." (4:86)

"...When you enter houses salute one another with a greeting from Allah, blessed and sweet... " (24:61)

Cooperation : "...Cooperate with one another for virtue and piety and do not cooperate with one another for sin and transgression..." (5:2)

"And hold fast together to Allah's rope (Islam) and do not be divided..." (3:103) "And the believers – men and women – are friends of one another, they command for the right and forbid the wrong, establish Salat and pay Zakat and obey Allah and His messenger..." (9:71)

Meetings : "O you who believe, when you are asked to make room in meetings, then make room. Allah will make room for you (in the Akhirat). And when it is said, "Move up" then move on. Allah will raise in rank those of you who believe as well as those who are given knowledge. Allah knows whatever you do." (58:11)

"Truly they are the believers who believe in Allah and His messenger and when they are with him on some common matter, they should not leave until they have asked him for permission to do so. Those who ask for such permission are the ones who believe in Allah and His messenger..." (24:62)

Talking : "Be modest in your behaviour and lower your voice. Truly the harshest of all voices is the voice of the ass." (31:19)

Seek Permission Before Entering Someone's House :

> "O you who believe! Do not enter houses other than your own without first seeking permission and greeting the people inside. That is better for you so that you may be heedful. And if you find no one therein, still do not enter until permission has been given..." (24:27-28)

Keeping a Promise: "O you who believe! fulfil your contracts (promises, covenants)..." (5:1) "... Keep your promise, every promise will be enquired into." (17:34) "Among the believers are men who are true to the contract they made with Allah..." (33:23) "...And (the pious are those) who honour their contracts when they make them..." (2:177)

Honesty : "And give full measure when measuring out, and weigh with proper scales..." (17:35)

"And give just weight and do not weigh unfairly." (55:9)

" Whenever you speak, speak justly even if a near relative is concerned... " (6:152)

Truthfulness : "O you who believe! Fear Allah and stand by those who are truthful." (9:119)

"That Allah may reward the truthful for their truth and punish the hypocrites if He wills..." (33:24)

"Truly Muslim men and Muslim women, believing men and believing women and obedient men and obedient women, and the truthful men and the truthful women... Allah has promised them forgiveness and a great reward. " (33:35)

"Allah said: This is the day (Day of Judgement) on which the truthful will benefit from their truthfulness, for them are the gardens underneath which the rivers flow where they will live forever. Allah is pleased with them and they are pleased with Him. That is the greatest success." (5:119)

Patience, Steadfastness and Forgiveness : ". ..Seek help from Allah and be patient, the earth belongs to Allah. He gives it as heritage to whom He wills from among His slaves..." (7:128)

"...Our Lord, fill us full of patience and make our feet firm. Help us against the disbelievers." (2:250)

"And anyone who acts patiently and forgives, that truly would be from the things recommended by Allah." (42:43)

"Tolerate patiently what (unbelievers) say and part from them in a polite manner." (73:10)

"O you who believe! Seek help in steadfastness (patience) and prayer. Surely Allah is with those who are steadfast (patient)." (2:153)

"...and those who are steadfast in poverty and illness and during the time of battle. Such are they who are on the right track and such are Allah-fearing (Muttaqun)." (2:177)

"O you who believe, endure and outdo all others in endurance, be firm in the battlefield, and observe your duty to Allah, so that you may be successful." (3:200)

"Be patient (O Muhammad) with the finest patience." (70:5)

"Then have patience (O Muhammad) as the most determined of the messengers (before you) had patience..." (46:35)

"Practise forgiveness, command decency and avoid ignorant people." (7:199)

Punctuality and Time-keeping : "...Surely Salat at fixed hours has been ordained on the believers." (4:103)

Courage : "Those to whom people said: Truly the people have gathered against you, so fear them. (The threat of danger) but it increased their faith and they said: Allah is enough for us! Most Excellent is He in Whom we trust." (3:173)

"And when the true believers saw the troops they said: That is that which Allah and His messenger promised us. Allah and His messengers told the truth. It strengthened their faith and obedience." (33:22)

Kindness : "It is because of mercy from Allah that you (Muhammad) were so gentle with them, for if you had been harsh and cruel-hearted they would have broken away from around you. Pardon them, seek forgiveness for them and consult them about the matter..." (3:159)

"... Be kind as Allah has been kind to you..." (28:11)

Trustworthiness : "Surely, I am a trustworthy messenger to you, so observe your duty to Allah and obey me."(26:101-108)

"Allah orders you to restore things entrusted (to you) to their owners..." (4:58)

Justice : "We surely sent Our messengers with clear proofs and revealed with them books and the balance (justice), so that people may deal with justice..." (51:25)

"Allah commands justice and fairness..." (16:90)

"...Let not the enmity and hatred of others make you avoid justice. Be just, that is nearer to piety..." (5:8)

Hijab and Chastity : "Tell the believing men to lower their gaze (from looking at forbidden things) and guard their private parts (from illegal sexual acts). That is purer for them. Surely Allah knows what they do." (24:30)

"And tell the believing women to lower their gaze and guard their private parts and not show off their beauty except which is apparent, to draw cloaks (head coverings) over their juyab (bosoms, bodies, necks and heads) and not to reveal their feminine beauty except to their husbands or fathers or husband's father or their sons or their husband's sons or their brothers or their brother's sons or sisters or their women or their maids or old male attendants having no sexual vigour or small children who have no sense of women's private parts. And let them not stamp their feet so as to reveal what they hide of their beauty. And turn to Allah together, O believers! In order that you may prosper." (24:31)

"O prophet! Tell your wives and your daughters and the women of the believers to draw their cloaks close round them (when they go out). That will be better, so that they may be recognised and not to be annoyed. Allah is ever Forgiving and Merciful." (33:59)

Bringing about Social Change : "...Surely Allah does not change the condition of a people as long as they do not change what is in themselves..."(13:11)

Generosity : "You will not attain righteousness (al-Birr) until you spend what you hold is dear to you..." (3:92)

"Those who spend their wealth (for the sake of Allah) night and day, both secretly and openly, will get their reward from their Lord, they shall have no cause to fear nor shall they grieve." (2:214)

Reliance on Allah : "If Allah is your helper none can overcome you and if He does not help you, who is there to help you? And on Allah let the believers rely." (3:160) "... He who relies on Allah, Allah is enough for him." (65:3)

Bad Conduct and Prohibitions : "... Give up the faith of worshipping idols and stop lying." (22:30) "... Allah's curse will be on him if he is of those who tell a lie." (24:1)

Backbiting, Spying and Suspicion : "O you who believe! Avoid much suspicion for indeed some suspicions are sins. And spy not, neither backbite one another. Would one of you love to eat the fresh of his dead brother? You hate that (so hate backbiting)! And keep your duty to Allah. Surely, Allah is Forgiving and the most Kind." (49:12)

Cheating and Fraud : "The cheaters will suffer terribly. Those who insist on full measure when they have people measure something for them; but when they have to measure or weigh things for others, they give less than their due..." (83:1-3)

Extravagance : "Do not squander (your money) extravagantly. Truly the extravagant are the brothers of devils, and the devil is ever ungrateful to his Lord." (11:2621)

Arrogance : "Do not walk in the earth arrogantly. Surely, you can never split the earth apart nor rival the mountains in height." (17:37) "... Allah does not love arrogant boasters." (57:23)

Hoarding : "And let the hoarders not think that what Allah has bestowed upon them from His bounty is better for them. But it is worse for them. That which they hoard will be a burden for them on the Day of Judgement..." (3:180)

"...Those who hoard gold and silver and do not spend them for Allah's sake, announce to them a painful punishment..." (9:34)

Mischief and Corruption : "... Eat and drink that which Allah has given you and do not act corruptly making mischief in the earth." (2:60)

Mockery and Ridicule : "O you who believe! No people should mock or ridicule other people, for the ridiculed ones may be better than those who ridicule them..." (49:11)

Hypocrisy : "And there are people who say: we believe in Allah and the Last Day but actually they do not believe." (2:8)

"When the hypocrites come to you (O Muhammad) they say: We testify that you are indeed Allah's messenger and Allah knows that you are His messenger and Allah declares that the hypocrites are liars indeed." (63:1)

Abortion and Fear of Poverty : "Do not kill your children in fear of poverty, We shall provide for them and you. Killing them is a big sin." (17:31)

Interest and Usury : ".. .Allah has permitted trading and forbidden interest and usury..." (2:275)

Wine and Gambling : "O you who believe! Wine (all kinds of alcoholic drinks) and gambling, stone altars and divining arrows are only a filthy work of Satan; give them up so that you may prosper." (5:90)

Fornication and Adultery : "And keep away from illegal sexual intercouse. Surely, it is a hateful filthy work and a very bad thing." (17:32)

"The man and the woman who commit illegal sexual intercourse flog each one of them with a hundred lashes..." (24:2)

Theft : "As for the thief, both male and female, chop off their hands. It is the reward of their own deeds and exemplary punishment from Allah. Allah is the Mighty and the Most Wise." (5:38)

Quotes from the Prophet

Hadith (pi. Ahadith) means news or information. It has a special meaning in Islam. It refers to the sayings and doings of Prophet Muhammad and the actions he approved.

Duties and Obligations

Jihad : "The most excellent man is the one who works hard in the way of Allah with his life and property." (al-Bukhari) "The best Jihad is to speak the truth before a tyrant ruler." (al-Bukhari)

Iman, Islam and Ihsan : "Faith (Iman) is that you believe in Allah (Tauhid) and His angels and His messengers (Risalat) and in the life-after-death (Akhirat).

Islam is that you worship Allah and not associate anyone with Him, keep up Salat, pay Zakat, and observe Sawm in Ramadan.

Ihsan is that you worship Allah as if you see Him and if you do not see Him, surely He sees you."
(al-Bukhari).

Love of the Prophet : "None of you has faith unless I am dearer to him than his father, and his son and all mankind." (al-Bukhari)

Salat and Taharah : "The key to Paradise is Salat and the key to Salat is (purification)." (Mishkat)

Parents : "A man asked the Prophet, "O messenger of Allah! Who deserves the best care from me? The Prophet said, "Your mother." The man asked, "Who then? "The Prophet said, "Your mother. 'The man asked once again, "Who then?" the Prophet said, "Your mother." (al-Bukhari)

A man came to the Prophet and said, "Messenger of Allah, I desire to go on a military expedition and I have come to consult you." The Prophet asked him if he had a mother, and when he replied that he had, the Prophet said, "Stay with her, for Paradise is at her feet." (an-Nasai)

"A father's pleasure is Allah's pleasure, a father's displeasure is Allah's displeasure." (al-Tirmidhi)

Wife : "The most perfect of the believers is the best of you in character, and the best of you are those among you who are best to their wives." (al- Tirmidhi)

Children : "He is not of us who has no compassion for our little ones and does not honour our old ones." (al-Tirmidhi)

"No father can give his child anything better than good manners." (al-Tirmidhi)

"Be careful of your duty to Allah and be fair and just to your children." (al-Bukhari)

"Whoever properly brings up two daughters until they reach maturity, that man and myself (the Prophet) will be as close in paradise as two adjacent fingers." (Muslim)

Guests : "He who believes in Allah and the Last Day should honour his guest." (al-Bukhari)

Neighbours : "By Allah, he has no faith (the Prophet repeated it three times) whose neighbours are not safe from his wickedness." (al-Bukhari) "He is not a believer who eats his fill while his neighbour remains hungry by his side." (al-Baihaqi)

"Jibbrail has been recommending good treatment towards the neighbours so much that 1 thought he would give them the right to inherit' (al-Bukhari)

Orphans : "The best house among the Muslims is the house in which an orphan is well treated and the worst house among Muslims is the house in which an orphan is badly treated." (Ibn Majah)

The Needy : "One who tries to help the widow and the poor is like a warrior in the way of Allah." (al-Bukhari)

Basic Qualities

Intention (Niyyat) : "Actions shall be judged only by intention, a man shall get what he intends." (al-Bukhari)

Truthfulness : "Guarantee me six things and I shall assure you of Paradise. When ycu speak, speak the truth, keep your promise, discharge your trust, guard your chastity and lower your gaze and withhold your hands from high-handedness." (al-Baihaqi)

"Surely truth leads to virtue, and virtue leads to Paradise." (al-Bukhari)

Keeping Promises : "Do not quarrel with your brother Muslim, nor jest with him nor make him a promise which you cannot keep." (al-Tirmidhi)

Tolerance : "There are two traits in me which Allah likes, toleration and deliberation in undertakings." (Ahmad, al-Tirmidhi)

Politeness : "Allah is polite and likes politeness." (condensed from Muslim)

Modesty : "Modesty (haya) is part of faith." (al-Bukhari, Muslim)

Brotherhood : "Each of you is a mirror of his brother, if you see something wrong in your brother, you must tell him to get rid of it." (al-Tirmidhi) "Believers are like the parts of a building to one another – each part supporting the others." (al-Bukhari) "None of you can be a believer unless he loves for his brother what he loves for himself." (al-Bukhari) "A Muslim is he from whose tongue and hands, other Muslims are safe." (al-Bukhari)

Charity : "Every good action is a charity and it is a good action to meet a friend with a smiling face." (al-Bukhari)

"There is a man who gives charity and he conceals it so much that his left hand does not know what his right hand spends." (al-Bukhari)

"Removing from a road that which is harmful is charity." (al-Bukhari)

Contentment : "Wealth does not come from abundance of goods but from a contented heart." (al-Bukhari, Muslim)

Learning : "The best of you is he who has learnt the Quran and then taught it." (al-Bukhari)

"The seeking of knowledge is a must for every Muslim man and woman." (Mishkat)

"The learned are the successors of the prophets. They leave behind knowledge as inheritance. One who inherits it obtains a great fortune." (al-Bukhari)

Kindness : "Allah is not kind to him who is not kind to people." (al-Bukhari, Muslim) "Those who are kind and considerate to Allah's creatures, Allah bestows His kindness and affection on them. Show kindness to the creatures on the earth so that Allah may be kind to you." (Abu Daud, al-Tirmidhi)

Thankfulness : "He who does not thank people does not thank Allah." (al-Tirmidhi)

Steadfastness : Sufyan bin 'Abdullah said, "I asked: 'O Allah's Messenger! tell me something which I should stick to.' He said: 'Say, my Lord is Allah, then remain steadfast.'" (an-Nawawi's Forty Hadith)

Repentance (Tawbat) : "By Allah, I (Muhammad) ask Allah's forgiveness and turn to Him in repentance more than seventy times a day." (al-Bukhari)

Gifts : "Give gifts to one another, for gifts take away malice." (Mishkat) "The messenger of Allah used to accept gifts and give gifts in return." (al-Bukhari)

Visiting the Sick : "Visit the sick, feed the hungry and free the captives." (al-Bukhari)

Manners

Meeting and Greeting : "When one of you arrives at a meeting where people are seated, he should say salam to them. And when he wishes to leave, he should say salam to them. " (Abu Daud)

"Do not sit between two men without the permission of both of them." (Abu Daud)

"Meetings are like, trusts, except three kinds of meeting: for shedding prohibited blood, or for committing adultery or for taking property unlawfully." (Abu Daud)

"When one of you meets his brother, he should say salam to him." (Abu Daud)

"The young should say salam to the old, the passerby to the one sitting and the small group to the large one." (al-Bukhari)

"The best (way) of saying salam is shaking hands." (al-Tirmidhi)

Talking : "He who truly believes in Allah and the last day should speak good or keep silent." (al-Bukhari, Muslim) "He who keeps silent, remains safe." (al-Tirmidhi)

Eating and Drinking : "The blessing of food is to wash hands at the beginning and washing after taking it." (Mishkat)

"Say Allah's name (Bismillah) and eat with your right hand and eat from near you." (al-Bukhari)

"When one drinks, he should not breathe into the vessel (glass)." (al-Bukhari)

Clothing : "Eat and drink, give sadaqah and wear good clothes as long as these do not involve excess or arrogance." (an-Nasir Ibn Majah)

"Indeed, he who wears silk in this world (will) have no share in it in the life-after-death." (al-Bukhari and Muslim)

"Gold and silk are lawful to the women of my Ummah and forbidden to the men." (al-Tirmidhi, an-Nasai)

"Allah's messenger cursed the men who put on women's clothes and the women who put on men's clothes." (Abu Daud)

"The Prophet said to Asma', the daughter of Abu Bakr .'When a woman reaches puberty, it is not right that any part of her body (should) be seen but this and this,' and he pointed to his face and two hands." (Abu Daud)

Leave that which does not Concern you : "An excellent Islamic practice is to give up what is not one's business." (Malik, Ahmad)

Bad Conduct

Lying : "Woe to him who tells lies to make people laugh! Woe to him! Woe to him!" (Ahmad, al-Tirmidhi)

"It is great treachery that you tell your brother something he accepts as truth from you, but you are lying." (Abu Daud)

Backbiting : "If anybody pledges to me that he will keep his tongue under control, guard his chastity, will not speak ill of others nor indulge in slander and backbiting and refrain from adultery and similar sins, I shall assure him of Paradise." (al-Bukhari)

Suspicion : "Beware of suspicion, for suspicion may be based on false information, do not spy on another, do not disclose others' hidden defects." (al-Bukhari)

Jealousy : "Keep away from jealousy for as fire burns wood, so jealousy consumes good actions." (Abu Daud)

"Nothing is more atrocious than injuring unjustly a Muslim's reputation." (al-Tirmidhi)

Anger : "He is not strong who throws down another, but he is who controls his anger." (al-Bukhari, Muslim)

"If anger rouses anyone, he should sit down and if that does not help, he should lie down." (al-Tirmidhi)

Pride : "If anyone has got an atom of pride in his heart, he will not enter Paradise." (al-Bukhari)

Abuse : "Abusing a Muslim is sinful and killing him is disbelief (kufr)." (al-Bukhari, Muslim)

Hypocrisy : "The signs of the hypocrite are three: When he speaks, he lies; when he promises, he breaks it; when any trust is kept with him, he misuses it." (al-Bukhari)

Taunting : "A believer neither taunts, nor curses nor speaks foul nor chats nor babbles." (al-Tirmidhi)

"Do not rejoice over the distress of a brother Muslim for Allah may relieve his distress and put you in his position." (al-Tirmidhi)

"Beware, in everybody there is a piece of flesh, if it is healthy, the whole body is healthy, and if it is sick, the whole body is sick. Beware, it is the heart." (al-Bukhari, Muslim)

Address of Friday

The Khutbah is the oration or sermon delivered in the mosque every Friday, and on the chief festivals,' after the meridian prayer. After the usual ablutions, the four Sunnat prayers are recited. The Khatib, or preacher, then seats himself on the Minbar (pulpit), whilst the Muazzin proclaims the Adaan; after which he stands up on the second step, and delivers the sermon, which must be in the Arabic language, and include prayers for "Muhammad, the Companions, and the King." There are several books of Khutbahs published for the use of preachers. The most celebrated of these preachers' manuals is the Majma Khitab, printed by Abdur Rahman of Kanpur. The sermons are arranged for every Friday in the year, and are the compositions of various Muslim divines. It is remarkable that short sermons are meritorious; for it is related that the "Prophet" remarked that, "the length of a man's prayers and the shortness of his sermon are the signs of his sense and understanding; therefore, make your prayers long and your Khutbah short."

The following is a translation of the third Khutbah in the book of sermons already mentioned; it is a fair specimen of an average Khutbah, both as to its length and matter:

"In the name of God, the compassionate, the merciful."

"Praised be God. Praised be that God who hath shown us the way in this religion. If He had not guided us into the path we should not have found it.

"I bear witness that there is no deity but God. He is one. He has no associate. I bear witness that Muhammad is, of a truth. His servant and His Apostle. May God have mercy upon him, and upon his descendants, and upon his companions, and give them peace.

"Fear God, O ye people, and fear that day, the day of judgement, when a father will not be able to answer for his son, nor the son for the father. Of a truth God's promises are true. Let not this present life make you proud. Let not the deceiver (Satan) lead you astray.

"O ye people who have believed, turn ye to God, as Nasua did turn to God. Veril God doth forgive all sin, verily He is the merciful, the forgiver of sins. Verily He is the most munificent, and bountiful, the King, the Holy One, the Clement, the Most Merciful."

The preacher then descends from the pulpit, and sitting on the floor of the mosque, offers up a silent prayer. He then, again, ascends the Minbar, as before, and proceeds thus:-

"In the name of God, the compassionate, the merciful.

"Praised be God. We praise Him. We seek help from Him. We ask forgiveness of sins. We trust in Him. We seek refuge in Him from evil desires and from former sinful actions. He who has God for his guide is never lost; and whomsoever He leadeth aside none can guide into the right path.

"We bear witness that there is no deity but God. He is one. He hath no partner.

"Verily we bear witness that Muhammad is the servant and apostle of God, and may God have mercy upon him, who is more exalted than any being. May God have mercy upon his descendants, and upon his companions. May God give them peace! Especially upon Amir-ul-Mominin Abu Bakr Siddiq (may God be pleased with him). And upon him who was the most temperate of the "friends" Amir-ul-Mominin Umar Ibn-ul-Khattab (may God be pleased with him). And upon him whose modesty and faith were perfect, Amir-ul-Mominin Uthman (may God be pleased with him).

And upon the Lion of the powerful God, Amir-ul-Mominin Ali ibn Abu-Talib (may God be pleased with him). And upon the two Imams, the holy ones, the two martyrs, Amir-ul-Mominin Abu Muhammad Hasan and Abu Abdullah Hussain (may God be pleased with both of them). And upon the mother of these two persons, the chief of women, Fatima-uz-Zohra (may God be pleased with her). And upon his (Muhammad's) two uncles, Hamza and Abbas (may God be pleased with them). And upon the rest of the "companions," and upon the "followers" (may God be pleased with all of them). Of Thy mercy, O most merciful of all merciful ones, O God, forgive all Musalman men and Musalman women, all male believers, and all female believers. Of a truth thou art He who wilt receive our prayers.

"O God, help those who help the religion of Muhammad. May we also exert ourselves to help those who help Islam. Make those weak, who weaken the religion of Muhammad.

"O God, bless the king of the age, and make him kind and favourable to the people.

"O servants of God, may God have mercy upon you. Verily, God enjoineth justice and the doing of good, and gifts to kindred; and He forbiddeth wickedness, and wrong, and oppression. He warneth you that happly ye may be mindful.

"O ye people, remember the great and exalted God. He will also remember you. He will answer your prayers. The remembrance of God is great, and good, and honourable, and noble, and meritorious, and worthy, and sublime."

The preacher then descends, and taking up his position as Imam, facing the Mihrab conducts two rakat prayers. The Khatib, however, does not always officiate as Imam.

In Turkey and Egypt, and in other countries under Muslim rule, it is the custom for the Khatib to deliver the Khutbah whilst he holds a wooden sword reversed.

The prayer for the reigning monarch, if he be a Muslim, would be offered up in the following manner:

> "O God, aid Islam, and strengthen its pillars, and make infidelity to tremble, and destroy its might, by the preservation of Thy servant, and the son of Thy servant, the submissive to the might of Thy Majesty and Glory, whom God hath aided, our master Amir Sher Ali Khan, son of Amir Dost Muhammad Khan, may God assist him and prolong his reign. O God, assist him, and assist his armies. O Thou God of the religion and Lord of the world, assist the armies of Muslims; frustrate the armies of infidels and polytheists, thine enemies, the enemies of the religion."

13

Right Way

Through Quotations

The Hadith (pl. Ahadith) is, as we have already remarked, the second part of the Muhammadan rule of faith. It forms the body of that oral law of the Arabian legislator which stands next to the Quran in point of authority, being considered by all Muhammadans, whether Sunni, Shia, or Wahabi, as a supplement to that book. The collections of these traditions are called Hadith, being records of the saying of the Prophet, but they are also called Sunna, a word which signifies custom, or regulation.

Muhammad gave very special injunctions respecting the faithful transmission of his sayings; for example, it is related by Tirmidhi, that the Prophet said, "Convey to other persons none of my words except those which ye know of a surety. Verily he who purposely represents my words wrongly, would find a place no where for himself but in fire."

Abu Daud received only four thousand eight hundred, out of five hundred thousand, and even after this careful selection he states that he has mentioned, "those which seem to be authentic and those which are nearly so." Out of forty thousand persons who have been instrumental in handing down traditions of "the Prophet," Bukhari only acknowledged two thousand as reliable authorities. Such being the case, it is not surprising that Ilm-i-Hadith, or the Science of Tradition, has become a most important branch of Muslim Divinity, and that the following canons have been framed for the reception or rejection of traditions.

I. With reference to the character of those who have handed down the tradition':-

> *Hadith-i-Sahih*, a genuine tradition, is one which has been handed down by truly pious persons who have been distinguished for their integrity.

Hadith-i-Hasan, a mediocre tradition, is one the narrators of which do not approach in moral excellence to those of the Sahib class.

Hadi-i-Zaif, a weak tradition, is one whose narrators are of questionable authority.

The disputed claims of narrators to these three classes have proved a fruitful source of learned discussion, and very numerous are the works written upon the subject.

II. With reference to the original relators, of the Hadith:-

Hadith-i-Marfu', an exalted tradition, is a saying, or an act, related or performed by the Prophet himself and handed down in a tradition.

Hadith-i-Mauquf, a restricted tradition, is a saying or an act related or performed by one of the ashab or companions of the Prophet.

Hadith-i-Maqtu', an intersected tradition, is a saying or an act related or performed by one of the Tabain, or those who conversed with the companions of the Prophet.

III. With reference to the links in the chain of the narrators of the tradition, a Hadith is either Muttasil, connected, or

Munqata', disconnected. If the chain of narrators is complete from the time of the first utterance of the saying or performance of the act recorded to the time that it was written down by the collector of traditions, it is Muttasil; but if the chain of narrators is incomplete, it is Munqata.'

IV. With reference to the manner in which the tradition has been narrated, and transmitted down from the first:

> *Hadith-i-Mutawatir,* an undoubted tradition, is one which is handed down by many distinct chains of narrators, and which has been always accepted as authentic and genuine, no doubt ever having been raised against it. The learned doctors say there are only five such traditions; but the exact number is disputed.

Hadith-i-Mashur, a well-known tradition, is one which has been handed down by at least three distinct lines of narrators. It is called also Mustafiz, diffused. It is also used for a tradition which was at first recorded by one person, or a few individuals, and afterwards became a popular tradition.

Hadith-i-Aziz-, a rare tradition, is one related by only two lines of narrators.

Hadith-i-Gharib, a poor tradition, is one related by only one line of narrators.

Khabar-i-Wahid, a single saying, is a term also used for a tradition related by one person and handed down by one line of narrators. It is a disputed point whether a *Khabar-i-Wahid* can form the basis of Muslim doctrine.

Hadith-i-Mursal (lit. "a tradition let loose"), is a tradition which any collector of traditions such as Bukhari and others, records with the assertion, "the Apostle of God said".

Riwayat, is a Hadith which commences with the words "it is related," without the authority being given.

Hadith-i-Mauzu, an invented tradition, is one the untruth of which is beyond dispute.

It is an universal cannot that no tradition can be received which is contrary to the Quran, and it is related that when' Aishah heard Umar say that Muhammad had taught that the dead could hear, she rejected the tradition as spurious, because it was contrary to the teaching of the Quran.

Whatever may be the difference of opinion as to the authority of the various traditions, it must be remembered that they form the groundwork of the different schools of thought of the Muhammadan religion. It is, therefore, impossible for European critics to form a just estimate of the Muhammadan creed without being acquainted with those traditions which are generally received as authentic and genuine.

European writers are unfortunately under the impression that the "Muhammadan revival" is a going back to "first principles," as expressed in the Quran, whereas, it is, as we have already remarked, a revival of the study of the traditions concerning their Prophet, which study has undoubtedly been promoted by the establishment of printing presses in Egypt, Turkey, and India. Not that we think Islam will present any fairer proportions even when deprived of those excrescences which are supposed to have been the preternatural growth of tradition, as long as the Pilgrimage has the so-called divine sanction of the Quran, and the position of women is regulated by the same "divine oracles."

The following are the six principal collectors of Hadith received by the Sunni Muhammadans :-

1. Muhammad Ismail Bukhari.'	Born, A.H. 194; died, A.H. 256.
2. Muslim-ibn-i-Hajjaj	Born, A.H. 204; died, A.H. 261,
3. Abu Isa Muhammad Tirmidhi	Born, A.H. 209; died, A.H. 279.
4. Abu Daud Sajistani	Born, A.H. 202; died, A.H, 275.
5. Abu Abdur Rahman Nasai	Born, A.H. 215; died, A.H. 303.

6. Abu Abdullah Muhammad, Ibn-i-Majah — Born, A.H. 209; died A.H. 273.

Some divines substitute the following for that of Ibn-Majah.

Muatta Imam Malik. — Born, A.H. 95; died, A.H. 179.

The following are the collections of Hadith received by the Shia:-

1. The Kafi, by Abu Jafar Muhammad, A.H. 329.
2. The Man- id-yastahzirah-al-Faqih by Sheikh Ali A.H. 381.
3. The Tahzib, by Sheikh Abu Jafar Muhammad, A.H. 466.
4. The Istibsar, by the same author.
5. The Nahaj-ul-Balaghat, by Syied Razi, A.H. 406.

Copies of the *Sihah-Sittah*, or "six correct" books of tradition received by the Sunnis, together with the seventh work by Imam Malik, have been lithographed, and can be purchased in the book shops of Delhi, Lucknow, and Bombay; but the work most read is the *Mishkat-ul-Musabih* (the niche for lamps), which is a collection of the most reliable traditions. This work was originally in Arabic; but it was translated into Persian in the reign of Akbar. It was rendered into English by Captain Matthews, and published in Calcutta in 1809. The English translation has been long since out of print, but efforts are being made by the author of these notes for its republication. The popular collection of Shia traditions arranged in the form of an historical narrative is the Hyat-ul-Qulub, a Persian work which has been translated by the Rev. J.L. Merrick (Phillips, Sampson, and Co., Boston, U.S., 1850).

The most trustworthy of the various collections of Sunni traditions is the one usually called Bukhari. It was compiled by Abu Abdullah Muhammad ibn-i-Ismail a native of Bukhara.

In obedience to instructions he is said to have received in a vision, he set himself to commence the collection of all the current traditions relating to Muhammad. He succeeded in collecting not fewer than six hundred thousand traditions, of which he selected only 7225 as trustworthy! These he recorded in his work; but it is said that he repeated a two *rakat* prayer before he wrote down any one of the 7275 traditions which he recorded. There is, therefore, every reason to believe that the compilers of the books of tradition were sincere and honest in their endeavours to produce correct and well authenticated traditions of their Prophet's precepts and practice; but, as Sir William Muir remarks, "The exclusively oral character of the early traditions deprives them of every check against the licence of error and fabrication."

But although the traditions of Muhammad are shrouded with a degree of uncertainty which is perplexing, to the student of history, still there can be no doubt as to the place they were intended to, and still do occupy in the theological structure of Islam. And everything Muhammad said with reference to religious dogmas and morals is believed to have been inspired by God; by a *"wahi ghair-i-mutlu,"* or an inspiration similar in kind to that which we believe to have been given to the inspired writers of our Christian Scriptures.

Giving Inspiration

According to Muslim theologians, inspiration is of two kinds, *Wahi* and *Ilham*. *Wahi*, is that which was given to the prophets, and is used especially for the Quran; Ilham being the inspiration to Walis, or saints.

Ilham is the word generally used by Christian missionaries for the inspiration of the sacred Scriptures, and we believe it is sometimes used by Arabic divines for a higher form of inspiration, but always in the compound form of Ilham Rabbani.

Sheikh Ahmad in his book, the Nur-ul-Anwar, defines inspiration as follows:- "Wahi,-or inspiration, is either Zahir (external), or Batin (internal). Wahi Zahir is divided into three classes:- (1) Wahi Quran, that which was given by the mouth of the angel jibbrail, and which reached the ear of the Prophet after he knew that it was Jibbrail who spoke to him. (2) Isharat-ul-Malak, that which was received from Jibbrail, but not by word of mouth, as when the Prophet said,' The Holy Ghost has breathed into my heart! (3) Ilham, or Wahi Qalb, that which was made known to the Prophet by the light of prophecy. This kind of inspiration is possessed by Walis or saints, but in their case it may be true or false. Wahi Batin is that which the Prophet obtained by analogical reasoning (qias) just as the enlightened doctors, or Muftahidin, obtain it."

The Isharat-ul-Malak, mentioned in the above quotation is never used for the inspiration of the Quran, but for certain instructions which Muhammad professes to have received direct from Jibbrail, and which are recorded in the Hadith, or Traditions.

Whatever may have been the actual impression upon Muhammad's mind as to the nature of the communications he professed to have received from God, it is evident that Muslim theologians have no conception of the World of God being given in the form of the Old and New Testament Scriptures. The most plausible objection raised against the New Testament, by Muhammadan controversialists of the present day, is that the Christians have lost the original Gospels and that our present book contains merely the Hadith or traditions, of Matthew, Mark, Luke, and John. It is, therefore, necessary to correct their common idea that the Gospel was revealed to Jesus in the same manner as the Quran is said to have been given to Muhammad; to show that it was the special office of the Holy Spirit to give the New Testament Scriptures, and that they came to man by the same method of inspiration whereby the Old Testament writings were given to the Prophets of old, the Quran being an exception to God's usual method of giving inspired writings to his Prophets.'

Consensus : Ijma is the third foundation of the Muhammadan rule of faith. It literally means collecting, or assembling, and in Muslim divinity it expresses the unanimous consent of the Mujtahidin (learned doctors); or, as we should call it, "the unanimous consent of the Fathers." A Mujtahid is a Muslim divine of the highest degree of learning, a title usually conferred by Muslim rulers. There are three foundations of Ijma: (1) *Itifaq-i-Qauli,* unanimous consent expressed in declaration of opinion; (2) *Itifaq-i-Faili,* expressed in unanimity of practice; (3) *Itifaq-i-Saquti,* when the majority of the Mujtahidin signified their tacit assent to the opinions of the minority by "silence" or non-interference.

The Mujtahidin, capable of making Ijma, must be "men of learning and piety, not heretics, nor fools, but men of judgement."

There is great diversity of opinion as to -up to what period in the history of Islam, Ijma can be accepted. Some doctors assert that only the Ijma of the Mujtahidin who were Ashab (companions); others, that of those who were not only "companions" but "descendants" of the "Prophet," can be accepted; whilst others accept the Ijma of the Ansars, (helpers) and of the Muhajirin (fugitives) who were dwellers in Medina with Muhammad. The majority of learned Muslim divines, however, appear to think that Ijma may be collected in every age, although they admit that owing to the numerous divisions which have arisen amongst Muhammadans, it has not been possible since the days of the Taba' Tabain, (i.e., the followers of the followers of the companions).

The following is considered to be the relative value of Ijma:-

That of the Ashab (companions) is equal to Hadith Muatwatir. That which, was decided afterwards, but in accordance with the, unanimous opinion of the Ashab, is equal to Hadith Khabar-i-Mashhur, and that upon which there was diversity of opinion amongst the Ashab, but has since been decided by the later Mujtahidin is equal to Hadith-i-Khabar-i-Wahid.

Amongst the Shias, we believe, there are still Mujtahidin whose Ijma is accepted, but the Sunnis have four orthodox schools of interpretation, named after their respective founders, Hanafi, Shafai, Maliki, and Hambali. The Wahabis for the most part reject Ijma collected after the death of "the Companions".

Inference : Qias (lit. "to compare") is the fourth foundation of Islam, and expresses the analogical reasoning of the learned with regard to the teaching of the Quran, Hadith, and Ijma.

There are four conditions of Qias: (1) That the precept or practice upon which it is founded must be of common (amm) and not of special (Khass) application; (2) The cause (il!at) of the injunction must be known and understood; (3) The decision must be based upon either the Quran, the Hadith, or the Ijma; (4) The decision arrived at must not be contrary to anything declared elsewhere in the Quran and Hadith.

Qias is of two kinds, Qias-i-Jali or evident, and Qias-i-Khafi or hidden.

An example of Qias-i-Jali is as follows:- Wine is forbidden in the Quran under the word Khamar, which literally means anything intoxicating; it is, therefore, evident that opium and all intoxicating drugs are also forbidden. Qias-i-Khafi is seen in the following example:—In the Hadith it is enjoined that one goat in forty must be given to God. To some poor persons the money may be more acceptable; therefore, the value of the goat may be given instead of the goat.

The Belief

Faith, Iman, is defined as "the belief of the heart and the confession of the mouth." It is of two kinds - Iman- i-Mujmal and Iman-i-Mufassal.

Iman-i-Mujmal is a simple expression of faith in the teaching of the Quran and the Hadith.

Iman-i-Mufassal is a belief in the six articles of faith, viz.:- 1. The Unity of God. 2. The Angels. 3. The Books. 4. The Prophets. 5. The Day of Judgement. 6. Predestination, or the Decrees of God.

Men of Letters and Piety

The Muslims have no hereditary priestly caste as the Hindus, nor have they a distinct order of clergy exactly corresponding with those of the Christian Church. But still there is a powerful hierarchy possessed of great political and religious influence.

In countries under muslim rule the religious dignitaries are appointed by the king, who is properly the highest spiritual authority in the kingdom. The Sheikh-ul-Islam at Constantinople unites in himself the functions of the Primate and Lord Chancellor.

The following are the chief religious functionaries, in a state governed according to Islamic law.

Qadi -The minister of justice, who passes sentence in all cases of law; religious, moral civil, or criminal.

Mufti-The law officer who expounds the law, and in difficult cases supplies the Qadi with "fatwas" or decisions.

There are still persons in India bearing the titles of Qadi and Mufti' , but the offices have ceased to exist under British Government. The Indian law, however, permits civil cases being decided by Muhammadan divines, if both parties consent to the arrangement.

Imam-The Arabic word Imam is said, by Sale, to answer to the Latin antistes, the president of the temple. It is also used for the four successors of Muhammad, the four great doctors of the four orthodox sects, the twelve great leaders of the Shias, and for any great religious leader. It is, however, commonly used for the person who leads the daily prayer, and is in receipt of the revenues of the mosque.

The titles of Qadi, Mufti, and Imam may be said to embrace the various appointments held by Muslim divines; but there are also numerous titles to denote doctors of Science and Divinity.

Tabib. A doctor of medicine.

Hakim. A doctor of philosophy, used also for a doctor of medicine.

Muhaqqiq. A very learned doctor in one or two sciences.

Maulawi, also Mulla. A doctor of divinity used for any person who has been educated in the Muhammadan religion, and assumes the office of teacher.

Faqih. A doctor of law.

Mutakallim. A doctor of theology.

Muhaddis. A doctor of the law of the traditions.

Mufassir. One learned in the commentaries on the Quran.

Madarris. An academical doctor, i.e., one educated in some school of reputation.

Doctors of Divinity are of three grades: Maulvi,' Alim (pl. Ulama), Mujtahid (pl. Mujtahidin). The title of Mujtahid is held by very few Sunni Muhammadans, but is more common amongst the Shias.

In addition to these titles, which express the degree of learning, there are others which denote the piety and sanctity of the individual. Pir and Wali are the common titles; but the following express certain degrees of reputed sanctity

Abid, one constantly engaged in the worship of God.

Zahid, one who leads a life of asceticism. The title of Faqir does not always denote one who has renounced the possessions of the world, but is applied to any one of a humble spirit, one poor in the sight of God, rather than in need of worldly assistance.

Qutbah and Ghaus, the highest orders of sanctity. According to tradition, a Ghaus is a saint whose ardour of devotion, is such, that in the açt of worship his head and limbs fall asunder! whilst a Qutbah is one who is supposed to have attained to the state of sanctity which reflects the heart of the Prophet.

There are four titles of respect which scarcely belong to either the religious or the learned classes, but are of more general use:-

Sheikh, an appellation which literally signifies an elder or aged person, It is a common title of respect, and is almost synonymous with our English "Mister". In Egypt and Arabia it appears to be used for the Hindustani and Persian Khan, or chief.

Miyan, (lit. "a master" or "friend") generally used for the descendants of celebrated saints, but also as a title of respect.

Sayyed, generally pronounced Syud (lit. "lord"). For the descendants of Prophet Muhammad (PBUH) from the daughter Fatima and her husband Ali. The word Sayyed is often used as part of a name, without reference to family descent from the Prophet; as Sayyed Ahmad, Sayyed Shah, & c.

Mir, also used for Sayyeds, but not exclusively.

Knowledge of Religion

Islamic theological literature is very extensive, and in consequence of the cheapness of lithographic printing, it is daily increasing.

The following are its chief divisions:

1. *Hadith*-Accounts of the precepts and practice of Muhammad. The collectors of Hadith may be numbered by hundreds, but the chief authorities are the six books known as the Sihah-i-Sita, or "six correct books". The popular work on the subject amongst the Sunnis of India being the Mishkat-ul-Musabih.
2. *Usul* (lit. "roots")-Treatises on the rules and principles of the four foundations of the Islam law, - being expositions of the exegesis of the Quran and Hadith, and the principles of Ijma and Qias. The most popular works on this subject are the Manar, by Abdullah ibn Ahmad, A.H. 710, and the Talwi' Tauzia,' by 'Ubaid-Ullah ibn Masud, A.H. 747.
3. *Aqaid* (lit. "creeds")-Expositions of scholastic theology, founded upon the six articles of faith. The most celebrated exposition of the Islam creed being that by Imam Ghazzali, A.H. 505. In India the work most read is the Sharah-i-Aqaid, by Maulvi Masud Sad-ud-din Taftazani, A.H. 792.
4. *Fiqah*-Works on Muhammadan law, whether civil or religious. The work most read amongst Sunnis is the Hidayah, written by a learned man named Ali, A.H. 593; part of which has been translated by the late Colonel Charles Hamilton. A smaller work, entitled the Sharah Waqaiah, by Abdul Haqq, is also much used.
5. *Tajsir*-Commentaries on the Quran. These are very numerous, and contain very many Jewish traditions of the most worthless character. One of the latest and most learned of these productions is said to be the short commentary by Shah Wali Ullah of Delhi, who died A.H. 1176.

The best known commentaries amongst the Sunnis are

Baizawi (A.H. 685), Madarik (A.H. 701), Jalalain (A.H. 911), Baghawi (A.H. 515), Mazhari (A.H. 1225), Hoseini (A.H. 900).

6. *Siyar*-Ecclesiastical history, i.e., the history of Muhammad and his successors. This branch of literature, Sayyed Ahmad Khan of Aligarh says, "is the one which requires the most emendation."

The chief authorities on the life of Muhammad and early days of Islam, in addition to the Hadith, are Ibn Ishaq, Ibn Hisham, Waqidi, and Tabari, whilst the most popular histories amongst the Sunnis of India are the Rawzat-ul-Ahbab, by Ataa Ullah ibn Fazl Ullah, A.H. 1000, and the Madarij-un-Nabuwat, by Sheikh Abdul Haqq, A.H. 1025.

In addition to his theological studies, the Muhammadan student is instructed in Mantiq (logic), Sarf (inflexion), and Nahw (syntax).

The text of a book is called Matan, the marginal notes Hashiyah, and its commentary Sharh.

14

Mosques in Islam

In Arabic it is called *Masjid* (the word is derived from the *'sajaj'* which means the place where one prostrates oneself placing his forehead on the floor). In different languages its names are Spanish, *Mosquita;* German, *Moschee;* English, *Mosque;* and Turkish, *Cami.* The Holy Prophet is reported to have said: "The whole of the earth has been made a Mosque for me." Therefore a Muslim is free to perform his prayer anywhere he likes. The need for a special place for prayer appeared very early and it is believed that the house of Muhammad (peace be upon him) was used as the first Mosque where the Muslims assembled for the Prayers and to listen to the Revolution. Later on, a part of it was roofed in by an awning so as to protect the worshippers from the sun's heat or foul weather.

The following injunctions are given in the Holy Quran regarding Mosques:

(a) Say: "My Lord hath commanded Justice; and that ye set your whole selves (to Him) at every time and place of prayer, and call upon Him, making your devotion sincere as in His sight: such as He created you in the beginning, so shall ye return."

(b) The Mosques of God shall be visited and maintained by such as trust in God and the Last Day, establish regular prayers, and practise regular charity, and fear none (at all) except God. It is they who are expected to be on true guidance.

Muhammad's (peace be upon him) injunctions regarding Mosques, as laid down in the *Ahadith,* are as follows.

(a) When you enter a *Masjid,* you must say, 'O Creator! open on us the doors of Thy compassion'; and when you leave the *Masjid,* say, 'O Lord! we supplicate thy munificence.

(b) It is a sin to spit in a *Masjid.*

(c) Do not read poetry in a Masjid, and do not buy and sell there, nor sit in a circle talking before prayers on a Friday.

(d) The prayers of a man in his own house are equal to the rewards of one prayer, but prayers in a *Masjid* near to his home are equal to twenty five prayers, and in a *Jama Masjid* they are equal to five hundred prayers, and in Jerusalem to five thousand, and in my Masjid (at Al-Medina) to fifty thousand, and at the Kaaba, to one hundred thousand.

The first Mosque erected by the Holy Prophet was at Quba, a place three miles south-east of Medina. It was the place where he had reached on Monday 23rd September, 622 A.C. during his Migration journey. This Mosque was without cupola, niche or minaret. It is said that the direction of the Qibla had been altered even before the crucial change was affected at Medina.

Liberty of Construction

Every Muslim is free to build a Mosque following the practice of the Holy Prophet. Abu Bakr, the first Caliph had erected a Mosque even in the courtyard of his house, while still at Mecca, in very early period. It was by the orders of Umar Farooq, the second Caliph, that large and beautiful

Mosques were built in every part of the empire. In the Arabian Peninsula alone some 4,000 Mosques were built during his reign.' He, also, issued orders for their proper management. He was so just a ruler that he demolished a Mosque simply because it had been erected over a piece of land forcibly acquired from a Jew. It was returned to its original owner.' Such an example of justice cannot be presented by any other religion or ruler of any other faith. How much particular was he in the observance of the Islamic injunctions in his foreign dealings can be judged from the following example.

During his visit to the Church of the Resurrection at Jerusalem the hour of the prayer approached. The Patriarch bade him to offer his prayer there, but he categorically refused and prayed on the steps of the Church of Constantine, saying, "for had I done so, the Muslims in a future age might have infringed the treaty, under colour of imitating my example." He strictly believed in the religious freedom of the non-Muslims. In one of the documents he wrote to Abu Ubaidah, the commander of the Syrian army, as follows:

> "And as for the procession of the cross in their feasts, do not prevent them there from outside the city, if it is without banners and standards, once a year, as they have requested you. As for the inside of the city between the Muslims and their Mosques, no crosses should appear. "

Whenever and wherever the Arabs founded their camp cities *(hirahs)* in the course of their conquest, first marked out the area of the Mosque. They maintained their tribal identity. They showed that they did not like centralization. Consequently each clan had its own settlement, its Mosques, markets and burial-ground. The result was the increase in the number of Mosques with their magnificent structures and designs. During the reign of Walid b. Abdul Malik 'Damuscus shone with the white domes and towers of innumerable palaces and Mosques.

He erected for himself a lasting monument in the great Mosque.' The erection of a Mosque was a social obligation on the ruler. As Islam spread governors built Mosques in their respective provinces.

The Muslims adopted all that was good in architecture. This is the reason that we see the impacts of the Byzantines, Goths, Greeks, Persians and Buddhists in the Muslim architecture. They took minarets from the Byzantines; pillars from the Goths; an unformed shape of domes from the Buddhists; mosaics and arabesque from the Persians and the Chinese Turks. They altered them according to their requirements and made them a part of their architecture. As Islam does not believe in territorialism, race and language therefore we see a mixture of all colours in the Muslim architecture. This very soul prevails upon the whole Muslim world.

Important Factors

The essential element of the Mosque is an open court with arcades on one or more sides. Usually the Mosque is a rectangular construction generally built of stones or bricks. The court is usually paved with enamelled bricks. Now a tendency has cropped up to sheath it in glistening patterned tiles. Sometimes trees and flower plants add to the beauty of their foliage to the ornamentation of the building. It symbolizes Paradise or at any rate an oasis. We know that the court of the Great Mosque of Cordova was planted with fruit trees. In its centre there is usually a large water tank where the worshippers perform their ablutions.

It becomes easy for a large number of worshippers to perform ablutions as some water tanks are very large, e.g., the water tank of the Badshahi Mosque of Lahore is 50 feet per side. Some Mosques have a large court. It is recorded on the annals of history that Timur intended that the Great Mosque of Bibi Khanum should be the largest Mosque in the world.

So its ground area was 548 by 358 feet with a court of 256 by 210 feet. The court of Ahmad Ibn Tulun Mosque measures 301 feet 10 inches per side. So it is square in shape. On the contrary, we know that the Al-Aqsa Mosque has no court at all and all the terrain, between it and the Dome of the Rock fulfills precisely that function. During the two centuries or so of the Seljuk rule, the court ceased to be a feature of the Mosque.

In compensation, a gallery was added to the facade. Its examples are the Aaeddin Mosque (1224 A.C.) in Nigde and the Ulu Mosque (1302 A.C.) in Ermenak. Similarly the Jama Masjid of Gulberga (South India) has no open courtyard as the whole structure is entirely covered in by a roof. This Mosque was completed in 1367 A.C. Structurally the prayer halls of such Mosques are supported by pillars which add to their beauty. Some Mosques have a swarm of pillars, e.g., the Adina Mosque has 1050 pillars. It was built by Ulugh Khan, Governor of Ala-ud-Din Khilji in 1300 A.C. The prayer hall of the Great Mosque of Cordova was covered with a forest of 850 pillars, each one composed of two columns.

Near the highly decorated entrance gate of the Mosque there is a low barrier, a few inches high, which denotes the sacred part of the Mosque. It is here that the worshippers remove their shoes, a custom dating from the reign of Umar Farooq (634-44 A.C.). But more certain is that it comes down from the second year after the Hijra of Muhammad (peace be upon him).

Al-Tabari (838- 923 A.C.) is of the view that the Caliph Walid bin Abdul Malik had issued orders that the new Mosques should measure 200 by 200 cubits, therefore a square like the house it replaced. With the passage of time it became customary to have arches supported by columns or other uprights. The court is often surrounded by galleries.

Usually the doors are covered with sheets of worked copper. They are sheltered by porches which are beautified with stucco or porcelain tiles. Now-a-days almost each city Mosque has a palatial hall which has direct entrance only through narrow cluster piercing the three walls. These walls are decorated with fine tile panels depicting flowers and trees. Sometimes they are covered with mosaics and stucco carvings.

Some Mosques have more than one hall, e.g., the Masjid-i-Jami of Isfahan has four prayer halls. They are inter-linked by the stories of iwan-loggias. In some Mosques the roofs are flat covered with lead or green tiles. The flat-roofed Mosques then assume various forms. The true or false vault is introduced. It is interesting to note that the roofs of the Neuji Mosque of Beijing (China) are hanging. Crowning glory of the Mosque construction lies in the shape and volume of its dome. First domical Mosque was the Mosque of Umar at Jerusalem, built in 687 A.C., although such Mosques were not commonly built about 13th century." Now it has become a fashion to have one or several domes." Some domes are of huge structure as the dome of the Great Mosque of Bibi Khanum measured 59 feet in diameter with its summit 131 feet above the floor.

The diameter of the dome of the Blue Mosque of Constantinople is 77 feet which reaches 141 feet at its highest point. The great triple domes of the Badshahi Mosque of Lahore are in their way superb examples of impressive design and workmanship. The Mosque of Bibi Mardun of Toledo has nine small ribbed cupolas, each different from the others. Whereas the Eski Mosque of Edrine has nine cupolas in three different types. The Great Mosque of Bibi Khanum has 288 cupolas. In the Mosque at Gulberga (South India) there are sixty eight bays roofed by a cupola besides a high and large dome.

Requisite the First

The first architectural requisite of every Mosque is the niche or arch which determines the spiritual axis of the Mosque. It points with mathematical precision to the sacred pile. It indicates the direction of the Kaaba which is the *Qibla* of the

Muslim *Ummah.* At first the Muslims used to say their prayers facing towards Jerusalem but in Rajb 2 A. H. the *Qibla* was changed to Mecca. It meant no localization of God. As the *Qibla is* the great 'sacrament' of unity for the Muslims therefore on that radius every Mosque is constructed. It is also a geographical expression of allegiance.

It symbolizes commitment to a set doctrines and ideological demands. To miss or ignore the *Qibla* is to destroy the prayer. Here the *Imam* stands whom the others follow while saying their prayer in congregation. Thus they follow the lessons of fraternity, discipline and social justice. It is interesting to note that the first *pucca mihrab* was built by Musailma bin Mukhlad during Muawiyyah's Caliphate in the Mosque of Amr bin-al-Aas in Egypt while making an extension in the Mosque. But the historians like Ibn-al-Afif (13th century), Al-Maqrizi (died 1442 A.C.), Ibn Taghribirdi (died 1456 A.C.) and as--Sayouti (died 1505 A.C.), agree that the first *mihrab* was built by Umar bin Abdul Aziz, the governor of Medina, who conducted the works at the Mosque of the Holy Prophet.

There are many shapes of arch-pointed ogival and keel arch. The keel arch was introduced in Egypt during the 12th century, in the Mosques of Al-Aqmar, Al-Salih Talai and Al-Azhar. But during the mid of the 13th century the architects of the Mosque of Baybars switched over to the pointed ogival arch. In the Turkish Mosques the keel arch was used very little.

The *mihrab is* generally semicircular with fluted roof and decorated with calligraphic inscriptions. It is usually situated in a covered sanctuary. This apsidal is more or less the result of indigenous workmanship. It is richly ornamented with marble, mosaics, stucco carvings or tiles. Sometimes the decoration extends to the entire wall around it and anointed with perfumes. Gradually the architects raised a cupola immediately before it. Such cupolas were to be built in all sorts of sizes, heights, complexities, and materials - wood, brick and stone. Writing about 1225 A.C. Al-Yaqut (1179-1229 A.C.) pronounced Great Mosque of Damuscus, built by Walid bin Abdul Malik, to be the most beautiful construction in the world. There is a real feeling of artistic enthusiasm in the description by Ibn Zubayr (1145-1217 A.C.) dating from slightly earlier: "This blessed Mosque was entirely adorned, outside as well as inside, with gilded mosaics and arrayed with the richest ornaments of a marvellous art............ Its *mihrab* is one of the wonders of Islam for its beauty and the rare excellence of its decorations; it sparkles all over with gold.................. The Qibla of this blessed Mosque, the three cupolas adjoining it, the brilliant light shed through the gilded and polychromed grilled windows, the sunbeams that stream down to become transformed into reflections of diverse colours dazzling the eye with their indecent rays, all this stretching across the entire south wall to reform a marvellous ensemble that defies descriptions: no words can match even a tiny part of the effect its form makes on the mind of the visitor."

Great Mosque of Damuscus was taken as model for most of the great Mosques of the Near East, notably in Harran, Rusafe, Aleppo and Harna. Its aisles run parallel to the *Qibla* wall crossed by an axial nave, a cupola preceding the *mihrab,* and porticoes around a very large court containing a small octagonal building. Prominent among such Cairo Mosques are the Salih Talai Mosque (160 A.C.), Baybars Mosque (1266 A.C.), Maridani Mosque (1340 A.C.), Al-Mahmudi Muayyad Mosque (1415-20 A.C.) and Yahya Zayn-al-Din Mosque (1448 A.C.). The *mihrab* of the Great Mosque of Cordova is an unique construction. It is a true and proper separate room behind its arch with mosaics. It is decorated with flawless marble reliefs and it reposes like a gem within its casket. Its incised and gilded stuccoes make it marvellous.

Some Mosques have several *mihrabs* because, generally there are multi-storied Mosques. The additional *mihrabs* are always smaller than the central niche. In the Great Mosque of

Damuscus three additional and much smaller *mihrabs* open into the Qibla wall. Among several other examples one is the Atala Mosque of Jaunpur (India) which was erected in 1408 A.C. by Ibrahim Lodi (1517-26 A.C.). Its lowest compartment has three *mihrabs.* The second stage is composed of eight decorated arches, four of them are squinches bridging across the angles.

Art in Islam

Mathematics has exerted a great influence on the Muslim art of architecture. It can be observed in the construction of *mihrabs.* "How the original parallel lines of the frontal art of niche appear, in later times, as the peripheries of two circles with superimposed centres. The stereotyped structural parts of the frontal arch which is pointed towards a centre lying along a line joining the two upper ends of the supporting columns, became in later times a point lying mid-way between the centres of the two constituent circular arches." Similarly the Moti Masjid of Delhi, built in 1654 A.C., is a matchless example of the felicitous proportioning of the arcades in the facade the skilfull contrasting of these with the colonnades of the cloisters and arched entrances, the delicate shape and melodic disposition of kiosks over the parapet, the subtle effect produced by raising the central dome on its drum, and above all in the flawless nature of the material, all of which have combined to give this building an appearance of rare and moving beauty.

In such a proportion and balance this Mosque really seems to be a pearl. Whatever the reason may be a majority of the earliest Mosques was square in plan. The Mosques of Kufa, Baghdad, Harran and Cairo were all square.

The *minbar* (pulpit) is usually set at right angles to the Mosque wall on the right side of the *mihrab.* It is approached by steps. The Holy Prophet ascended the pulpit for the first time on a Friday and delivered the Friday sermon. In the beginning there was no *minbar* and he leaned against one of the palm trunks of the Mosque. It was only two years before his death that the *minbar* was introduced.

It was a platform of a wooden erection two yards high, with two steps, each a yard ḥigh, and a flat surface of one yard which was square shaped. The Holy Prophet invested it with great sanctity. All oaths regarding disputed rights were taken close by it." Under the Pious Caliphs the significance of the Mosque for the State was embodied in the *minbar*. Here the installation of the Caliph used to take place. After the death of the Holy Prophet, Abu Bakr ascended the *minbar* and delivered an address. After this oath-taking ceremony he assumed the leadership of the Muslims. It was the same with the other Pious Caliphs.

The antique *minbar* of the Holy Mosque of the Kaaba was a wooden erection mounted on wheels. The second Mosque with a *minbar* was erected by Amr bin-al-Aas in Egypt. The Caliph Muawiyyah had the armchair raised higher by setting it on a base of abony with six steps. It was in the reign of Marwan 110 32 A. H./749 A.C.) that the general use of *minbar* came into practice. Under the Umayyads it grew into a ladder of nine steps, the lowest of which surmounted by an arch. The movable pulpits were, during the week pushed back against the wall of the *Qibla* and were pulled into the place for the celebration of the ritual prayer. As the time lapsed fixed pulpits were introduced. These were erected of wooden, stone or marble.

Special artistic tendencies were developed in the meanwhile. Some *minbars* were most aesthetically and constructionally competent manifestation of architecture. The *minbar* of the Great Mosque of Kairouan is a magnificent specimen in carved wood. The Holy Prophet held a javelin in his hand while delivering a *khutbah*. In time it was replaced by a sabre. During the 19th century it was replaced by a wooden facsimile. The Turks, also, used a bow as an insignia of command. There was, also, a custom to adorn the *minbar* with a green standard under the Umayyads, black under the Abbasides.

The *minbar* is occupied only by the *khatib* either on Fridays or *Eids.* It means that it is a 'place of authoritative declaration of allegiance.' As there is no clergy in Islam the *minbar* became the symbol of political, military and financial powers too. It is true that the large strides have been taken in the modernization of curricula, buildings and student conditions, but it takes a longer time and patience to modernize the prepossessions. So the Mosque pulpit still tends to be a mirror of the minds of its occupants and in turn of the pattern of their education.

Minarets are, also, a special feature of the Mosque. After the adoption of towers in Medina, they became the minarets without which one can scarcely imagine a Mosque. Generally they contain stairs. There are, also, minarets with external staircase winding round them e.g. Mosques of Samarra and Ibn Tulun. The minarets contribute much to the picture squeness of the Mosque. They become more graceful and 'show delicate articulations and gradations tapering from the square to the polygon and cylinder with skilfull use of "stalactite" or pendentive treatment of angles and transitions and support for the balconies.' They are crowned by a gallery and before the invention of loudspeakers the muezzin used to call for prayer from there. They play an important role of communication between interior and exterior space. They make it a 'symbolic form designating the intercommunication of two spaces and two worlds' as some minarets are very tall, e.g., the minaret of the Mosque of Hassan (Rabat) culminates at a height of 2621/2 feet.

Some Mosques have only a single minaret as the Masjid--i-Pa. Minar of Zaware (Iran, 1068 A.C.) and the Kalayan Masjid of Bukhara (1127-29 A.C.). But large Mosques have several minarets usually placed at their corners. The Blue Mosque of Constantinople has six minarets. Four of them have three balconies, each above the corners of the prayer hall; two with two balconies each at the north corner of the court. The minarets are found in Mosques of the later Saracenic style. Their shape, decoration and the materials used vary from country to country. Both bricks and stones are used in their construction with tiles and mirrors.

Similarly sometimes they are 'ornamented by blind arches with delicate little pillars, and by windows, loggias and lisenas; while the terminal turrets are enlivened by a lining of many-coloured fence.' In 11th and 12th centuries elaborate minarets were built in Egypt, Syria and in the West. Prominent examples of square minarets are those of Walid's Great Mosques of Damuscus and Medina, Bishr at Kairouan and Mosque of Hakim. They contained rooms that could be used as dwellings. In Iran and Turkey they are cylindrical in shape. The Mosques built in Islamabad have, also, cylindrical minarets. The Iranian minaret rises from a square or octagonal base and culminates in a balcony capped by a roof and a small cupola. Even the minarets of Cairo were to have all sorts of direct ancestors: square bases from Syria, cylindrical towers and polygonal shafts from Iran, minaret balconies support on stalactites from Anatolia and the shape of the window from elsewhere.

The Moors managed to make minaret towers of imposing massiveness at Masura of proud splendour in Marrkesh: the Hassan tower in Rabat, and the Giralda of Servile, noted for its unexcelled grace and elegance. Under the Almorvaids was built the Great Mosque (1135-38 A.C.) which shows the advance the Moors made in the domain of architecture. The round columns are replaced by quadrangular pillars and the horseshoe by cusp arches.

Gradually another element appeared in the Mosque, i.e.,

the *maqsura*. The Holy Prophet did not place any barrier between himself and the Muslims. The first Caliphs, also, practised the same thing. But unfortunately Umar Farooq, Uthman and Ali were assassinated. Amir Muawiyyah was, also, assaulted but he escaped. After his recovery he erected the first *maqsura*. In the later times in the Turkish Mosques the *maqsura* was replaced by a gallery reserved for the rulers and their intimates. "It is remarkable that the *maqsura* has no religious importance rather it shows a social hierarchy among the faithful."

The *Iwan is* a hall with one side open. 'It was Iran that was to make an almost exclusive use of the *Iwan* in a very original and totally different way. It was to serve as three dimensional module for earlier facade as well as for those facing the court in the *madrasas* and *madrasa*-Mosques.' In the Mosques of Egypt, the *Iwan* was not to play such an important part as it had in Iran. The name *liwan* simply came to be applied to the entire prayer hall. Then a new custom arose to erect a monumental portal in front of the Mosque.

The portals of the Iranian Mosques and madrasas enclose a huge keel arch which is very deep. Credit goes to the Iraninas for introducing the *pishtaq* which is a huge rectangular portal framing a recessed porch within a keel arch. In Egypt and Syria the proportions of the portal itself were completely altered. In Turkey, the portals are always centered in the middle of the main facade while in Cairo the composition is exactly opposite of it. 'The huge portal looks like a triumphal arch extending a splendid and pressing welcome into the Mosque.' The Iranians, also, developed a system of successive squinches called *muqarnas*. During the 12th and 13th centuries they were being used in the Syrian and the Seljuk Mosques. In Anatolia the *muqarnas* are of triangle in shape subsequently they do not extend upward with the amplitude one sees in Egypt. On the political and social plane such portals were, also, a visual translation of the grandiose idea of themselves that the princes who built them wished to impose upon their subjects.

Adjoining the Mosques are latrines with running water and special installations for performing ablutions.

There is an enormous difference between a city Mosque and a village Mosque. The former speaks of a bourgeois conception of wordily prestige and grandeur. Marble is luxuriously used in it. Its hall is large and it is colonnaded around all the sides. Generally crystal chandeliers hang from its ceiling. The entire building is faced in colourful tiles with white, black and gold motifs. On the contrary, a village Mosque is simple but well built, well white-washed and well-swept. It is generally dwarfed by an enormous tree which provides protection from the scorching sun. It has, usually, no minarets and consequently the *adaan is* delivered at the door of the Mosque. Friday prayers are not held in a village Mosque.

A Mosque is a spiritual centre of the Muslims where they assemble five times a day for worship. It is narrated by Uthman that the Holy Prophet said, "Who builds a Mosque for Allah, He will construct an abode for him in the Paradise. Abu Hurrayrah reported that the Holy Prophet said, "The portions of land that are dearest to Allah are the Mosques and the parts most hateful to Allah are the markets." As the Muslims subjugated different lands it became necessary to provide Mosques for the soldiers. In the beginning it used to be an open space fenced in with a palmy reed which could be transported when the army moved.

Afterwards the area was determined by four arrows shot from a central point and a ditch around the space thus defined. With the lapse of time covered colonnades were erected around the open space. Anyhow it should be borne in mind that whether a Mosque exists or not the very place where God is faithfully worshipped is equally pure. Because the theme of the prayer is always self-humiliation, the glorification of the Giver of all good, and reliance on His mercy. "It is one of the glories of Islam that temples are not made with hands, and that its ceremonies can be performed anywhere upon God's earth or under His heaven. The only condition is that he must direct himself towards the Kaaba and make the prayer ritual ablutions to purify himself in order to pray. During the 13 years of Muhammad's stay in Mecca *Baitul Muqaddas* (Jerusalem) served as the *Qibla*. It continued to be the *Qibla* even after his *Hijrat*. But after 17 months of the *Hijrat* the *Qibla* was changed over to *Masjid-al-Haram* in Mecca and a Divine injunction was revealed to this effect. 'This change of direction during prayer has a deeper significance than might at first sight appear. It was really the beginning of the National Life of Islam: it established the Kaaba at Mecca as a religious centre for all the Muslim people, just as from time immemorial it had been a place of pilgrimage for all the tribes of Arabia.'

What is the Best Place?

The Mosque is the best place in the world therefore no worldly proceedings are allowed to be conducted there except relating to the welfare of the Muslim community. It is obligatory for a Muslim to let his right foot first of all enter the Mosque. The Holy Prophet would say when he entered the Mosque:" I seek refuge in God, the Magnificent, in His Glorious Self, and in His Eternal Dominion, from Satan the Outcast." Sometimes he would pray: "In the name of God, Blessings and peace be upon the Messenger of God! My Lord! Forgive me my sins, and open unto me the gates of Thy mercy!" He would say when he came forth from the Mosque. "O God! Behold, I beg of Thee Thy bounty."

On some occasions he would say in these words: "In the name of God, Blessings and peace be upon the Messenger of God! My Lord! Forgive my sins, and open unto me the doors of Thy bounty!" He hated images sternly. Every Mosque in the world bears witness to this effect. According to the chronicles when Qutub-ud-Din Aibek entered Delhi, its vicinity was freed from idols and idol-worship and then the Mosques were raised.

Another factor essential for the construction of a Mosque is the simplicity which has been stressed upon in these words: "I have not commanded to raise the Mosques high." To this Ibn Abbas adds: "You will surely adorn them as the Jews and the Christians adorn their places of worship." The Apostle has been reported to have said, "The hour of doom (al saah) will not come till people vie with one another in (the building of) Mosques. We know that the Mosque of the Holy Prophet was of simple construction. It was made of unbaked bricks. Its roof was covered with palm-leaves. People used to prostrate on the muddy floor during the rains. All the Mosques built during the reign of Umar Farooq in Basra, Kufa, Fustat, Madain, Damuscus and Jerusalem were of simple structure.

It was during the reign of Walid bin Abdul Malik that the Mosques were built massively of stone and with luxurious decoration. The major portion of the courtyard was now roofed and a solid enclosing wall was also built. It was designed solely to isolate the interior space from the world outside. Luxuriousness and ostentation in Mosques became the salient features of the Mosque. To keep out pack animals Umar bin Abdul Aziz (717-20 A.C.) proposed to hang chains across the entrance because at that time the Mosques were not provided with doors of any sort. Generally the Muslims adopted the architecture in vogue in each land and made use of the local craftsmen. A ceaseless architectural activity began which was fine and at the same time admirable.

The erection of a Mosque has had been the task of the rulers, administrators, notables and public. We see that the Moorish School produced the huge Mosques at Cordova (built 8th-10th centuries). The Persian Mosques are characterized by pointed bulbous domes and gorgeous tile decoration. The Turkish School converted the Byzantine architecture to the Islamic values. It is exemplified by the Mosque of Sulaiman at Constantinople. It was built during the years 1550-57 A.C. by the great architect Sinan.

During the 11th and 12th centuries Egypt became the centre of architectural activities where a distinctive tomb Mosque was developed. The feature of a great dome was introduced by Saladin's successors, e.g., the dome of the tomb-Mosque of Al-Shafiy in the Karafa. According to S. Khuda Bakhsh the Mamluks were dome-builders *par excellence.* The Mamluk Mosques are indeed among the most beautiful Muslim buildings of pure architectural aesthetics. They gave the local architects a free hand in the development of Mosques. On the contrary, in Syria the Zangiah and Artukids were satisfied with classical architecture.

The Seljuks brought with them the typical architecture. The Mosques of the Ottoman Turkey rank among the finest achievements of the Muslims, or indeed, world architecture. The Ottomans introduced a new type of basilican Mosque. Its example is the Sultan Orhan Mosque (1339-40 A.C.) of Basra. Constantinople was the gem of jewel of the Ottoman Mosques. It was ('dream in the hearts of the Crusaders, thorn in the hearts of Pope, obsession in the hearts of Tsars, jewel-of jewels in the hearts of Sultans, lodestone of mastery in the hearts of novelists.................. end of the vision for Alexander the Great, whose sarcophagus is still there.'

The Indian School retained bulbous domes and round minarets of the Persian School with the deviation that stone and marble were used for exteriors. There are Mosques with "battering walls and pointed arch with spear-head fringe of the early Tughlaqs, the arch - lintel-bracket combination of Firuz, the 'boat- keel' dome and pyramidal roof of the Lodis, besides several other structural practice and decorative motifs. Under the Mughals were built such magnificent Mosques as Pearl Mosque at Agra. From Persian and Greek buildings were collected, and, without regard to uniformity or size, were utilized in the Formulation of arcades. In the words of the Emperor Babar (1526-1530 A.C.). "Whatever work a man took up he aimed and aspired to bring it perfection." So how could the descendants of the such great people do imperfect works! The number and arrangement of the columns in a Mosque now assume importance. Thus the number of columns in the Amr-Mosque must have been more numerous than the number of days in the year. In recent years the greatest activity in building new Mosques has been in Turkey, Indonesia and Pakistan. Steps have been taken towards emancipation from traditions and a fresh career has been started in this regard. Now-a-days a large number of Mosques reflect in architecture and decoration much more the qualities that the Greeks would associate such an edifice and would embody in its ground plan, proportion, construction and decoration. Here it seems appropriate to mention the Muslim Masjid of Lahore in which the prayer hall, court and water tank all are located on the first floor. On the ground floor are shops and dispensary.

The Value

The enormous symbolic and practical importance of the Mosque makes it both signs of the *Ummah* and the rulers. We see that the people do the same as do their rulers. After the conquest of Mithra, Sultan Mahmood erected a Mosque at Ghazna. Only marble was used in its erection. It came to be known as *Urus-i-Falk*. His nobbles, in his imitation, raised several Mosques.

Sometimes a Mosque or a part of it is known by the name of some important personality for one or the other reason. For example the cloister of the Great Mosque of Damuscus is still called the *Zawiah* of *Imam Ghazzali* as he had lectured over there. The Wazir Khan Mosque of Lahore is known by the name of its founder as the chronograms inscribed on the portal of the Mosque show:

The Muslims had penetrated into the sea-coast of Bombay and Sind during the reign of Umar Farooq. It was in the time of Walid bin Abdul Malik that Muhammad bin Qasim conquered Sind in the beginning of the eighth century. The provincial government at Basra earmarked a large sum for him to build Mosques throughout the subjugated territory. It was due to the religious tolerance of the Muslims that even the non-Muslims showed respect to the Mosques. It is narrated that when the Hindus recaptured Sindan, they left the local Mosque in the possession of the Muslim population which did not vacate the region. The Muslims could hold their Friday service and even pray for the Caliph.

In 750 A.C. the Abbasides defeated the Ummayyads and celebrated their triumph by a general massacre. Luckily a grandson of the Caliph Hisham, Abdul Rahman bin Muawiyyah, succeeded to escape to Spain. After five years of wandering adventure he occupied Seville and made himself master of the capital. The importance of the Mosque can be judged by this incident that on the same evening he presided, as Governor of Spain, over the citizens assembled for public worship in the Great Mosque.

Al-Mansur, the second Abbaside Caliph, laid the foundation of the city of Baghdad. It was circular in shape and surrounded by double walls. The palace stood in the centre with the chief Mosque adjacent to it. He erected several Mosques. One of them was close by the palace of Al-Zahab. Its size was half than the palace, i.e., 200 by 200 yards. Its roof and pillars were wooden. When Harun-ur-Rashid ascended the throne he ordered to rebuild it with bricks and limestone. Al-Mutazid bullah, the sixteenth Caliph of the House of Abbas, made an extension in the Mosque by demolishing the palace and incorporating its area into it.

It was the daily routine of Al-Mansur (754-75 A.C.) that after the evening prayer, he listened to the dispatches of the day. He took counsel with his ministers and then retired to rest when one-third of the night was spent. He slept a very little, and arose early for the morning prayer. Throughout the Abbasid Caliphate almost each Caliph erected at least one magnificent Mosque in the capital. After the return of the Caliphate from Samarra, Al-Mamun (813-33 A.C.) erected the great Mosque of the palace *(Jami-al-Kasr).* It was surrounded by two other palaces, namely the *Firdaus,* upstream and the *Taj,* downstream. As the Abbaside Caliphate was despotic therefore the secret agencies of the Caliph kept a very close watch on the leaders of the Mosques. Once Tahir bin Hussain prayed in his Friday *khutba* for the welfare of the *Ummah* instead of the Caliph.

The incharge of the Secret Service of that province, immediately, informed the Caliph through the incharge of the Postal Service. The Abbaside Baghdad had sixty thousand public baths *(hamams)* and each *hamam* had five Mosques. It means that Baghdad had three lac Mosques. If we suppose that five persons performed their prayers in each Mosque then the total population of Baghdad was fifteen lacs. These Mosques, also, provided shelters to the fugitives at the time of the Crusades (498 A. H/ 1104 A.C.). An annalist has written about the 10th century Cordova in these words: "The city extended twenty four miles one way and six on the other, and the whole space was occupied by houses, palaces, Mosques and gardens along the banks of the Guadalquiver." Syed Amir Ali adds that beyond the city walls stretched the suburbs, divided into twenty seven quarters, inhabited a thriving population. In each division there were Mosques, markets and baths.

Whenever Sultan Tughril Beg, the founder of the Seljuk dynasty, took a city he erected a Mosque and a school in commemoration of his victory. He had given the orders for public imprecation on heretics from the pulpits of the Mosques. The Sultan himself professed the Hanafite orthodoxy but his vizier Abu Nasar Mansoor Kunduri was a Mutazalite. He included the Asharites in the imprecation and started a persecution of the most prominent *Imams* and doctors among the disciples of Al-Ashari. To erect the Mosques was a practice with every religious-minded ruler. During the reign of Malik Shah the cities were adorned with colleges, hospitals, Mosques and palaces. Isfahan under the rule of Shah Abbas was an enclosed city within mud brick walls and it held some six lac people and 162 Mosques and 48 religious colleges. Same was the practice with Sultan Mahmood (1000-30 A.C.) of Ghazna. When he returned to Ghazna after the conquest of Kannauj in 409 A. H. he ordered for the construction of a Jama Masjid and a madrasa. When Sultan Muhammad Tughlaq (1325-51 A.C.) laid the foundation stone of a Khurramabad a Mosque and a madrasa were erected within the walls of the fort.

Ibn Batutah (1304-78 A.C.), who visited coast towns in China towards the middle of the 14th century, reported that: "In every town there is a special quarter for the Muslims inhabited solely by them, where they have Mosques, they are honoured and respected by the Chinese. They strictly followed their religious injunctions. No one could dwell among them who did not visit the Mosque. Their Mosques were built conforming to the Chinese architecture. Although they enjoyed religious freedom yet every Mosque was obliged by law to have a tablet to the emperor, with the inscription on it, 'The Emperor, the Immortal, may he live for ever.'

The new-converts to Islam were more enthusiastic regarding the erection of Mosques. It was about 1501 A.C. that the Raja Pra Ong Mahawangsa of Malay archipelago accepted Islam on the invitation of a learned Arab named Sheikh Abd Allah. His name was changed to Sultan Muzlaf-al-Shah. He built Mosques wherever the population was considerable and directed that to each Mosque should be attached forty four of the inhabitants at least as a settled congregation, for a smaller number would have been few for the duties of religion. So Mosques were erected and great drums were attached to them to be beaten to call the people to prayer on Fridays.

At this juncture, it seems appropriate to refer to the Emperor

Akbar and his *Din-i-ilahi.* It was neither beneficial for the Muslims nor for the Hindus. It, simply, added to the intellectual, moral and sectarian confusion. According to Sir Wolseley Haig, "During his last days, Akbar, had started victimising the Muslims and destroying the Mosques."

In the beginning of the Islamic history, the State used to make arrangements for the management of the Mosques. But with the conception of separation between religion and politics; downfall of the Muslims in certain lands and the lost of State interest in administering the Mosques, the local communities themselves devolved upon this responsibility. A Mosque generally has a staff consisting of a mutawalli an Imam, a khatib and a muezzin.

A mutawalli or trustee is charged with the management of a Mosque by those who endowed the Mosque. He is, also, known as Nazir or warden. He is a salaried person if he was not the founder himself. The administration of the Mosques and madrasas founded during the Mamluk period was to remain in the hands of the descendants of the founder. During the Mughal period many Mosques were under the system of mutawalliship, e.g., the Wazir Khan Mosque had a mutawalli. His descendants functioned as mutawallis in the years to come. The mutawalli 'may function either singly or with a board of some members of the congregation.' He has the right to appoint the Imam, but he cannot prohibit anyone to enter the Mosque on account of sectarian differences. He can dismiss the Imam if he feels that he is not doing justice with his job.

The Imam is the main functionary in each Mosque. He leads the prayers at the prescribed times including the congregational prayers. Imam is an Arabic word and it answers to the Latin Antites. It signifies to aim at or to follow after. It means an examplar or one whose example ought to be imitated. In this sense it is applied to Muhammad (peace be upon him) and Pious Caliphs in civil and religious matters. It is, also, applied to the heads of the four orthodox sects, namely; the Hanafi, the Shafi, the Maliki and the Hanabli.

During his life Prophet Muhammad (peace be upon him) led the prayers himself except a few days of his serious illness. He, also, appointed his different Companions throughout the State to lead prayers. An Imam is expected to be a man of sterling character piety and learning. There is no clergy in Islam therefore it is not obligatory that he should also perform such functions as that of a priest in Christianity e.g; a newly-born baby is baptised by him.

The office of the Imam is not in 'any sense a sacerdotal one. He is not being set apart with any ceremony, as is the case of a Christian presbyter, nor the office being hereditary, as in the case of the Hindu Brahmins. The position of Imam in this sense is not unlike the shaliach, or *legatus,* of the Jewish synagogue, who acted as the delegate of the congregation, and was the chief reader of prayers in their name.' In Islam any Muslim can lead the prayers, provided he is a pious man; even though he may not be an alim. The Muslim community does not need a mediation to obtain forgiveness for his sins because every Muslim can go directly to God for a remission of his sins. There was a time when Imam used to practise any profession in his private life. Although the practice has been changed now-a-days and the Imam is generally paid for his services from the Mosque's endowment fund. This practice of having paid Imams is to a very large extent responsible for the degeneration of the Muslims.'

The first and foremost condition is his learning so that he should impart true knowledge of Islam to his co-religionists. Abu Masud-al-Ansari says that the Holy Prophet said: 'Let him act as Imam to a congregation who knows the Quran thoroughly; and if all present should be equal in that respect, then let him perform who is best informed in the rules of prayer; and if they are equal in this respect also, let him act as Imam who has fled for the sake of Islam; and if equal in this likewise, let that person act who is oldest; but the governed must not act as Imam to the governor." Similarly it was said that: "Those who are well-grounded in knowledge and possess the greatest excellence are most entitled to imamah or the leadership of prayer." Accordingly the Holy Prophet, on his death-bed, appointed Abu Bakr to lead the prayers in his place.

Anyone else can lead the prayer during the absence of the Imam. Even a woman can lead the prayer while men followed her though it was in her own house. Aishah and Umm-i-Salma are reported as leading obligatory and *tarawih* prayer for women. Abu Hurrayrah reports that the Holy Prophet said: "When any of you acts as *Imam* to others, he must be concise in his prayers, because there are decrepit, aged, and sick persons amongst them, and when any one of you says his prayers alone, he may be as prefix as he pleases."

In the early days of Islam the *Imam* was also the leader of the community, politically and militarily. This was the practice during the reign of the Pious Caliphs. Even the governors enjoyed the same very position. During the Ummayyad reign (661-750 A. H.) Muawiyyah, Abdul Malik and Umar II presided over the Friday service and the daily prayers. But the others shrieked from their duty. Anyhow their presence was indispensable at the Friday service when he delivered the pontifical sermon. Usually, they wore white clothes with a pointed cap sometimes adorned with jewels. After prayers they used to deliver a sermon.

Sometimes even the Caliph was represented by an important functionary of his court; as Yezid II (702-24 A.C.) was often represented by the chief of the body-guard *(Sahib-ush-Shurta).* Once Walid II (743-44 A.C.) 'sent to the Mosque, enveloped in his cloak, a beautiful lady of the *harem* with whom he had been entertaining himself; and who entered fully into the spirit of the joke, to preside at the Friday service in his stead. Under the Ummayyads the governor or the chief Qadi, also, presided over the public prayers.

The Abbaside Caliphs, with rare exceptions, attended and presided at the Friday service and often delivered the usual sermon themselves. The Caliph's *cortege* was usually impressive. Syed Amir Ali has drawn a colourful scene of such occasions. Troops marched in front with banners flying, drums beating, and trumpets sounding, then followed the princes of the royal blood on splendidly caparisoned horses, and behind them came the Caliph on a milk-white horse, followed by his principal dignitaries. The rest of the body-guard brought up the rear. On these occasions he was dressed in a black or violet-coloured *Kaaba* reaching below the knees, with a shawl-girdle or jewelled belt round the waist, a rich black mantle over the shoulder, and wearing a high-peaked hat called *kalansueh.*

The *kalansueh* was usually ornamented with a single diamond of great value. The signet and staff of the Prophet was indispensable accompaniments. Generally a golden chain studded with gems hung round the neck, and the shoes had jewelled buckle. The *Kaaba,* which closely fitted the body, came below the knees and was worn open at the neck, showing the embroidered *khaftan* underneath. The sleeves were worn buttoned till Mustain set the fashion of wearing them loose; and his *Kaabas,* we are told, had sleeves three cubits wide.

People of the Staff

In Central Asia, it is usual to set apart a learned man by binding the turban round his head, the act being performed by a leading scholar.

Every Mosque has a *muezzin* who gives the call for prayers. Custom requires that he should have a sonorous voice. Bilal was the first *muezzin* in the history of Islam. A *muezzin* may be assigned some other menial duties as well such as cleansing the Mosque. Sometimes there are one or two *muezzins,* someone to light lamps during the night and sweep and keep it clean.

The large Mosques may have *khatibs* whose functions are to deliver the *khutbah* or formal sermon at the Friday congregational prayer. *Khutbah is* delivered acquainting them with the various injunctions of the Holy Quran and the precepts of the Holy Prophet. Its context is fixed—in addition to the praise of God and a blessing of the Holy Prophet, it must offer a prayer for the Muslim community, a recitation from the Holy Quran and an admonition to piety. Imam Abu Hanifa considered the recitation of the prayer and *khutbah* lawful and valid in any language. Abu Yusuf and Muhammad (both are disciples of Abu Hanifa) hold that when a person does not know Arabic he may validly offer his devotions in any other language.

Now we come to *waqf.* It is a term which signifies the appropriation or dedication of property to charitable uses and the services of God. It has played an important role in the history of the Mosque. The institution of *waqf* originated during the period of the Ummayyad Caliphate and spread rapidly throughout the Muslim world. It met a real social need for a long time in the Muslim society. Properties were assigned in perpetuity for their maintenance by a ruler or sometimes by a wealthy private individual.

The Abbaside Caliphs set up an endowment in the form of lands for the *Harmaen* and other Mosques. Mugtadar billah (908-32 A.C.) allotted several estates of Baghdad and Sawad, on the advice of Ali bin Isa, for the *Harmaen.* Thirteen thousand dinars were got from the estate of Baghdad and eighty thousand dinars from Sawad per annum. The whole amount was spent on the maintenance of the *Harmaen."* The *waqf* provided funds for the repair and maintenance of the Mosque, and also for the salaries of the staff attached to it. The *Al-Aqsa* Mosque had 135 houses which supported the Mosque requirements of their rent. After the war of 1967, the Israelis demolished them. Wazir Khan, the founder of the Wazir Khan Mosque of Lahore, allotted all the shops and houses on either side of the street extending from the Mosque to the Delhi Gate as *waqf* for the Mosque. The income of this *waqf*, together with that of the sarae and the baths close to the Delhi Gate, bequeathed permanently to support the Mosque and establishment attached to it.

Similarly the Masjid Nila Gumbad of Lahore has several shops attached to it. Their rent meets out the maintenance requirements of the Mosque. So in the past the public *waqf* were managed by a *nazir* or a *mutawalli* who generally received a salary for his services, if he was not a founder of the *waqf* himself. The administrators were men of high positions. Usually they were *Qadi's* who were particularly in charge of the madrasa trusts where they often used to teach. The *nazirs* (administrators) were, also, the incharge of the supplies of materials and appointed porters, sweepers, lamp cleaners, etc. Sometimes the Caliphs directly appointed *imams, khatibs* and even *muezzins* in the principal Mosques. In far flung areas the princes or the Qadis appointed such functionaries.

In the Mughal India there were officials to look after the management of charitable endowments. The finance minister *(diwan)* looked after such revenues. The district judge *(sadr kachari-i-sadarat)* issued cheques for stipends and daily allowances and passed bills for payment. There was an important department to look after the distribution of alms............ The officials of this department - *Amin, Darogha* and Mushrif - were appointed under the seal of *Mir-i-Saman.*

There are different rules regarding the erection and *waqf* of Mosques. The objects of such an endowment must be of a perpetual nature. Immediately after the building of a Mosque the right of an individual over it ceases when he allows even a single person to say his prayers in it. If a person appropriates land for building a Mosque he cannot afterwards resume or sell it. According to Imam Yusuf, if the place where a Mosque is situated should become deserted or inhabited, in as mush as there is no further use for the Mosque still the property does not revert to the original owner and founder.

Because once a Mosque, always a Mosque. But Imam Muhammad alleges that in such a case the land and the material again become the property of the founder or his heir. If any place is used, temporarily, for performing a prayer, it does not become a Mosque. It is generally that if a man makes a Mosque on the condition that he shall have an option, the *waqf* is lawful and the condition is void.

15

Society vs Polity

Politics in Islam

Politics is a part of Islam. It cannot be separated from it. Indeed, the separation of religion and politics is meaningless in Islam. We have already learnt that Islam is a complete system of life, and politics is very much a part of our collective life. Just as Islam teaches us how to say Salat, observe Sawm, pay Zakat and undertake Hajj, so it teaches us how to run a state, form a government, elect representatives, make treaties and conduct trade.

The Islamic political system is based on the following main principles:

Sovereignty of Allah : Sovereignty means the source of power and authority. In Islam, Allah is the source of all powers and laws (3:154; 12:40; 25:2; 67:1). It is Allah Who knows what is good and what is bad for His servants. His say is final. Human beings should not and must not change His Law. For example, the Quran says, "As for the thief male and female, chop off their hands. It is the reward of their own actions and exemplary punishment from Allah. Allah is Mighty, Wise." (5:38) According to Islam, this order cannot be changed by any ruler or government claiming to be Islamic (5:44; 2:229). There are many laws in the Quran concerning our life, and those laws must be put into practice by an Islamic state for the greater good of all human beings.

Khilafat of Mankind (Vicegerency of Man) : Man is the vicegerent, the agent or the representative of Allah on earth (2:30; 6:165). Allah is the sovereign and man is His representative. Man should do as Allah commands him to do. Man can choose either to obey or disobey Allah, but because of this freedom of choice he will be answerable to Allah on the Day of Judgement. In the political sense, Khilafat means that human beings should implement the will of Allah on earth as His deputy or agent, on His behalf as a trust (Amanah). An agent is always expected to behave as his master wants him to behave (10:14).

Legislation by Shura (Consultation) : Islam teaches us how to run a government, to legislate and to arrive at decisions by the process of Shura. Shura means "to take decisions by consultation and participation" (3:159; 42:38). This is an important part of the Islamic political system. There is no room for tyranny in Islam. Shura must be based on the Quran and the Sunnah. It must not contradict or attempt to overrule the Quran and the Sunnah.

Accountability of Government : The Islamic political system makes the ruler and the government responsible firstly to Allah and then to the people. The ruler must work for the welfare of the people according to the Quran and the Sunnah of Prophet Muhammad. In Islam the ruler is a servant of the people. Citizens of an Islamic state have the right to question the ruler and the government about any matters that concern them. In turn, the people must obey their ruler, so long as he follows the Quran and Sunnah.

Both the ruler and the ruled are the Khalifah of Allah. They will appear before Allah and account for their actions on the

Day of Judgement. The responsibility of the ruler is heavier than the ruled.

Independence of the Judiciary : In the Islamic political system, the judiciary is independent of the executive. The head of the state, the government and any member or employee of the government can be called to the court when necessary. They would be treated no differently from other citizens. The Quran has many injunctions about justice. One of the main functions of the Islamic state is to ensure justice for all citizens (4:58,135; 5:8). The ruler and the government have no right to interfere in the system of justice.

Equality before the Law : The Islami" political system ensures equality for all citizens before the law. It does not discriminate against anyone on the basis of language, colour, class, race, religion or sex. Allah distinguishes between us on the basis of Taqwa (piety or fear of Allah). One who fears Allah most is the noblest in Islam (49:13).

Concept of Ideal State

The duty of an ideal Islamic state is to establish Salat and Zakat; promote the right and forbid the wrong (22:44). The state is responsible for the welfare of all citizens – Muslims and non-Muslims alike. It must guarantee the basic necessities of life (food, clothing, housing, medicine and education). All citizens of the Islamic state should enjoy freedom of belief, thought, conscience and speech. Every citizen should be free to develop his potential, improve his capacity, earn wealth and own such wealth within the limits set by the Quran and the Sunnah. A citizen should enjoy the right to support or oppose any government policy which he thinks right or wrong with the following in mind:

a. The Islamic state is duty bound to implement the laws of the Quran and the Sunnah. The Quran strongly denounces those who do not decide their matters by Allah's revelations (5:42-50).

b. An ideal Islamic state should ensure a fair distribution of wealth. Islam does not believe in equal distribution as it is against the law of creation and basic human nature and instinct.

There is not a perfect Islamic state in the world today. There are many Muslim countries. An Islamic state is based on the model of Prophet Muhammad's state in Medina while a Muslim state is one which has a majority Muslim population and some Islamic features.

However, organised efforts are being made in many parts of the world to establish an Islamic system of government to implement the laws of the Quran and Sunnah. Notable among the organisations which have been working to Islamise society are: al-Ikhwanul Muslimin in the Middle

East, Jamaat-e-Islami in Pakistan, Bangladesh and Kashmir, Milli Salamat Party (renamed Rifah Party and now banned) in Turkey, Dewan Dakwah Islamia (DDII) in Indonesia, Islamic Salvation Front (FIS) in Algeria, National Islamic Front in Sudan (now defunct), Parti al-Islam se-Malaysia (PAS), and

Hizb an-Nahdah in Tunisia : There are many more Islamic organisations which have also been working towards the Islamisation of societies. The efforts for Islamic revival in Egypt, Pakistan, Sudan, Iran, Turkey, Malaysia, Bangladesh, Algeria and elsewhere have generated great hope and enthusiasm among Muslim adults and youth all over the world. This hope can only become a reality when Muslims make actions match their words. Only then will Almighty Allah guarantee their success. It is hoped that a real Islamic state will emerge from these efforts which will guide the world towards justice, happiness and peace.

Government in Islam

Management of the State and government is a baffling subject that has averted attempts by statesmen and politicians at various periods of history to deal with effectively. This is a very complex subject which concerns itself with practically all aspects of human society.

The primary concern of the State and government is the organisation of the various institutions of the State. Fair and quick dispensation of justice, equitable distribution of national wealth and decentralization of state power go to contribute considerably to a smooth running of the government, which in turn vitally helps in utilising the natural resources of a country for development of the wealth of the state. The process of utilisation of these resources helps to increase developmental activities of the citizens of the state through State participation in social and economic development. It raises the standard of living and intellectual capabilities of citizens thus increasing their technical know-how and health standards.

The political process, which constitutes the main thrust that propels social, economic and cultural growth of a nation, is one of the main concerns of a state. Economic development too is dependent upon a rightful fruition of the political process. If the political process is carried out on strictly democratic lines, it must ensure that the process has been rightly initiated and is proceeding in the right direction; that the dignity and authority of the weaker sections of society is ensured; that a certain ratio is maintained in the highest and lowest incomes of the citizens and they are provided equal opportunities of economic development.

A state and government run on these constructive lines guarantees to each individual the basic necessities of life and human rights. They work for freedom from exploitation of the weaker sections of the society by the upper classes, alleviation of poverty, human suffering and oppression, creation of widespread political awareness, arranging maximum participation of the people in developmental activities, developing democratic institutions, raising educational standards, establishing high moral and ethical standards, setting up a progressive and foolproof electoral system, doing away with narrow nationalism and racialism, linguistic and sectarian hatreds and concentration of wealth in few hands, boosting trade and industry, introducing a benevolent tax system, preventing wasteful expenditure by the government, living an austere life, bringing about unity among human beings, and bestowing happiness to one and all.

Keeping these requisites in view we enumerate below the basic issues that need to be addressed seriously, and translated into action, for a better running of the state and government.

The basic issues, according to our understanding of the duties of the state and government, are in line with the true concept of an Islamic State based on the teachings of all the Prophets and the Holy Books. They will amount to a fruition of our faith in God Almighty – the Creator of the universe and the Sustainer of all creation – and are central to the formation of a development-oriented society.

Basic Issues

1. Guaranteeing "basic necessities of life." (health, housing, education, employment) to everyone.
2. Safeguarding "basic human rights" of all citizens of the state without any discrimination of caste, colour, creed, religion or sex. All human beings to be treated as equal in status and dignity.
3. Providing freedom from all kinds of exploitation by the upper classes and equal opportunities of progress in all areas of life.
4. Ending monopolies of the means of production by extending public ownership over all rural and urban lands.
5. Alleviating of human suffering and oppression in all fields of life.

6. Making every country a truly democratic and welfare State by securing for the ordinary people the right to rule and to frame laws through creation of widespread political awareness among the masses, by transferring to them maximum administrative authority from the central to the provincial, district and local levels and by developing in them the capability to use this authority in the best manner and to the best interests of the people. To give them maximum participation in the country's political process and the government's policy-making and developmental activities.
7. Reconstructing all institutions on democratic lines and developing "democratic culture" at the individual, family and social levels.
8. Setting up high standards of political leadership giving due importance to educational standards, a good record of public service, a good moral standard and strength of character, a certain amount of goodwill amongst the people and firm commitment to the cause of the lower and middle classes.
9. Formulating foolproof electoral system with clear-cut parameters that would ensure fair and free elections, and guarantee a true democratic Order.
10. Demarcating clearly the duties and rights of both the government and the Opposition in every country and giving the Opposition due importance in the running of the State as it is the "government in waiting."
11. Giving full importance to legislative business. Enacting all laws through the legislature and not by promulgation of Presidential Orders.
12. Doing away with narrow nationalism and fanaticism, keeping within limits all kinds of racial, linguistic, sectarian and religious biases, getting rid of religious elitism and monopoly in all its forms and instead develop-

ing the concept of human unity and dignity, and working for creating "unity of humankind on the bases of moral and ethical values formulated by the Prophets."

13. Bringing about a consensus regarding the basic issues faced by the nation and devising therewith programmes and methodology for national development and prosperity.
14. Basing politics on mutual consultation, cooperation and collective interest, and ridding it of palace intrigues and confrontation for securing personal ends and for amassing wealth, so that politics could be made a means of serving the masses, and freeing them from all forms of exploitation and oppression.
15. Setting up an autonomous commission on a permanent basis for accountability of politicians and government servants.
16. Acquiring for women a respectful position in society by securing for them equal rights with men, making them economically independent, getting for them high positions in the educational field, and arranging their equal participation in the political process through effective representation in the legislature.
17. Establishing close relationship with all the nations world.
18. Promoting economic justice and alleviating poverty and deprivation among the hard pressed workers and peasants.
19. Basing the country's economy on the principle of "self-reliance" with least reliance on foreign loans.
20. Initiating a process of realistic and effective land reforms for ending *jagirdari* and absentee-landlordism, by fixing a land ceiling and by providing few acres of land in ownership to every landless peasant for cultivation. Giving incentives to small farmers with a view to increasing agricultural production.

21. Fixing a limit on urban property.
22. Stopping concentration of wealth in few hands, and preparing a mechanism by which to spread it out among the different sections of the population, so as to increase the purchasing power of the common man. Spending whatever is in excess to one's genuine needs for the public good considering it to be an act of worship.
23. Boosting trade and industry in the private sector while providing full safeguards to the consumer and the industrial workers, while paying special attention to raising the standard of living of the workers. Also developing basic and heavy industry in the public sector.
24. Building the necessary infrastructure – highways, electric trains, seaports, airports – for the development of trade, industry and agriculture.
25. Regulating the economic and fiscal system of the country on the basis of justice and benevolence *(adl-o-ehsan)* as envisaged by the Islamic system of Zakat and sadaqat and getting rid, as soon as possible, of the interest system *(riba)* introduced by Capitalism.
26. Realising taxes from the people strictly in accordance with their incomes, be they from agricultural or urban properties. A minimum of indirect taxes be imposed so that the taxpayer is least burdened.
27. Avoiding wasteful government expenditure, minimising non-developmental expenditure and censuring pomp and show by politicians and government dignitaries. Stopping forthwith unnecessary foreign tours with large entourage.
28. Bringing the ratio of the highest and the lowest incomes to minimum possible.

System of Economy

Islam is a complete way of life. No part of the life of an individual or a community is left out of Islam. The economic aspect is an important part of life, so Islam gives detailed guidelines for the conduct of our economic life. It concerns mainly how we earn and use our wealth. The Islamic system is balanced and places everything in its right place.

Earning and spending money is essential for our living, but we do not live only for this. Man needs bread to live but he does not live for bread alone. We have a greater purpose in life. We are Allah's agents (Khalifah) on earth. We not only have a body but we also have a soul (Rah) and a conscience. Without a conscience, our behaviour would be worse than wild animals and would create enormous problems in society.

Everything in Islam is for the benefit and welfare of humanity. The economic principles of Islam aim to establish a just society in which we behave responsibly and honestly, not selfishly fighting for the biggest possible share of something without regard for honesty, truth, decency, trust and responsibility. The economic system of Islam is based on the following principles:

Earning and Expenditure by Halal Means : Muslims are not allowed to earn and spend in any way they like. Islam has laws, based on the Quran and the Sunnah, to regulate earning and expenditure:

a. Earnings from the production, sale and distribution of alcoholic drinks are unlawful, as are earnings from gambling, lotteries and from Riba (interest or usury) transactions (5:90-91; 2:275).

b. Earning by falsehood, deceit, fraud, and theft is unlawful (Haram). Taking orphans' property deceitfully has been particularly forbidden (2:188; 4:2; 6:152; 7:85; 83:1-5).

c. Hoarding food stuff and basic necessities, smuggling and the artificial creation of shortages are unlawful (3:180; 9:34–35).

d. Earnings from brothels and from other immoral sources which are harmful to society are also unlawful (24:23). Islam strikes at the root of evil and wants to establish a just and fair society. A Muslim must earn his living in Halal ways and he should always bear in mind that whatever he does is known to Allah. He will be accountable for his actions on the Day of Judgement. He cannot hide anything from the knowledge of Almighty Allah.

Unlawful expenditure is not allowed in Islam. A Muslim should not spend his money irresponsibly. Rather, he should spend it wisely and thoughtfully. Extravagance and waste are strongly discouraged (7:31; 17:26; 19:27-31; 25:28).

Right to Property and Individual Liberty : In Islam a person has a right to his earnings. The Islamic state does not interfere with the freedom of speech, work or earnings of an individual provided this freedom does not harm the greater good of society. Every individual will be answerable to Allah for his or her actions on the Day of Judgement (4:7; 36:71; 16:111).

System of Zakat (Welfare Contribution) : Compulsory payment of Zakat is one of the basic principles of an Islamic economy. Every Muslim who has sufficient wealth must pay the fixed rate of Zakat to the Islamic state. Zakat helps to narrow the gap between the rich and the poor. It is a form of social security. An ideal Islamic state is responsible for providing the basic necessities of food, clothing, housing, medicine and education for every citizen. No one should have any fear of insecurity, poverty or hunger (9:69, 103; 98:5).

The giving of charity (Sadaqah) is greatly recommended in Islam. It is a further means of helping the poorest and most vulnerable in society. It encourages those blessed by Allah with more than they need, to show consideration for the less fortunate and exercise social responsibility.

Prohibition of Riba (interest or usury) : An Islamic economy prohibits all transactions involving Riba (interest or usury). In Islam there is no distinction between interest and usury. Islam allows only a zero rate of interest, that is, no interest at all. Whatever the name used, interest or usury, it is prohibited in Islam.

Interest is neither a trade nor a profit. It is a means of exploitation and concentration of wealth. The Quran says:

> "They say, 'trade is like interest.' But Allah has allowed trade and forbidden interest." (2:275)
>
> "Whatever you pay as interest, so that it may increase in the property of (other) men, it does not increase with Allah." (30:39)
>
> "O you who believe, do not take interest, doubling and multiplying, and keep your duty to Allah, so that you may prosper." (3:130)
>
> "O you who believe, observe your duty to Allah and give up what remains (due) from interest, if you are believers. But if you do not do it, then be warned of war from Allah and His messenger; and if you repent, then you shall have your capital. Do not exploit and be not exploited." (2:278-279)

Interest (Riba) is an integral part of modern free-market economies. Unlike Zakat, which distributes wealth from the rich to the poor, interest takes wealth from the poor to the rich. Modern economies depend on interest; it is assumed to be impossible to live without it. This false assumption is challenged by the successful interest-free facilities offered by Islamic banks and investment companies throughout the world, including the UK.

A fully-fledged interest-free economy is not yet a reality. It is a complex situation. Nevertheless, we should work towards an interest-free economy to ensure social justice and equal access to opportunities for everyone in the world. An interest-free economy is only possible when an Islamic government carefully and systematically plans and implements the economic system of Islam.

Law of Inheritance (Mirath) : The Islamic law of inheritance (Mirath) is a wonderful system that ensures the fair distribution of wealth after someone dies. It details the rights of relatives over the property of the deceased person. Suratun Nisa' of the Quran deals with the law of inheritance in great detail (4:7-12,176).

Some Instructions

Islam has laid down many more rules and guidelines about economic life. All human and natural resources should be put to good use in an Islamic state. Corruption and all immoral pursuits must be rooted out, even if they are economically lucrative. Some individual freedoms may have to be sacrificed for the greater good of society.

Islam encourages simplicity, modesty, charity, mutual help and cooperation. It discourages miserliness, greed, extravagance and unnecessary waste.

Life and Society

Family Life in Islam : Family is the basis of Islamic society. Its origin goes back to the beginning of the creation of man and woman – Adam and Hawwa' (Eve). So, it is an institution founded by Allah's will. Allah says in the Quran:

> "O mankind! be mindful of your duty to your Lord who created you from a single soul and from it created its mate and from the two created many men and women." (4:1)

Marriage is the basis of the Islamic family. A good and sound society can only grow if a man and a woman are bound in a solid relationship through the sacred contract of marriage.

Marriage develops love, care and cooperation between the husband and wife. It gives peace of mind and provides a secure and solid basis for the growth and progress of the whole human race. Without marriage, the human race would come to a standstill. Marriage was the practice of most of the prophets including Muhammad.

Marriage (Nikah) : Marriage is a sacred social contract between a bridegroom and a bride. A great deal of thought is necessary therefore before a man and a woman decide to marry.

> Piety should come before all other considerations. Prophet Muhammad said, "Do not marry only for the sake of beauty, maybe the beauty becomes the cause of moral decline. Do not marry even for the sake of wealth; maybe the wealth becomes the reason of disobedience; marry rather on the grounds of religious devotion." (Ibn Majah) "A woman is married for four things: her wealth, her family status, her beauty and her religion. So you should marry the religious woman (otherwise) you will be a loser." (al-Bukharf)

A Muslim man is expected to marry a Muslim woman although in some cases chaste Jewish and Christian women can be married. However, a Muslim woman is not allowed to marry a non-Muslim man. In Islam, marriage is a religious and social institution and not simply a sexual relationship.

Muslim marriages are traditionally arranged by parents but the final say lies with the man and the woman. Islam does not allow free mixing of grown-up boys and girls, nor does it allow sex outside marriage. The Islamic way of life does not approve of the boyfriend/girlfriend system, or mixed parties of grown-ups and the like.

Islamic society is based on submission and obedience to the Will of Allah. Husband and wife, bound by marriage, are Allah's servants and representatives (Khalifah). Marriage must not conflict with the purpose of life (seeking Allah's pleasure), rather it should lead towards its achievement.

Divorce is allowed but is regarded as the least desirable of all lawful acts. Prophet Muhammad? said, "Of all things which have been permitted, divorce is the most hated by Allah." (Abu Daud, Ibn Majah) Islam encourages adjustment reconciliation and happiness but when living together is impossible, Islamic law does not prohibit divorce (Talaa).

Status of Women : Women are an important and integral part of Islamic society. Unlike a number of other religions, Islam holds a woman in high esteem. Her importance as a mother and a wife has been clearly stated by Prophet Muhammad.

> A man came to the Prophet and said, "Messenger of Allah, I desire to go on a military expedition and I have come to consult you." The Prophet asked him if he had a mother, and when he replied that he had, he said, "Stay with her, for Paradise is at her feet." (an-Nasai)
>
> Once a person asked the Prophet, "Who deserves the best care from me?" The Prophet replied, "Your mother (he repeated this three times), then your father and then your nearest relatives." (al-Bukhari)

In his farewell speech at 'Arafat in the tenth year of the Hijrat, the Prophet said, "O people, your wives have certain rights over you and you have certain rights over them. Treat them well and be kind to them, for they are your partners and committed helpers."

> The Prophet also said, "The best among you is the one who is the best towards his wife." (at-Tirmidhi)

These sayings clearly prove the important position given to women in Islam yet there are people, especially in the West, who have misgivings about the status of women in Islam. To these people, the Muslim woman is seen almost as 'a prisoner within the four walls of the house', a 'non-person', and 'someone who has no rights and living always under the domination of a man'. These notions are totally wrong and are based on ignorance rather than correct knowledge of Islam.

One of the rites of Hajj is a fast walk between as-Safa and al-Manwah, which is observed to remember the event of Hajar (Hagar), mother of Prophet Isma who ran between these two hills to find water. This is another proof of the importance and respect given to women by Islam.

In order to judge the incorrect ideas held by western people, it would be useful to survey the attitudes to women in different societies in the past.

During the Roman civilization, for example, a woman was regarded as a slave. The Greeks considered her a commodity to be bought and sold. Early Christianity regarded women as temptresses, responsible for the fall of Adam from Heaven'.

In India, the Hindus until recently considered their women worse than death, pests, serpents or even Hell. A wife's life ended with the death of her husband. In the past, a widow had to jump into the flames of her husband's funeral pyre.

> In pre-Islamic Arabia, a woman was treated as a cause for grief and unhappiness and baby girls were sometimes buried alive after birth. This is mentioned in the Quran when Allah says: "And when the female (infant) buried alive (as the pagan Arabs used to do) is questioned. For what sin was she kitted?"
>
> (81:8-9)

In France, in 587 CE, a conference was held to study the status of women and to determine whether a woman could truly be considered a human being or not! Henry VIII in England forbade the reading of the Bible by women and throughout the middle ages the Catholic Church treated women as second-class citizens. In the universities of Cambridge and Oxford, male and female students were not given the same rights until 1964. Before 1850, women were not counted as citizens in England and English women had no personal rights until 1882.

If we keep this status in mind and look into the position of the women in Islam, we must conclude that Islam liberated women from the dark age of obscurity, insecurity and being non-entities fourteen hundred years ago!

Islam is a religion of common sense and is in line with human nature. It recognises the realities of life. This does not mean it has recognised equality of man and woman in every respect. Rather, it has defined their duties in keeping with their different biological make-up (2:228). Allah has not made man and woman identical, so it would be against nature to try to have total equality between a man and a woman.

That would destroy the social balance. Society would not prosper but would instead have insoluble problems such as broken marriages, children born outside marriage and the break-up of family life. These problems are already rife in Western society. School girl pregnancies, an increase in abortions, divorce and many other problems have resulted from a permissive outlook and the so-called freedom of women championed by feminists.

Rights of Women : Allah has created every living being in pairs, male and female (51:49), including mankind. Allah has honoured the children *of Adam* – both male and female (17:70). Men and women who believe are friends of one another (9:71). Allah will reward both men and women in the life-after-death (3:195). In Islam a woman has a distinct and separate identity. She is not just an appendage of her husband. Islam has given her the right to own property. She is the owner of her earnings. No one (father, husband or brother) has a right over them. She can dispose of her earnings and property as she wishes, within the bounds of Halal (lawful) and *Haram* (unlawful).

Islam has given women a right to inheritance. She has a claim on the property of her dead father, husband or childless brother (4;7,32,176). A woman has the right to choose her husband. No one can impose a decision on her against her will. She has the right to seek separation *(Khul)* from her husband if their marriage becomes impossible to sustain.

If any man falsely questions a woman's chastity, that man is declared unfit for giving evidence (24:4).This shows how a woman's honour is safeguarded from false accusations.

The *Quran* asks the Muslims to treat women kindly (4:19). It makes Muslim husbands responsible for their wife's maintenance. Women, in return, are expected to remain loyal and chaste (4:34).

A woman has a right to develop her talents and to work within the limits of Islam. Islam allows a non-Muslim married woman to retain her religion and her husband cannot interfere in this freedom. This applies to Christian and Jewish women with Muslim husbands.

Duties of a Woman : Islam is a fair and balanced system of life. While it specifies the rights of women it also lays down duties. A Muslim woman is expected to observe the following:

1. Belief in Tauhid and the practice of Islam should be her first duty. A Muslim woman must perform her Salat, observe Sawm, pay Zakat on her own wealth (if it is applicable) and go to farj if she can afford it. She is exempted from Salat and can defer Sawm during her monthly period, but she must make up the days lost afterwards. Friday prayer (Salatul Jumuah) is optional for women.
2. She is required to maintain her chastity at all times. She must not have any extramarital relationship. The same is the case with men.
3. It is her duty to bring up children according to the rules

of Islam. She has to look after the family and has almost absolute control over domestic affairs, although the family is run by mutual consultation and cooperation. She is the queen of the family and is the manager of household affairs.

4. She should dress modestly and should put on Hijab (covering cloak) while going out and meeting adult males beyond her close relatives (33:59, 24:30-31). She should not dress as a man.
5. She is her husband's helpmate. A faithful wife is like a garment, a source of peace, love, happiness and contentment for her husband (30:21,2:187).
6. If she is asked to go against the commands of Allah, she must defy even her husband, father or brother.
7. She is expected to guard her husband's property and belongings in his absence.

Islam considers a husband and a wife as complementary to one another. Neither dominates the other. Each has his or her own individual rights and duties – together they form a peaceful and happy family which is at the core of a sound, stable and peaceful society.

Man and woman are not exactly equal in Islam. They have different physical and biological features. Islam recognises the leadership of a man over a woman (4:34,2:228) but that does not mean domination.

An average man is usually stronger, heavier and taller than an average woman. Women can become pregnant and bear children but men cannot. Women tend to be sensitive, emotional and tender while men are comparatively less emotional. Allah has given different qualities to a man and a woman and they are expected to love, support and help one another to build a happy family.

Throughout history, men and women have never been

treated the same. Islam has given women the right position and has not attempted to violate divine laws. Other religions and philosophies have failed to define the exact and appropriate role of women. In the West, women have been reduced almost to a plaything of enjoyment and fancy. Women have tended to degrade themselves probably unwittingly in modern times for the sake of real or imaginary equality. They have become objects of exploitation by men and the slogans of liberty and equality have virtually reduced them to playful commodities. They have neither gained liberty nor achieved full equality; rather they have lost their natural place in the home.

The natural balance, fairness and mutuality have been disturbed. The outcome has been horrendous for social peace and stability. The natural peace at home should be restored.

The Polygamy : Islam is a practical religion. It can answer all human problems. Islam allows restricted polygamy – marriage to more than one woman (polygyny), with a maximum of four. The normal Muslim practice is monogamy – one man married to one wife; polygamy is the exception.

The Quran has imposed strict conditions for marrying several wives: "And if you fear that you will not deal justly with the orphans, marry of the women who seems good to you, two or three or four; and if you fear that you cannot deal justly (with them), then one only or (slaves) that your right hands possess. Thus it is more likely to prevent you from doing injustice" (4:3) This verse says that in order to marry more than one woman, a man must be able to be fair and just to each of them. If he is not able to be so, he should marry only one woman.

Another verse of the Quran says: "You will not be able to deal fairly between wives, however much you wish. So do not incline too much to one of them so that you leave another in suspense, if you come to a friendly understanding and fear Allah, Allah is ever Forgiving and most Merciful." (4:129) This further emphasizes fair treatment. But in special circumstances Islam allows polygamy. These situations are:

1. When a wife is barren and cannot bear children but the husband wants children. It is better to have a second wife than to divorce the barren one. However, a barren wife has the option to seek separation from her husband if she wishes, on the grounds of the second marriage of her husband.
2. If the first wife is chronically ill and she is unable to carry out her marital and household chores, the husband may marry another woman and thus help restore family stability.
3. Polygamy may be the solution to the problems of a society which has more women than men. This happens especially after a war. The verse in the Quran allowing more than one wife was revealed after the battle of Uhud in which many Muslim men were martyred.

The proportion of women to men increased considerably in the countries which took part in the First and Second World Wars. A solution to such a situation is marriage to more than one woman by those men who are able to and can be fair to each wife. This is better than leaving a large number of unmarried women.

Islam strictly forbids any sexual relationship outside marriage. There is no such thing as a mistress in Islamic society. Islam has given dignity to women by marriage and has protected them from exploitation of greedy and selfish men. Having more than one wife is better and more dignified than having a number of mistresses. Islam holds you responsible for your actions. You cannot just enjoy women and avoid the responsibilities of fatherhood. This is inhuman and unjust.

There should be no one-parent families or illegitimate children in an ideal Islamic society. It is only possible in a cultural climate of irresponsible and uncontrolled permissiveness. A woman who is going to be a second wife can refuse to marry the man on the grounds that he already has a wife. But if a woman happily consents to her husband marrying again and the second wife agrees, why should anyone else object to it?

The overwhelming majority of Muslims are monogamous—they have only one wife. The fact that some Muslims have more than one wife has become a matter for propaganda against Islam and such propaganda can give a misleading impression of the Islamic way of life. This is especially so when non-practising Muslims are given prominence in this propaganda.

As opposed to polygamy, the case of polyandry (a woman having more than one husband) may be raised. The case of polyandry is impractical and it creates problems rather than solving them. How will paternity be decided? Which husband would claim the fatherhood of the child? How would inheritance be decided? Such questions have no answer in polyandry.

Furthermore, it is possible for a man to live with more than one wife and have children from all of them. But for a woman to please more than one husband seems almost impossible. A woman can bear children from only one husband at a time. Polyandry is forbidden in Islam.

Islam is a practical way of life. It has responded to reality and necessity. It has also put a check on human tendencies and ensured balance. The system is full of wisdom and is perfectly scientific and fair, completely logical.

Allah, the All-knowing, has prescribed what is best for us. We should not be apologetic in our approach. Islam provides the best answers to all problems. We cannot blame Islam if we do not know it or fail to understand it. We need to look at Islam as a whole, not only at a part of it. This is because Islam views life as a whole and does not divide it into different parts.

All areas of life are inter-related; the status of women, marriage and family life are essential aspects of the whole Islamic system. One has to take a holistic view of Islam, there is no room to "pick and choose'.

Some other Dimensions

> ***Food and Drink :*** Food and drink affect us in many ways, such as our health, growth and state of mind. Islam has given regulations about our food and drink. Islam aims to establish a healthy and moral society. It allows all wholesome and pure things to be taken as food and drink. The Quran says: "O Mankind! eat the lawful and good things from what is in the earth and do not follow the foot steps of the devil. Surely, he is your open enemy." (2:168)

It follows from this that Islam has forbidden only what is impure and harmful. Lawful things are called Halal and forbidden things are known as Haram in Islamic law. Islam forbids eating the meat of the following:

(a) dead animals (i.e. those which died naturally');

(b) animals slain without invoking Allah's name;

(c) animals strangled to death;

(d) pigs;

(e) carnivorous animals;

(f) animals devoured by wild beasts;

Islam also forbids the eating of the blood of an animal (2:173; 5:3; 6:145; 16:115).

Islam teaches respect and consideration for the life and welfare of animals. It is one of the many favours of Allah that He has created animals for mankind to eat by His permission, provided we slaughter them in the way He has commanded. Islamic law requires an animal to be slaughtered by a sharp knife penetrating the inner part of the animals neck, ensuring it dies quickly and allowing the maximum drainage of blood. Allah's name must be mentioned at the time of slaughter.

The meat and by-products of animals not slain in this way are Haram. Efforts should be made to obtain Halal meat from Muslim butchers. If there is no Muslim butcher nearby, then the 'Kosher' meat of the Jews is regarded as Halal for Muslims.

There are now plenty of Muslim butchers in most of the European countries, USA, Canada, Australia and New Zealand. In case of doubt, Muslims can eat vegetarian food.

Fish and vegetables are lawful. All kinds of intoxicating (alcoholic) drinks such as beer, wine and spirits are prohibited. Alcoholic drinks are not at all conducive to a healthy society. The Quran says:

> "O you who believe, intoxicants and gambling, idols and divining arrows are filthy tricks of Satan; avoid them so that you may prosper. Satan wants to incite enmity and hatred among you by means of wine and gambling and prevent you from remembering Allah from Salat. So will you not give them up?"
>
> (5:90-91)

Drinking alcohol causes serious social problems in society. It leads to many vices and sins. Islam aims to root out all evils to ensure that society remains healthy and peaceful. Islam also forbids the taking of drugs except for medical purposes.

Muslims begin their meals by saying Bismillahir Rahmanir Rahim (In the name of Allah, the Most Merciful, the Most Kind) and should finish by reciting the following dua:

Alhamdu lillahil ladhi atamana wa saqana wa ja alana minal muslimin.

All praise is for Allah who gave us to eat and to drink and made us Muslims.

Prophet Muhammad asked us to eat with the right hand and to wash our hands before and after meals. It is better not to eat so much so as to fill the stomach. The Prophet also asked us not to drink water and other soft drinks in one go; rather, we should pause whilst drinking and it is better to have three pauses.

The Islamic system of life has very beneficial regulations. We should try to follow these rules as best as we can. We should not find excuses to avoid Islamic laws and regulations, rather we must make serious efforts to follow Allah's commands.

Dress : Islam asks us to make our society nice and decent. Allah has created man in the best of forms and He wants His servants to dress nicely and decently. We should bear in mind that we are the best of all creatures and our dress should reflect this. Proper dress helps prevent indecency, immoral behaviour, and adds beauty to our personality.

The Quran says: "O children of Adam! we have revealed to you clothing to conceal your private parts and as a thing of beauty. But the garment of Taqwa (piety) is the best of all." (7:26)

Islam does not recommend any particular dress for us. However, there are guidelines which include:

1. Men must cover their body at least from the navel to the knees.
2. Women must cover their whole body except the face, hands and feet while inside. But they are also required to cover their whole body including a part of the face while going out or meeting adult males, outside close relatives. Some Islamic jurists allow the face to remain uncovered

3. Men and women must not wear clothing that arouses base feelings. This includes clothing that is see-through, skin-tight or revealing.
4. Men are not allowed to wear pure silk, clothes decorated with gold or gold jewelry.
5. Men are not allowed to wear women's clothing and vice versa.
6. Muslims are not allowed to wear dress that symbolises other religions. Islam encourages simplicity and modesty. Forms of dress expressing arrogance are disliked. The style of dress depends on local custom and climatic conditions but the above guidelines still apply.

Festivals : Like all other religions, Islam has a number of special occasions of celebration. These occasions are observed with devotion to seek the pleasure of Allah, not just for pleasure.

The festivals are occasions of thanksgiving and happiness. The two major occasions in Islam in each year are 'Eid-ul-Fitr and 'Eid-ul-Adha.

'Eid-ul-Fitr is observed on the 1st of Shawwal (the tenth month of the Islamic calendar), the day after the month of Ramadan. On this day, after a month of fasting, Muslims express their joy and happiness by offering a congregational prayer, if possible in an open field, otherwise in Mosques or hired halls. They express their gratitude to Almighty Allah for enabling them to observe a month of fasting.

The day is generally observed as a holiday in Muslim countries. Special dishes are prepared and it is customary to visit friends and relatives and to give presents to children. Muslims generally wear their best clothes on this day.

Eid-ul-Adha is on the 10th of Dhul Hijjah (the twelfth month of the Islamic calendar)' and is followed by three further days of celebrating called Aiymut Tashriq. Eid-ul-Adha commemorates Prophet Ibrahim's readiness to sacrifice his son Ismail (Ishmael) following the command of Allah.

Allah accepted Ibrahim's devotion and obedience and asked him to sacrifice a ram instead. This occasion of great importance comes every year during the days of Hajj (Pilgrimage to mecca) and is observed by offering congregational prayer, as in 'Eid-ul-Fitr.

After the prayer, Muslims who can afford it sacrifice animals like goats sheep, cows or camels to seek Allah's pleasure. The meat of the sacrificial animal is eaten and shared among relatives, neighbours and the poor. This sacrifice expresses the inner feeling of a Muslim that, if need be, he will sacrifice his most loved possession for Allah. This is the lesson of the occasion.

We must remember that what Allah wants is not the animal nor its meat or blood; rather He wants our devotion and submission to His command (22:37).

Other festive occasions include Lailatul Qadr (Night of Power), the day of 'Arafat (9th of Dhul Hijjah), and 'Ashurah (10th of Muharram).

The Salatul jumuah on each Friday may also be regarded as a weekly festival for Muslims, when they gather together for congregational prayer.

Islamic festivals are observed according to the Islamic calendar which is based on lunar months. The lunar year is shorter than the solar year by about eleven days. Festival dates are determined by the sighting of the new moon.

A practising Muslim in today's world genuinely feels unhappy when he sees injustice, inequality and oppression. Muslims in some parts of the world are under bad leadership and suffer from hunger and poverty.

In other parts of the world Muslims are persecuted and killed for their beliefs. So, even on festival days, Muslims feel some sadness in their hearts when they think of those less fortunate than themselves. Sometimes, in countries where Muslims are a minority, the sighting of the moon is a controversial issue and 'Eid is observed on different days.

The unity of Muslims is less visible when we do not celebrate together. Muslims should ask Almighty Allah to help them to resolve this unhappy situation. When Allah's mercy and blessings flow, peace and happiness will be established in society and Muslims will be able to enjoy their festivals which are meant to make them happy and joyful.

Bibliography

Adams, C.C. : *Islam and Modernism in Egypt,* Oxford University Press, New York, 1953.

Ahmad, Bherhan : *The Mujaddid's Conception of Tauhid,* Feroz Pub., Lahore, 1940.

Ahmad, Imtiaz : *Divorce and Remarriage among Muslims in India,* Manohar Publishers, New Delhi, 2003.

Ahmad, K. N. : *Muslim Law of Divorce,* Kitab Bhavan, New Delhi, 1988.

Ahmad, Manzuruddin : *Islamic Political System,* Kitab Bhavan, New Delhi, 1991.

Ali, Chiragh : *The Proposed Political Legal and Social Reform under Muslim Rule,* Popular Prakashan, Bombay, 1883.

Badrul, S. : *Muslim Behaviour,* Kitab Bhavan, New Delhi, 1991.

Bahedur, Kalim : *The Jamaat-i-Islami of Pakistan,* Progressive Books, Lahore, 1978.

Baksh, S. K. : *Politics in Islam,* Kitab Bhavan, New Delhi, 2003.

Bawer, Raymond : *The New Man in Soviet Social Psychology,* Oxford, New York, 1990.

Berger, M. : *Islam in Egypt Today : Social and Political Aspects of Popular Religion,* MacMillan, London, 1970.

Bernier, Francois : *Travels in the Mogul Empire*, MacMillan, London, 1916.

Bukhsh, S. K. : *Contribution to the History of Islamic Civilization*, Kitab Bhavan, New Delhi, 2000.

Charles, Howard : *The Constitutionalism*, Great Seal Books, New York, 1947.

Chave, F. : *Islamic Histroriography*, Cambridge University press, New York, 1990.

Davids, Waines : *An Introduction to Islam*, Cambridge University Press, New Delhi, 1995.

Durrani, F.K.K. : *Muhammad (PBUH) the Prophet*, Oxford, New York, 2001.

Enayat, Hamid : *Islam in the Political Process*, Cambridge University Press, Cambridge, 1993.

Engineer, Asghar Ali : *A Rational Approach to Islam*, Gyan Books Pvt. Ltd., New Delhi, 2001.

———: *Islam : Challenge in Twenty-first Century*, Gyan Books Pvt. Ltd., New Delhi, 2004.

Guillaume, A. : *The Traditions of Islam*, Khayats, Beirut, 1966.

Hassan, Ali : *Observations on the Musulmauns of India*, Macmillan & Co., London, 1832.

Helmut, Reifeld : *Islam in South Asia : Adaptation, Accommodation and Conflict*, Social Science Press, New Delhi, 1999.

Houtsma, T. : *Encyclopaedia of Islam*, Macmillan, London, 1934.

Irfan, Habib : *The Agrarian System of Mughal India*, Popular Prakashan, Bombay, 1963.

Jafar, Sharif : *Islam in India*, Oxford, New Delhi, 1972.

James, Burges : *The Muhammadan Architecture of Ahmadabad*, Bernard Quaritch, London,1900.

Jha, V. : *Indian Society: Historical Probings*, Rawat Pub., Delhi, 1974.

Joseph, and Bosworth, C.E. : *The Legacy of Islam,* Oxford University Press, New York, 1979.

Karl, Jaspers : *Man in the Modern Age,* Routledge & Kegan Paul Ltd., London, 1997.

Katharine, Scarfe : *Perception of the Islamic Word,* Cambridge University Press, New Delhi, 1992.

Lewin, Roger : *In the Age of Mankind,* Simithsonian Books, Washington, D.C., 1956.

Lewis, Richards : *Universe,* Harmony Books, New York, 1973.

Martin, Lings : *A Sufi Saint of the Twentieth Century,* Century Pub., London, 1971.

Mirza, Waheed : *The Life and Works of Amir Khusrau,* Kaveri Pub., Calcutta, 1935.

Mortimer, Edward : *Faith and Power, the Politics of Islam,* Oxford, New York, 2002.

Muhammad, Iqbal : *Six Lectures on the Reconstruction of Religious Thought in Islam,* Royal Pub., Lahore, 1930.

Nabith, A. : *The Foundations of the Articles of Faith,* Feroz Pub., Lahore, 1963.

Nasr, Seyyed H. : *An Introduction to Islamic Cosmological Doctrines,* Cambridge, 1964.

Nicholson, R.A. : *Literary History of the Arabs,* Kitab Bhavan, New Delhi, 1994.

Nusservanji, D. : *Zoroastrian Civilization,* Oxford, New York, 1922.

Oage, Charles H. : *The Society,* Macmillan & Co., London, 1959.

Padwick, C.E. : *Muslim Devotions,* MacMillan & Co., London, 1960.

Phillips, O. Hood : *Reform of the Constitution,* MacMillan & Co., London, 1970.

Pierce, R.A.: *Russia in Central Asia, 1867-1917,* University of California, Berkeley, 1960.

Qadir, Abdul, : *Criminal Law of Islam,* Kitab Bhavan, New Delhi, 1999.

Qazi A. Qadir : *The Changing World of Islam,* Royal Pub., Lahore, 1992.

Rizvi, Hasan Askari : *Islami Reassertion : a Socio Political Study,* Progressive Publishers, Lahore, 1981.

Robert, D. : *Exploring our Living Planet,* National Geographic Society, Washington, 1989.

Saukat, S. : *Human Rights in Islam,* Kitab Bhavan, New Delhi, 2001.

Sharma, Arvind : *Women in World Religion,* New York Press, New York, 1990.

Syed, M. H. : *History of Muslims in India,* Anmol Publications, New Delhi, 2003.

———— : *Islamic Terrorism : Myth or Reality,* Gyan Books, New Delhi, 2002.

Tarn, W. W. : *The Greeks in Bactria and India,* Cambridge, London, 1938.

Thomas, Arnold : *The Legacy of Islam,* Oxford University Press, New York, 2000.

Thompson, H.R. : *Sculptures and Inscriptions of Darius the Great on the Rock of Behistan,* Oxford, London, 1907.

Tritton, A.S. : *The Caliphs and their Non-Muslim Subjects,* Oxford, New York, 1930.

Tutsch, Hans E. : *Facets of Arab Nationalism,* Wayne State University Press, Detroit, 1965.

Underhill, E. : *Mysticism : a Study in the Nature and Development of Man's Spiritual Consciousness,* Oxford, New York, 1956.

Usmani, J.M. : *The Authority of Sunnah,* Kitab Bhavan, New Delhi, 1998.

Von, Edmund : *Modern Islam,* University Press, Los Angeles, 1952.

Von, Grunebaum : *Unity and Variety in Muslim World,* Oxford, New York, 2003.

Waheed, Akhtar : *Sufi Approach to the Problem of Alienation,* Wilson & Co., New Delhi, 1975.

Weiner, Myron : *Sons of the Soil : Migration and Ethnic Conflict in India,* University Press, Prineton, 1978.

Williams, Michael : *Outlines of World Military History,* Oxford, New York, 1996.

Wilson, Lambron : *Traditional Modes of Contemplation and Action,* University Press, Tehran, 1977.

Wolfson, H.A. : *Glimpses of Medieval Indian Culture,* Popular Pub., Bombay, 1959.

Yahanan, Friedmann : *Tolerance and Coercion in Islam : Interfaith Relations in the Muslims Traditions,* Cambridge, New York, 1990.

Yazbeck, Haddad : *Islamic Values in the United States,* Oxford, New York, 1997.

Zaehner, R.C. : *Hindu and Muslim Mysticism,* Oxford, London, 1960.

Zahid, Malik : *Subjects of Quran,* Kitab Bhavan, New Delhi, 1998.

Zahurul, Hasan : *Tarikb-i-Sufiya-i-Gujarat,* Jamil Academy, Ahmadabad, 1981.

Zaki, Azam : *The Ideas of Arab Nationalism,* Cornell University Press, New York,1956.

Index

H

I

K

L

M

N

O

P

Q

R

S

T

V

W

Z

□□□